This thought-provoking book is a major contribution to the international body of knowledge in strategic communication. Traditional rules of the game are changed by the way digital naturals gather information, build opinion, and make decisions and organisations need to understand the new power structures. Building competencies for listening to stakeholders and participating in emerging discourses on the web is a major challenge. Readers will be inspired by this research.

Ansgar Zerfass, *Professor and Chair in Strategic Communication, University of Leipzig & Editor of the* International Journal of Strategic Communication

These authors help clarify the role strategic communication plays in promoting democracy through social media. That daunting undertaking requires insightful exploration of platforms as well as examination of concepts such as relationships, democracy, social change and marketing opportunities and pitfalls. Focusing attention on digital naturals, the book ponders whether people shape social media, or social media shapes how they work and live.

Robert L. Heath, *Professor Emeritus, University of Houston, USA*

This new and exciting book, written by an international team of scholars within strategic communication, explores the changing nature of the online environment and introduces the *digital naturals*, the true citizens of the network society. Read it before your stakeholders do!

Winni Johansen, *Professor, Aarhus University, Denmark*

Finally, a book that foregoes easy generalisations for judicious evaluations around specific issues. The editors and authors are enthusiastic users who are not just consistently informed but clear-eyed, sceptical and alert to new developments, current theories, and professional challenges alongside a concern for equity. It sets standards for 21st-century social media democracy – buy this collection to become a better 21st-century citizen.

David McKie, *Professor, The University of Waikato, New Zealand*

Strategic Communication, Social Media and Democracy

Today almost everyone in the developed world spends time online, and anyone involved in strategic communication must think digitally. The magnitude of change may be up for debate, but the trend is unstoppable, dramatically reconfiguring business models, organisational structures and even the practice of democracy.

Strategic Communication, Social Media and Democracy provides a wholly new framework for understanding this reality, a reality that is transforming the way both practitioners and theoreticians navigate this fast-moving environment. Firmly rooted in empirical research, and resisting the lure of over-optimistic communication dreams, it explores the potential that social media offers for changing the relationships between organisations and stakeholders, and critically analyses what has been achieved so far.

This innovative text will be of great interest to researchers, educators and advanced students in strategic communication, public relations, corporate communication, new media, social media and communication management.

W. Timothy Coombs is Professor in the Department of Communication at Texas A&M University, USA.

Jesper Falkheimer is Professor in Strategic Communication at Lund University, Sweden.

Mats Heide is Professor in Strategic Communication at Lund University, Sweden.

Philip Young is a lecturer and researcher at Lund University, Sweden.

Routledge New Directions in Public Relations and Communication Research
Edited by Kevin Moloney

Routledge New Directions in Public Relations and Communication Research is a new forum for the publication of books of original research in PR and related types of communication. Its remit is to publish critical and challenging responses to continuities and fractures in contemporary PR thinking and practice, and its essential yet contested role in market-orientated, capitalist, liberal democracies around the world. The series reflects the multiple and interdisciplinary forms PR takes in a post-Grunigian world, the expanding roles which it performs and the increasing number of countries in which it is practised.

The series will examine current trends and explore new thinking on the key questions which impact upon PR and communications, including:

- Is the evolution of persuasive communications in Central and Eastern Europe, China, Latin America, Japan, the Middle East and South East Asia developing new forms or following Western models?
- What has been the impact of postmodern sociologies, cultural studies and methodologies which are often critical of the traditional, conservative role of PR in capitalist political economies, and in patriarchy, gender and ethnic roles?
- What is the impact of digital social media on politics, individual privacy and PR practice? Is new technology changing the nature of content communicated, or simply reaching bigger audiences faster? Is digital PR a cause or a consequence of political and cultural change?

Books in this series will be of interest to academics and researchers involved in these expanding fields of study, as well as students undertaking advanced studies in this area.

Public Relations and Nation Building
Influencing Israel
Margalit Toledano and David McKie

Gender and Public Relations
Critical perspectives on voice, image and identity
Edited by Christine Daymon and Kristin Demetrious

Pathways to Public Relations
Histories of practice and profession
Edited by Burton Saint John III, Margot Opdycke Lamme and Jacquie L'Etang

Positioning Theory and Strategic Communications
A new approach to public relations research and practice
Melanie James

Public Relations and the History of Ideas
Simon Moore

Public Relations Ethics and Professionalism
The shadow of excellence
Johanna Fawkes

Power, Diversity and Public Relations
Lee Edwards

The Public Relations of Everything
The ancient, modern and postmodern dramatic history of an idea
Robert E. Brown

Political Reputation Management
The strategy myth
Christian Schnee

Corporate Social Responsibility, Sustainability and Public Relations
Negotiating multiple complex challenges
Donnalyn Pompper

Challenging Corporate Social Responsibility
Lessons for public relations from the casino industry
Jessalynn R. Strauss

Strategic Communication, Social Media and Democracy
The challenge of the digital naturals
Edited by W. Timothy Coombs, Jesper Falkheimer, Mats Heide and Philip Young

Strategic Communication, Social Media and Democracy

The challenge of the digital naturals

**Edited by W. Timothy Coombs,
Jesper Falkheimer, Mats Heide and
Philip Young**

LONDON AND NEW YORK

First published 2016
by Routledge
2 Park Square, Milton Park, Abingdon, Oxon OX14 4RN

and by Routledge
711 Third Avenue, New York, NY 10017

First issued in paperback 2017

Routledge is an imprint of the Taylor & Francis Group, an informa business

British Library Cataloguing in Publication Data
A catalogue record for this book is available from the British Library

Library of Congress Cataloging-in-Publication Data
Strategic communication, social media and democracy : the challenge of
   the digital naturals / edited by W. Timothy Coombs, Jesper Falkheimer,
   Mats Heide and Philip Young. — 1 Edition.
      pages cm. — (Routledge new directions in public relations and
communication research)
   Includes bibliographical references and index.
   1. Social media—Economic aspects.   2. Public relations.
3. Organizational behavior.   I. Coombs, W. Timothy, editor.
   HM742.S87 2015
   302.3'5—dc23
   2015007024

ISBN 13: 978-1-138-49741-2 (pbk)
ISBN 13: 978-1-138-84116-1 (hbk)

Typeset in Times New Roman
by Apex CoVantage, LLC

Contents

Notes on contributors

Marja Åkerström is an associate professor at the Department of Strategic Communication (ISK) at Lund University, Campus Helsingborg. Her main research fields are within strategic communication, political communication, digital media and democracy, organisational communication and crisis communication. Her doctoral thesis in media and communication science (Lund University: *Cosmetic democracy*, 2010) is about democracy in local politics of Sweden and strategies used on- and offline by citizens, politicians and journalists in order to exercise influence and power. Earlier research projects include studies of social movements like Attac within the EU context, studies on the discourse of registrations of political opinions of Swedish citizens, environmental communication and studies on risk communication on a national level.

Cecilia Cassinger lectures at the Department of Strategic Communication, Lund University, Campus Helsinborg. Her research interests are in the area of marketing communication, branding, culture and politics. She has written on research methodology, consumption practices and the relationship between narrative and image in a business context.

W. Timothy Coombs (PhD from Purdue University in public affairs and issues management) is a full professor in the Nicholson School of Communication at the University of Central Florida, the second largest university in the United States. He received the 2002 Jackson, Jackson & Wagner Behavioral Science Prize from the Public Relations Society of America, the 2013 Pathfinder Award from the Institute of Public Relations in recognition of his research contributions to the field and the practice, and the 2014 Dean's Distinguished Researcher Award in the College of Sciences. Coombs has won multiple PRIDE awards from the Public Relations Division of the National Communication Association for both books and research articles. He is also a member of the Arthur W. Page Society. Coombs was a Fulbright scholar in Estonia in the spring of 2013. In the fall of 2013 he was named a NEMO professor at Lund University, Helsingborg Campus. Coombs has worked with governments, corporations and consulting firms in the United States, Asia and Europe on ways to improve crisis communication efforts for themselves and their clients.

Jesper Falkheimer (PhD) is a professor in strategic communication at Lund University, Campus Helsingborg. For several years he has combined research with university management positions and has been rector of Campus Helsingborg since 2011. His research interests are within the fields of strategic communication, public relations, crisis management and media studies. Falkheimer is author and editor of 11 books and anthologies and several international articles and chapters – for example in *The Routledge Handbook of Critical Public Relations* (2015), *The Routledge Handbook of Strategic Communication* (2014), *The Handbook of Crisis Communication* (2010) and *Public Relations and Social Theory* (2009). He is associate editor of the forthcoming *International Encyclopedia of Strategic Communication* (eds. Robert Heath and Winni Johansen). He is also an executive board member of the Swedish Public Relations Association, the PR agency Gullers Group AB and the media cluster Media Evolution AB; a member of the advisory boards of European Communication Monitor and Corporate Communication International (New York); and programme director for the Communication Executive Programme at IFL, Stockholm School of Economics.

Nils Gustafsson is a senior lecturer at the Department of Strategic Communication at Lund University, Campus Helsingborg. He received his PhD in political science in 2013. His doctoral thesis dealt with social network sites, political participation and equality. Research interests include political communication, political participation, democratic theory and media history. Currently he is conducting research on the political participation of young people in an age of social media.

Mats Heide is a professor in strategic communication at Lund University. His research interests are within the fields of strategic communication and organisational communication, and he has focused especially on change communication and crisis communication. During the last few years he has worked on a research project about internal crisis communication together with Charlotte Simonsson, funded by the Swedish Agency for Contingency Management. At present he is involved in a research project about communicative organisations, focusing on the importance and value of communication. Heide is author and co-author of 12 books (in Swedish) and several articles and edited chapters in anthologies, such as *The Routledge Handbook of Strategic Communication* (2014), *Encyclopedia of Public Relations II* (2014), *Handbook of Crisis Management* (2013) and *The Handbook of Crisis Communication* (2010).

Sherry Holladay (PhD) has research interests including crisis communication, corporate social responsibility, activism, reputation management and stakeholder relations. Her scholarly work has appeared in *Public Relations Review, Management Communication Quarterly, Journal of Communication Management, Journal of Public Relations Research, International Journal of Strategic Communication, Public Relations Inquiry, Journal of Communication* and *Encyclopedia of Public Relations.* She is co-author of the books *It's Not Just*

PR: Public Relations in Society, Public Relations Strategies and Applications: Managing Influence and *Managing Corporate Social Responsibility.* She is co-editor of the *Handbook of Crisis Communication.* Holladay has presented her work at numerous national and international conferences.

Henrik Merkelsen is associate professor at the Department of Strategic Communication, Lund University, Campus Helsingborg. His research is centred on risk management and public relations, and his work has been published in the fields' leading journals, such as *Risk Analysis, Journal of Risk Research* and *Public Relations Review.* Apart from his academic work he has worked for the past 15 years as a public relations advisor, and he is a frequent speaker at seminars for business leaders and public relations professionals.

Veselinka Möllerström (PhD) is lecturer and researcher at the Department of Strategic Communication at Lund University, Campus Helsingborg. Her research interests are spatial communication, storytelling, discourse analysis and media representations. She teaches graduate and postgraduate students in different subject areas within the field of strategic communication.

Howard Nothhaft (PhD) is an assistant professor in strategic communication at the Department of Strategic Communication, Lund University, Campus Helsingborg, Sweden. His research interests lie in the area of communication strategy and the implications of strategic communication for democracy. He has received several awards, and his work is published in various journals and handbooks.

Hagen Schölzel holds a PhD in political science from Leipzig University, Germany. He is currently lecturer at the Faculty of Law, Social Sciences and Economics at the University of Erfurt, Germany. He was associated researcher at the NEMO Research Group at Lund University, Campus Helsingborg. His research interests lie in the fields of sociology of communication, especially political communication, and cultural theory. He is author of the monograph *Guerillakommunikation: Genealogie einer politischen Konfliktform* (Guerrilla Communication: Genealogy of a Mode of Political Conflict) as well as author and co-author of several journal articles and book chapters. In the field of public relations research, his work includes co-authoring with Howard Nothhaft the article "(Re-)reading Clausewitz: The Strategy Discourse and Its Implications for Strategic Communication", which appeared in the *Handbook of Strategic Communication*, edited by Derina Holtzhausen and Ansgar Zerfass.

Jens Seiffert is a postdoc at the Department of Communication at Vienna University. In 2014 he finished his PhD thesis *Trust Within Media Society* at the University of Leipzig, where he worked as a research associate since 2009. During that period, he has spent a research semester at George Mason University, Virginia, United States, and was an affiliate researcher at Lund University, being part of the NEMO research project. He studied communication and media science, and political science at the University of Leipzig and Charles University in Prague, Czech Republic. He was a fellow of the Frederick Ebert Foundation between 2003 and 2007, and from 2009 to 2013 he was a scholarship holder at the Foundation for the Promotion of PR Science at the University of Leipzig. Beyond public trust, his fields of research are general PR theory, communication strategy and management, PR history and computer games.

Åsa Thelander is an associate professor and senior lecturer in strategic communication at the Department of Strategic Communication, Lund University, Campus Helsingborg. Thelander has recently published research about international retailing image, strategic communication in the cultural sector and methods in social science communication research.

Sara von Platen is a senior lecturer at the Department of Strategic Communication at Lund University, Campus Helsingborg. Her research covers areas such as the roles and functions of communication consultants, change communication and sense making during strategic change processes, self-referential communication and member identification in organisations. She has also been engaged in third-party research concerning communication strategies and environmental issues and is a regular speaker and seminar leader at events organised by Sveriges Kommunikatörer (Swedish Public Relations Association). At present she is engaged in the pioneering research project The Communicative Organization. The purpose of the project is to explore the processes, structures and actors that constitute communicative organisations and nuance some of the optimistic ideals that are currently associated with the concept of the communicative organisation.

Philip Young is a lecturer and researcher at Lund University, Campus Helsingborg, and was project leader for NEMO: New Media, Modern Democracy. He has investigated the impact of social media on public relations practice for over a decade, and is co-author with David Phillips of *Online Public Relations* (2nd ed.).

Acknowledgement

The NEMO: New Media, Modern Democracy project at Lund University, Campus Helsingborg, was made possible by the generous support of the Anne-Marie and Gustaf Anders Foundation for Media Research.

Preface

Everyone believes they live in extraordinary times, and that the speed of techno-logical and social change they are experiencing is more dramatic than that expe-rienced by earlier generations. Anyone working in strategic communication today uses tools and techniques that would be unrecognisable a decade or so ago.

Or at least that is the way it sometimes seems. The Internet can appear to have changed everything, from retail business models to the smartphone in everyone's pocket. Everything is instant, and everybody is connected.

The battle to understand the speed of these changes, to assess the true impact of apparently dazzling upheaval, presents a huge challenge for those trying to explain the processes, effects and implications of digital media for strategic communica-tion. What is revolution, what is evolution, and what is merely a passing fad? Are some developments so significant that they can be explained only by new theory, or are they merely new practices that have little fundamental significance?

At the beginning of 2012 researchers at the Department of Strategic Communi-cation (ISK) at Lund University, Campus Helsingborg, launched a research pro-gramme, NEMO: New Media, Modern Democracy, which would encourage and support investigations into a range of topics linked to these changes. Sweden offered a promising centre for study, distinguished by a strong sense of social responsibility and an embrace of online technologies that makes it one of the most connected countries in the world. Working in collaboration with researchers from across Europe and the United States, NEMO embarked on a series of related and continuing studies, many of which are reflected in this book. They bring together a range of new ideas and approaches to emerging social and cultural patterns that will have significant impact not only on strategic communication but also on wider issues of democratic engagement and social change.

Many of the chapters embrace the concept of *digital naturals*, a formulation pioneered by NEMO to describe actors who are comfortable in the new online environment, who possess a range of communicative and knowledge-gathering skills and who have sophisticated expectations for their relationships with organ-isations and institutions.

The book chooses a complex rather than a simplistic approach, reflected in the range of topics and methods, the levels of analysis and the inclusion of theory and practice. The spectrum of strategic communication topics is broad, from activism to city branding, from crisis communication to political engagement. The critique is applied at levels of analysis ranging from organisation-stakeholder, internal stakeholders, and local community to society as a whole; its focus is on relations between organisations and society, but is considered to be more society-centric than organisation-centric. The chapters use a variety of theories and in some cases begin to craft new theory.

Structure

Reflecting NEMO themes, the book has two sections, with Part I considering new media and strategic communication, and Part II broadening the discussion to include topics linked to modern society.

In **Chapter 1, Meet the Digital Naturals**, Philip Young and Marja Åkerström show how the digital naturals framing helps to explain and understand the rapidly evolving communication landscape, and why it is time to finally reject the outdated notion of 'digital natives'. By placing emphasis on experience, aptitude and 'propensities' rather than artificial constraints of age and chronology, and rejecting the digital dualism that distinguishes online from offline, they establish a robust setting for what is to follow.

Chapter 2, The Role of Communication Professionals in the Digital Age, by Henrik Merkelsen, Veselinka Möllerström and Sara von Platen, analyses the way in which practitioners use social media to explore their underlying understanding of the nature of public relations. Specifically, they apply Luhmann's concept of paradox to expose tensions in its self-conception, and conclude that it is difficult for the practice to uphold a consistent identity.

Further tensions between the rhetoric of public relations and its practical applications are identified in **Chapter 3, Exploring the Language of Social Media in the Discourse of Public Relations**. Philip Young, Timothy Coombs and Sherry Holladay begin by showing how the discourse of social media gurus has shaped the presentation and packaging of public relations, but question the extent to which aspirations to conversation and engagement have truly impacted practice. They go on to suggest that even when interacting with digital naturals, organisations establish parasocial relationships rather than developing something that could be properly described as interpersonal.

Chapter 4, Rotation Curation on Instagram, by Cecilia Cassinger and Åsa Thelander, looks at the way digital naturals contribute to creating an image of a mid-sized Swedish city. Exploiting technologies that have only recently become available, civic authorities in Landskrona are encouraging an ever-changing cast of smartphone photographers to take charge of an Instagram account to share their impressions of the city. With echoes of the paradoxes exposed in Chapter 3, their analysis reveals routines and hierarchies that both bring forward new voices but also limit social inclusion; asymmetries in power, predicated by social and cultural capital, impact strongly on efforts towards transparency and engagement.

The next two chapters look at ways in which the move online has impacted on two strategic communication disciplines. Firstly, in **Chapter 5** Mats Heide examines **Social Intranets and Internal Communication**, and then in **Chapter 6** Timothy Coombs and Sherry Holladay discuss **Digital Naturals and Crisis Communication**. The two studies show contrasting responses to the emerging dominance of digital naturals: whereas crisis communication practitioners are compelled to recognise the challenges of instant, networked communication for reputation, Heide's verdict is that organisations (and theorists) have been slow to exploit the social potential of internets. Paradoxically, although organisations can be quick to cast digital natural employees as cultural ambassadors to external stakeholders, they have done less to evolve internal communication techniques that complement the outside work experience. Echoing elements of Chapter 3, Coombs and Holladay identify the increasing incidence of paracrises, and highlight the role of digital naturals in moving the arena of crisis management from the private to the public stage.

Part II, **Modern Democracy**, opens with **Chapter 7**, **The Dream of Enlightenment Within Digital Reach?** Introducing the major themes of the second section, Nothhaft asks whether it is reasonable to expect that the emerging digital technologies will lead to greater democracy, and thus a 'better' society. His exploration identifies three understandings. The first is the *optimisation paradigm* in which democracy has already been realised, the way forward being to carefully and sensibly integrate new media into the existing democratic framework and to adapt institutions, structures, discourses and practices accordingly. The second understanding sees the *ideal* of democracy – what democracy *really* is – as lost and in dire need of recovery. In this *catalytic paradigm* digital media can expose and outmanoeuvre false forms of democracy. The third understanding holds that a new age has dawned. The current disaffection with politics is due to a fundamental lack of *fit between contemporary society and the established democratic practice*. The great hope is to find the way to an entirely new, as yet unthought of, future that would not be possible without technological innovation.

Against this backdrop, in **Chapter 8**, **What Do Digital Naturals Demand From Democracy?**, Marja Åkerström and Philip Young explore attitudes expressed in focus groups comprising motivated strategic communications students. Although taking connectivity, instant access to unrivalled quantities of information and opinion sharing as routine, these digital naturals could at first glance be seen as having conservative and disengaged views on democracy. Closer scrutiny is suggested.

Contrasting views as to the utility of and impact of social networking emerge in **Chapter 9**, **Social Media and Parliamentary Infighting: digital Naturals in the Swedish Riksdag?**, Nils Gustafsson's pioneering study of ways in which Swedish MPs use social media for intra-party competition. Resonating with Heide's findings on internal communications, Gustafsson's respondents showed inconsistencies between the perceived values of digital media as an external channel and as an interpersonal relationship with colleagues, rivals and peers.

In **Chapter 10, 'Swarming' for Democracy**, Howard Nothhaft and Hagen Schölzel examine the events which brought about the downfall of a leading German politician who was accused of plagiarism in his PhD thesis, Defence Minister Karl-Theodor zu Guttenberg.

Chapter 11, Deliberation and Adjudication as Democratic Practice in Post-Fact Society, by Marja Åkerström, looks at the controversy surrounding an Afghan boy who sought asylum in Sweden. Reporting of the case was driven by online platforms, and the discourse polarised along ideological divides. Although many voices were heard, Åkerström found that truth became negotiable; for her, the discourse facilitated by online technologies did not build collective intelligence, but rather it promoted pluralistic ignorance.

In **Chapter 12, The Gamification of Democracy**, Howard Nothhaft and Jens Seiffert argue that computer games are powerful tools for strategic communication that deserve much more attention from academics. Hugely popular computer games deploy what Bogost terms 'procedural rhetoric' in ways which have the potential to strongly influence political attitudes and expectations. If political engagement among the young is the greatest problem facing Western democracy, decoding the media logic of digital naturals becomes the key to the future.

Finally, in **Chapter 13, Digital Media and New Terrorism**, Jesper Falkheimer looks at the way technology offers boundless communication possibilities for terrorists, levelling the playing field with 'legitimate' political actors. Drawing on a study of the use of digital media by the Islamic State, the chapter poses serious questions that arise from the hybridisation of media strategies, whether used by corporations, governments, activists or terrorists.

So, chapter by chapter, this book demonstrates how it is becoming increasingly difficult to sustain a meaningful distinction between life online and offline. Social media and other forms of online communication – from Facebook, Twitter, Instagram and YouTube to cloud-based platforms, such as Wikipedia, multiplayer games and geolocation services – are transforming many aspects of social and organisational life in ways that have significant implications for democracy and civic engagement. Many of the changes are forcing a radical overview of public relations theory.

Digital technologies mean that reputations and relationships are negotiated in real time. In theory at least, power balances are being challenged and business models disrupted but, despite the optimism of digital evangelists, even in egalitarian Scandinavia the claimed benefits of a more inclusive, more representative public sphere remain elusive. The new reality appears still to be shaped by dynamics of power, access and media literacy.

The emerging dominance of digital naturals represents a clear 'turn' in the underlying assumptions and framings that underpin much strategic communication thinking.

1 Meet the digital naturals

Philip Young and Marja Åkerström

The emergence of the Internet and related technologies has brought profound economic and social change, arguably on a scale paralleled only by the invention of the printing press. As with printing, the most significant changes have concerned the ability to exchange information.

Printing enabled those with access to the technology to distribute information in a manner that had permanence and scale. Although there was cost associated with the replication and distribution of printed documents, this was far less than that associated with handwritten documents. There were also particular skills associated with accessing the information – the receiver needed to be able to read (or be read to).

But although those who could read a handwritten text could read a printed text, those who couldn't read a handwritten text were no more able to read printed text. The division between literacy and illiteracy was almost entirely dependent on access to education, determined by the intertwined parameters of social class and economic means. Age had very little influence, and it is hard to imagine anyone defining their competences with reference to the invention of the printing press. Likewise, the spread of printed materials could be reasonably measured and expressed only across centuries, with huge variations in adoption by geographical location.

With the Internet, it has all been rather different. It is beyond question that the information experience of someone living today in a highly developed industrial nation, such as Sweden, is profoundly different to that of a person living 20, 30 or 40 years earlier. Any organisation concerned with strategic communication is obliged to assume that Internet-enabled technologies will have significant influence on its ability to achieve objectives.

The speed of change has been dramatic, but it is still surprising to see professional communicators and academic researchers employing the terminology of "digital natives" and "digital immigrants," outmoded and unhelpful concepts that are linked to equally unhelpful framings that stress a divide between online and offline interaction.

It is time to move forward. Meet the digital naturals, *individuals who are comfortable in an online environment, being equipped through experience and exposure to both its cultural norms and the technological competencies required to operate effectively.*

The framing reflects the degree to which the technologies of digital communication have become commonplace, an accepted, almost unnoticeable and no longer noteworthy part of everyday life; for many interactions, the distinction between online and offline is no longer applicable (Jurgenson, 2011). This acceptance that to be digital is the natural state in a twenty-first-century developed economy does, however, open up for exploration the ways in which "naturalness" can be expressed, ranging from competence, literacy, acceptance and availability to the degree to which individuals are comfortable in the environment. At the same time, it demands that we recognise the new pressures, fears and uncertainties that it brings. To be at home in an environment does not imply that we therefore feel safe or secure there, or even that it is a place we really want to be.

As we will see, there are many reasons for rejecting the notion of natives, and they can often concern the unintended consequences of exclusion. At the same time, communicators and communication theorists are constantly required to differentiate among audiences, stakeholders, publics or whatever else. Very few messages are designed to reach a global audience, and differentiation and segmentation are integral to the vast majority of communication activities. Age is quite obviously an important criterion when delineating many groupings, but that is no justification for drawing a strong causal connection between birthdate and digital competence and acceptance. Furthermore, the digital natural framing pays little regard to the distinction between online and offline, and the redundancy of digital dualism is regarded as a natural and swift development for which age has little relevance.

As William Gibson, the science fiction writer who coined the phrase cyberspace, has observed, "The future is here – but is not evenly distributed." Something very similar could be said about the digital naturals.

Deconstructing the digital native

As the following section explains, the term 'digital natives' arose from a need to capture what appeared to be a significant change in learning habits that was being driven by new technology. Once coined, the framing gained traction and began to have some influence on debate, sometimes in positive ways, but as shown, by placing significant emphasis on chronological age, 'natives' began to distort perceptions in ways that can be seen as unhelpful.

Background

In 2001 Marc Prensky published 'Digital Natives, Digital Immigrants' (in *On the Horizon*, 2001). His intention was to focus attention on the changing expectations of university students, and to alert educators to the challenges of teaching the first generation to have grown up with new technology: "They have spent their entire lives surrounded by and using computers, videogames, digital music players, video cams, cell phones, and all the other toys and tools of the digital age" (p. 1).

He believed the change represented "a really big discontinuity" and a "singularity" and made a strong call for action. He sought to divide the world into *digital natives* and *digital immigrants*, claiming those born from the 1980s on had grown up with skills that older people would have to learn, often with difficulty and little prospect of fluency.

Prensky wasn't the first to use the term digital natives (that was probably Barlow, who published *A Declaration for the Independence of Cyberspace* in 1996), but the coinage gained traction. Indeed, for a short time it provided a useful lens for focusing a new debate, but the terminology has been appropriated to suggest a divide between those who are deemed by birthright to enjoy a privileged relationship with online technologies and those who are forever outside. For Prensky, the digital immigrants would learn – some better than others – to adapt to their environment, but they would always retain, to some degree, their "accent" . . . their foot in the past.

The "native" position was strongly expressed in 2008 by Palfrey and Grasser in *Born Digital*, which is subtitled *Understanding the First Generation of Digital Natives*.

Five years later, Brian Solis (2013) was claiming,

> Gen Y and Z were born with digital in their DNA. While that may seem like a given, it is the very detail that separates them from their parents, teachers, businesses, governments, and any organization other than those already run by Gen Y and Z.

He concluded, "As a result, our society splits into two camps, those who "get" these connected generations and those who do not or will not."

Bennett, Maton and Kervin (2008) identify two main assumptions in the literature on which the emergence of digital natives is based: First, that young people of the digital native generation possess sophisticated knowledge of and skills with information technologies, and second, that as a result of their upbringing and experiences with technology, digital natives have particular learning preferences or styles that differ from earlier generations of students.

There is certainly some truth in the observation about learning styles, but it becomes problematic when inflated to embrace a much broader change. As Jenkins notes in *Reconsidering Digital Immigrants* (2007):

> Talk of "digital natives" helps us to recognize and respect the new kinds of learning and cultural expression which have emerged from a generation that has come of age alongside the personal and networked computer. Yet, talk of "digital natives" may also mask the different degrees access to and comfort with emerging technologies experienced by different youth. Talk of digital natives may make it harder for us to pay attention to the digital divide in terms of who has access to different technical platforms and the participation gap in terms of who has access to certain skills and competencies or for that matter,

certain cultural experiences and social identities. Talking about youth as digital natives implies that there is a world which these young people all share and a body of knowledge they have all mastered, rather than seeing the online world as unfamiliar and uncertain for all of us.

Implications

The digital native framing necessarily encourages the notion of the digital immigrant. Unfortunately, immigrant is seldom used to convey notions of enhanced status; rather it carries associations with colonialism, perhaps racism and certainly "othering". Few people emigrate to reduce their status, opportunities or quality of life: the implication is that migrants either are escaping challenging circumstances or believe they have identified an opportunity for advancement. From the outset, the new arrival must begin a process of assimilation, to adjust to and accept the cultural norms of the adopted environment, by embracing its language, customs and norms. In many situations, the immigrant who fails to assimilate, for whatever reason, is criticised, even ostracised by those who consider themselves to be native.

Continuing with this literal interpretation of the terms leads to two further understandings. Sometimes, the number of immigrants comes to greatly exceed the number or power of the native population, causing great damage to the indigenous population. But as Jenkins observed earlier, there are dangers in assuming that natives have the competence and awareness to maintain their position in society, never mind enjoy benefit and privilege. Furthermore, the Prensky framing – the *singularity* – seems to imply a clear and abrupt change which scarcely reflects the fast moving nature of technology. The digital ecology of 2001, which he believed to be so novel, has long been left behind. Prensky's 'native' had yet to experience Facebook, YouTube, smartphones, Wi-Fi and high-speed broadband, and would no doubt feel disorientated and lost if catapulted forward to 2014.

As boyd (2014, p. 177) observes, the notion of digital natives has political roots, mostly born out of American techno-idealism; 15 years on, it is quite clear that chronological age offers few insights that deepen understanding of communicative behaviour.

In a paper delivered to the seventh International Political Marketing Association conference in Stockholm in September 2013, we made the case for a more constructive grouping. The concept of digital naturals was initially coined to describe a cohort of students brought together to discuss the implications of new media for democracy (see Chapter 8). This was a group of young people (under 30) whose experience of democracy was developed over a time when social media and digital technologies were becoming commonplace. From a social constructivist perspective, it was reasonable to conclude that the way the cohort accessed information – be it news or propaganda – and the way they shared and discussed opinion would be significantly influenced by digital platforms and channels. Interestingly, the majority of respondents did appear to believe that their use of digital networks gave them a superior knowledge of the world, and they made frequent reference to the perceived differences. They were naturals insofar as they were comfortable with technologies employed to access and discuss political issues, but the most obvious distinction between them and the (older) researchers was that they could not remember a time before digital.

Age does matter

The digital naturals framing does not deny that the use of technologies has an age dimension, but argues that this has very little to do with chronology of adoption, and a great deal to do with natural life cycle. Yes, teenagers use social media in different ways than, say, those in their fifties, but they conduct most of their social activities differently, too. They may well wear different clothes, and wear them differently, have different hairstyles, listen to different music, have different sleep patterns and so forth, but this is due to an interplay between the need to construct an individual identity and the need to negotiate new types of social relationships that just happen to coincide with fashion or available technology.

The construction of identity through the exchange of opinion and the need to establish broader and deeper relationships are particularly strong in adolescence and early adulthood, so it is entirely to be expected that those at this life stage share more information through social networks. The acts of sharing are part of a social calibration, linked to peer esteem and positioning, that has always existed. The difference is that some facets of this process are more visible to those outside the groupings, and as would be expected, the interactions are mediated by digital affordances. If a 15-year-old uses Facebook more regularly than a 50-year-old, it is more likely to be a result of social pressures and circumstances than a native affinity for the technologies.

As danah boyd and others explain, teenagers have a different view of privacy than do other age groups. Although they are seen to be willing to put more online, they spend more time creating personal space, shared to some degree with peers, but jealously protected against the intrusion of adults.

Defining characteristics of the digital environment

The term 'digital naturals' has conceptual and operational uses. As a theoretical framing it allows investigation across a range of interests and particularly encourages examination of individual behaviours linked to values. For those concerned with operational issues it opens opportunities for a more sophisticated analysis of stakeholder interactions, not least by highlighting competences linked to character and experience rather than technological affordance.

The changes brought about by digital communication can be categorised in a number of different ways. Some refer to logistical qualities, including *reach* and *timelessness* (identified by Fawkes & Gregory, 2000), to implications that highlight evolutions in notions of *transparency* and *porosity*, and those relating to the accumulation of knowledge, including *aggregation* and *curation*, which have seen expression in loosely defined concepts such as *groundswell* (Li & Bernhoff, 2008) and *crowdsourcing*, which are linked to user-generated content and co-creation of meaning. This has in turn fostered an emerging language of social media, which privileges conversation, engagement, openness and interactivity. (The value and authenticity of such terminology are discussed in Coombs, Holladay and Young in Chapter 3.)

The adjustments to reach and timelessness can be considered commonplace; there can be few people in the developed Western nations who are not aware that given access to the appropriate technologies, messages can be transmitted and received almost simultaneously by people in any part of the world and, increasingly, at no perceptible cost. Some may use these technologies to keep in touch with friends and relatives a continent away; almost all will accept that news of an event of global significance will be visible to global audiences within a very short time of occurrence. The networked and aggregated elements of reputation and understanding may be more opaque, but the vast majority of those who access online content will have used a search engine, and thus encountered an element of aggregation.

Engagement with Facebook means engagement with what Fuchs (2014) describes as *participatory culture*, and this interaction is facilitated by "spreadable media" (Jenkins, 2007). Even the most limited interaction takes the user into areas associated with peer review, endorsement and value sharing.

The very act of logging on to a social network involves a renegotiation of notions of privacy. Any activity conducted in the digital space involves leaving tracks and traces that are discoverable, searchable and subject to analysis, or remediation, and this is intrinsically linked to identity construction. That few people have any real appreciation of how much personal information they are surrendering, or to what use that information might be put, leads to reconsiderations of long-held attitudes towards privacy, and may well lead to increasing unease. There is no easy way of proving this, but it is almost certain that few Westerners feel *more* comfortable in the knowledge that their thoughts and opinions are increasingly revealed to external observers. Being comfortable in a digital environment appears to necessarily demand either a lack of curiosity or a willingness to ignore troubling factors in return for immediate utility.

Characteristics of the digital natural

For many people, regular access to the Internet is an almost indispensable part of daily life, with devices such as smartphones performing a range of practical or diverting roles that complement our cognitive and communicative skills. Looking to science fiction for metaphors, some see parallels between smartphone dependency and the fusion of man and machine exemplified by RoboCop. Borrowing terminology from Donna Haraway's 1985 essay *A Cyborg Manifesto*, it is possible to see the digital natural as an individual whose mental powers – particularly memory, but also speech and sight – are enhanced by technology that is so closely embedded as to blur the boundary between human and machine.

Certainly, smartphones and other Internet-enabled devices encourage us to outsource memory (why memorise facts when they are instantly accessible, and verifiable on, say, Wikipedia, or captured in image and film, on Instagram or YouTube?), and the convergence and miniaturisation of accessories, such as a camera, calendar, notepad, maps, music player, television monitor, radio set and – yes! – telephone, into one device encourage the feeling that technology is disappearing and becoming prosaic. Memory artefacts (photographs, videos, text notes) are increasingly stored "in the cloud," joining music and book collections that no longer have a physical presence. Ownership becomes a blurred issue, with more in common with rental than purchase.

Instant access to news (from world events to family gossip) and information (whether practical or esoteric) erodes concepts of distance and promotes a 24-hour news cycle that means events can play out to observers in real time. For interpersonal communication, e-mail, instant messaging, Skype and FaceTime mean there is little difference in terms of cost per conversation or convenience in talking to someone in the same room or in Australia or Sweden.

Social networks, such as Facebook and Twitter, are keen to promote both the sharing of information and weak interaction, such as liking or rating. Likewise, business models such as those adopted by Amazon, TripAdvisor, and news outlets, be they BuzzFeed or the *Daily Mail*, encourage rating and commenting, routine behaviours that build community, allow for individual expression and create data that can be harvested for demographic and behavioural insights.

So digital naturals can be characterised as experiencing the world with radically redefined concepts of space and time, with a greater reliance on external information and content than ever before. The individuals who populate this world will then behave in ways which, to a greater or lesser degree, reflect propensities that have evolved in experience that is conceptualised with shrinking regard to notions of online and offline.

For communicators, especially at an operational level, the urge to segment behaviours and propensities has encouraged a causal linkage between youth behaviours and emerging technologies. Adolescents are seen as having different appreciations and concerns about personal privacy, the sharing of information (and property) and the propensity to comment on and review the actions and performance of peers, often coloured by a growing sense of self-importance. Such behaviours can be amplified by social media, but they are more the product of age, of life cycle, than an inherent aptitude for particular technologies. An individual is not excluded from being considered a digital natural simply for not having, or no longer having, the same intense – natural – teenage and young adult concerns that are an essential part of growing up.

One of the problems of the natives and immigrants framing is that it assumes that those born after 1980 somehow have a mixture of knowledge, literacy and competence that older people can never quite attain. This overconfidence does a disservice to young people. As boyd (2014, p. 177) points out, "It is dangerous to assume that youth are automatically informed."

There are significant concerns that need to be addressed concerning social class, but conclusions drawn mainly from age need to be treated with some degree of caution. The assertion is made that 14-year-olds are same as 40-year-olds. For example, Ofcom, the regulatory authority for the UK communications industry, introduced its 2014 communications market report by explaining *that a 'millennium generation' of 14–15-year-olds are the most technology-savvy in the UK.*

> The research – part of Ofcom's eleventh Communications Market Report – measures confidence and knowledge of communications technology to calculate an individual's 'Digital Quotient' score, or 'DQ', with the average UK adult scoring 100.
>
> The study, among nearly 2,000 adults and 800 children, finds that six year olds claim to have the same understanding of communications technology as 45 year olds. Also, more than 60% of people aged 55 and over have a below average 'DQ' score.
>
> http://stakeholders.ofcom.org.uk/market-data-research/
> market-data/communications-market-reports/cmr14/

Throughout it is most important to bear in mind that the OfCom commentary appears to be based on self-assessment and self-image. It may work well when considering the comfort element of the digital naturals framing, but understandably struggles to encompass the challenges presented by young people who overestimate their competences (they don't know what they don't know) or by older people who fear that they have less ability than they do in fact possess.

Digital acceptance

Two of the more significant factors limiting acceptance of digital technologies are usability and cost. Both the software and hardware which underpin digital communication have evolved rapidly, and the direction of change has been towards disappearance: although few users of an iPhone will be aware of all its features, and still fewer will actually use them, most will have been able to operate the device without having to read a manual (which is just as well, as Apple doesn't feel the need to include one in its stylish packaging). The first generation of digital natives, should they have taken delivery of a Windows 95 PC, would have spent some time loading programmes from disk, and may well have used the accompanying handbook, which would have been several centimetres thick: contrast this with the experience of a three- or four-year-old, who intuitively appreciates how to swipe a new game on an iPad. As Chip Bruce argues in *The Disappearance of Technology*, when a high degree of fluency is achieved, tools simply become invisible.

Although still expensive, both the price of hardware and the operating costs of being connected to the Internet have tumbled; certainly the utility offered renders the price acceptable, and may encourage a redistribution of spending priorities. (The Ofcom 2014 survey reports less Internet usage in lower-income social classes, but it appears smartphone ownership is sufficiently attractive for it to replace other items in the allocation of a tight budget.) It should not be forgotten that inequalities in economic status and proximity to equipment persist in creating what Jenkins calls the "participation gap" between digital haves and have-nots.

boyd (2014) reports that by 2011 95% of US youth had some form of Internet access. By 2013 a third of the UK population used Facebook every day, and of the daily users some 20 million – 83% – used a smartphone or tablet to check updates on Facebook (Halliday, 2013). She makes many telling observations around the reality that lies beneath the headline figures: access to the Internet is valuable thing, but there is a great difference between occasional use of a PC in a public place, such as a library or Internet café, and owning a smartphone and tablet, both with unlimited data plans.

Digital literacy

Much communication theory leans heavily on gaining an understanding about who is saying what, to whom and with what purpose. This same appreciation is an important life skill, not least for the digital natural, but the ability to identify the purpose(s) behind a communication is acquired with experience; a 15-year-old with quick fingers is unlikely to have as much expertise in assessing the credibility of a source or decoding a marketing or propaganda message, and so forth, than a less dexterous 55-year-old. As boyd discovered in her research for *It's Compli-cated: The Social Lives of Networked Teens* (2014), "Many teens I met assumed that someone verifies every link that Google shares" (p. 184).

Whatever age the individual, to be a natural – to be effective and comfortable in the environment – requires both the capability to think critically and the skills to communicate effectively. The more optimistic promoters of the digital dream (e.g. the cyber utopians discussed in Chapter 8) routinely overlook or sidestep issues surrounding literacy. At the very least, the negative messages that can be conveyed by poor spelling, punctuation and presentation are amplified and crystal-lised by online expression that is, for the moment, largely text-driven.

Practical applications

PR strategists put a lot of effort into categorising audiences and segmenting "pub-lics", and a key demographic characteristic for many campaigns is age. It may be fairly obvious that the target group for some products and services will be defined by how old they are, but the majority of campaigns need to consider quite a broad age span. Others might place emphasis on gender, education, income or lifestyle.

After defining a target demographic, the next stage is to try to identify which plat-forms and channels they are likely to use. Here it becomes useful to consider the extent to which the targets are likely to be digital naturals.

To recap, the characteristic features associated with being a digital natural include:

• Routine access to online platforms (owning a smartphone, having home broadband, etc.)
• Regular use of online platforms for news, conversation and information seeking

- Propensity to share information, opinions and emotions
- Digital aptitude, including the ability to critically assess sources and content, reading and writing skills and motor and sensory skills

Individuals will score differently against these broad groupings, and the groupings, or *propensities*, will need to be subdivided in ways tailored to the behaviour the campaign is designed to influence.

The strategist can then decide to what extent people who share similar values that are linked to the campaign target are likely to be considered digital naturals. If these propensities are expressed strongly in a target group, the ways to reach them will become clear. If the targets are unlikely to be considered naturals, the reason can be identified. For example, certain individuals might be strongly disinclined to share information on social networks but still have ready access to a range of platforms and channels, whereas others may be keen to share but don't have the economic means to participate. The possibility of these two positions, polar opposites, explains why there is no binary negative to the digital natural (compare this with the native/immigrant divide, which is presented as stark, and fixed, based on birth year and associated assumptions which are increasingly hard to justify).

Conclusion

We will no doubt soon reach a stage where the vast majority of people are digital naturals, and the term will lose utility. Digital dualism, the contrived distinction between offline and online, is disappearing, and it is certainly arguable that quite soon no one will think it worth making the distinction. In the unlikely event that the word 'smartphone' is still being used in 50 years' time, the connection with a telephone will be as opaque as the connection between a car's horsepower and riding a horse.

But what is and will remain of significance, even in a world where the vast majority of people can reasonably be described as digital naturals, is the extent to which they feel comfortable with a range of factors, ranging from literacy to the surrender of their privacy.

We must be aware of an apparent paradox in the definition of digital naturals, which is to assume that being competent to operate in the new environment is the same as being comfortable there. Many digital naturals will make good and effective use of online tools and resources but will be only too aware of the trade-offs they make in terms of personal privacy and accountability. The natural athlete may be very good at a particular sport, but he or she will also be aware, even fearful, of the risk of injury.

To be a natural does not mean to be happy, content or secure: the changes we are experiencing are too swift, and the future too uncertain.

Part I

New media and strategic communication

2 The role of communication professionals in the digital age – old paradoxes, new distinctions?

Henrik Merkelsen, Veselinka Möllerström and Sara von Platen

Questions concerning what PR is and ought to be have been debated extensively in literature over the past decades (see e.g. Edwards, 2012, for a recent overview), and the field's failure in terms of establishing a distinct domain of its own, especially in relation to marketing and advertising, has been labelled as an identity crisis (Hutton, 1999). Despite the persistence of these identity struggles, it was not until recently that they were linked to the academic literature on identity. In advocating a new identity for public relations, Ihlen and Verhoeven (2012) have made a first step in this direction. However, discourses on identity are likely to encounter paradoxes (Luhmann, 1995a), and in the empirical study of how social media has affected public relations practice we encountered some paradoxes related to the public relations identity.

In this chapter we summarise central theoretical foundations and results from a study of public relations consultancy in Scandinavia. The study uses the impact of social media on PR practice as an external factor that challenges taken-for-granted assumptions among PR consultants about the nature of their practice. Thus, social media is not the object of our study. Rather, we use social media as a methodological vehicle for gaining insights about what constitutes the core of PR practice – that is, how PR consultants define their own *identities*, *roles* and *practices*. The use of social media by digital naturals drives the need to consider this media influence on the practice.

The empirical foundation of the study is 20 semi-structured interviews with Scandinavian PR consultants and discourse analysis of selected practitioner literature, as well as the content of courses about social media offered by consultancy firms. The reasons for selecting consultants are that they have a clear role as *intermediaries*, their work involves considerable aspects of *commodification* and, since consultants are often first movers in adopting new practices and technologies, they were likely to be *digital naturals*. The general question that motivated the research was to study *how communication professionals in Sweden and Denmark perceive the challenges and opportunities of social media and how this affects their professional role*.

The chapter has three distinct themes: (1) the interplay between theory and practice, which uses paradox theory to advance arguments concerning the *identity* of the overall field of public relations; (2) how PR consultants reconstruct their professional *role* as expert advisors; and (3) the latent issue in PR research of the commodification of PR knowledge.

Paradoxes as a theoretical foundation for public relations identity

While public relations as a scholarly field was born out of practice, recent trends imply a wider societal perspective (Gregory, 2012). Thus, the traditional scope of research in terms of serving practice has been extended to also addressing wider societal implications of public relations practice (Ihlen & Verhoeven, 2012). In assisting this wider perspective a plethora of (mainly sociological) theories have been introduced to the public relations field (Ihlen, Van Ruler & Fredriksson, 2009). These attempts to connect public relations to a wider domain of social theory are highly relevant as practice cannot be fully understood unless its societal implications are taken into consideration. This is evident in ongoing debates concerning public relations' contribution to a fully functioning society (Heath, 2006).

However, when attempting to explain public relations within a wider societal context, it is evident that public relations theory is not an exception when it comes to what Luhmann has described as fundamental challenges of modern societal self-descriptions (Luhmann, 1988). In addressing society, and especially the conditions for social sciences to establish an adequate theory about it, he argues that society is a self-observing system that constantly makes self-descriptions (Luhmann, 1995b). Such self-descriptions are based on the paradox that the system cannot have access to its environment yet it manages to make a distinction between the system and the environment (Luhmann, 1995a). In fact, this distinction is a prerequisite for observation itself. In Luhmann's terminology observing is the act of making a distinction, and this distinction between the system and its environment is then internalised so the system becomes the distinction. This unity is a paradox, and Luhmann concludes, "The world is observable *because* it is unobservable" (1995a, p. 46). As Luhmann notes, from a logical perspective this does not make sense. The system can work with paradoxes through de-paradoxification; only logic is paralysed by the impossibility to dissolve them.

As social science is also a system – that is, a system that observes how other observers observe – the societal self-descriptions produced by social science are also paradoxical. More precisely they are either tautological or paradoxical, the former being a special case of the latter. At the most abstract level Luhmann connects the tautological self-description 'society is what it is' with a traditional positivist sociology trying to account for latent structures and underlying causes of anomalies in society, so that society can again become what it is. In contrast, the paradox of 'society is what it is not' is connected to the more progressive and critical sociology that points out the mechanisms that prevent society from being what it is (or ought to be) (see also Luhmann, 1994).

A pure paradox as a foundation for (any) identity is, of course, unsatisfactory. Paradoxes efficiently block the operations of a system in the sense that meaningful observations require distinctions. But the aforementioned tautology (society is what it is) and paradox (society is not what it is) fail to create meaningful distinctions. The tautology creates unity and thus identity by negating its own distinction, while the distinction made by the paradox simultaneously includes what it excludes.

These sterile conditions for societal self-descriptions are nevertheless bypassed by imposing a self-referential distinction between society and what is not society (e.g. state or individuals). The tensions observed in the relations between society-state or society-individual then offer a wide array of possible self-descriptions based on ideological foundations provided by, for example, functionalist or critical theories. Ideologies serve as de-paradoxication since they successfully overcome the sterility of the paradox. Similar to values, they are immune to empirical evidence and criticism and thus provide a stable foundation for an elsewise hyper-contingent and therefore meaningless reality. In this way ideologies allow the system to be productive and continue its self-descriptions while at the same time blocking insights into the unity of the difference created (e.g. that the distinction between society and individual is a distinction within society).

However, since second-order observations (observing how other systems observe) cannot take place from a privileged position outside society, they are at the same time also just first-order observations. Consequently, for Luhmann paradoxes are unavoidable prerequisites for observing, and the important question becomes how to conduct productive rather than pathological de-paradoxications in order to generate meaningful societal self-descriptions and to acknowledge that this operation renders the paradox opaque but does not resolve it. The paradox may reappear – for instance, when ideology is no longer in touch with reality.

In public relations theory similar self-descriptions based on the aforementioned tautologies and paradoxes have been reproduced for decades in attempts to define public relations and explain its practice. The Excellence tradition and later theories that emphasise public relations' capacity for and obligation to contribute to a fully functioning society share common ideological assumptions that enable them to advance beyond the tautology that 'society is what it is', and similarly the critical voices in our field rest on ideologies that permit de-paradoxication.

Public relations theory thus bases its descriptions on existing ideologies, while controversies between different scholarly positions in the field tend to focus on fundamental distinctions that seek to distinguish public relations from what it is not: public relations vs. marketing, dialogue vs. manipulation, ethical guardian vs. corporate mouthpiece and so forth. While such debates certainly have contributed to "the field's self-reflective institutionalization" (Christensen & Langer, 2009, 129) substantial theoretical progress has been sparse (Merkelsen, 2011), perhaps as a result of pathological rather than productive de-paradoxication.

While Luhmann's constructivism is 'radical', the organisation literature has a more pragmatic approach when using the detection of empirical paradoxes to stimulate theorising. These paradoxes have been broadly categorised in terms of *belonging, performing, organising* and *learning*, and tensions that occur between these facets of social enterprise (Smith & Lewis, 2011). However, despite the more specifically empirical focus on organisational paradoxes, the conclusions about the permanence of paradoxes are strikingly similar to Luhmann's: a paradox can disappear temporarily but will remain latent and is likely to become manifest again.

Contrary to a discipline such as corporate communication that seeks normative solutions to eliminate organisational paradoxes between identity (belonging) and behaviour (performing) (e.g. Cornelissen, 2014; van Riel, 1995; see also Christensen, Morsing & Cheney, 2008, for a critique), paradox literature in organisation studies embraces paradoxes in order to understand their productive forces. And rather than normatively pursuing a fixed, stable identity, the literature is attentive to the condition that identity is paradoxical.

This paradoxical nature becomes evident in attempts to develop theories that seek to account for the unfolding relational dynamics of identity. From the perspective of organisational identity introduced by Albert and Whetten (1985), Ybema *et al.* (2009) notice that the very concept of identity seems to draw these attempts back into essentialism and static thinking. While more flexible concepts, such as roles and role expectations, have been proposed (e.g. Simpson & Carroll, 2008), the problem is not easily solved, neither in organisation theory nor in the broader domain of social sciences, where concepts like identity and ontology continue to trouble the advancement of theories that emphasise the dynamic, relational character of the social (see e.g. Emirbayer, 1997).

Accepting paradoxes as a theoretical starting point may thus be a viable path for public relations literature as well. As Poole and Van de Ven (1989) warn, the quest for internal consistency when developing theories often comes with a high price when seeking to explain a multifaceted social reality.

New media destabilises old distinctions: insights from the study

The advent and rapid diffusion of new media technologies, advanced by digital naturals, change our social realities. New distinctions, such as online vs. offline, become meaningful points of orientation, while other distinctions lose their significance. In this section we present three themes from our study that point to the implications of these changes for public relations.

The paradox of public relations identity

Both in practice and in theory, public relations has sought to distinguish itself from marketing in order to establish a distinct identity for the discipline (e.g. Ehling, White & Grunig, 1992). However, changes in the media landscape with the rise of social media and decline of traditional newspapers affect practice and render this distinction contestable. One of the most significant empirical findings from our study was that although PR consultants emphasised this distinction when defining their professional identity, they were unable to uphold that distinction when accounting for their actual practice. This section argues that the distinction between public relations and marketing has always been based on a paradox: this has been de-paradoxified by the establishment of a conglomerate of distinction, in which the PR/marketing distinction serves as a master distinction.

Old distinctions . . .

It is no secret that the discipline of public relations is characterised by an awkward marriage between theory and practice (Cheney & Christensen, 2001). Discussions about how initial attempts to establish a theoretical core of public relation were intricately interwoven with attempts to legitimise the profession are now old hat (L'Etang, 2006; Merkelsen, 2011). And perhaps it is also time to discard the distinctions that these discussions are based on. But distinctions are resilient and often survive, although their raison d'être has been outpaced by reality. The distinction between public relations and marketing is a legacy from a past where its generative force was to establish a distinct identity for the field of public relations that both in theory and in practice could separate it from its identical twin.

This fundamental distinction has been accompanied by a number of similar distinctions. At the overall arena level where public relations is practised we find a distinction between *society* and *market*. At the actor level we find distinctions between *citizens* (as publics, constituents or stakeholders) and *consumers* (as target groups). At the text level we find distinctions between *dialogue* and *one-way communication*. Such distinctions correlate with similar distinctions between *editorial content* and *advertising*; between *mutual understanding* and *one-sided persuasion*; and between *transparency* and *sugar-coating* and so forth. As a normative foundation we find a distinction between the *democratic ideals* and *market mechanisms*.

These distinctions are not, of course, unique to public relations. But what defines public relations is the way these distinctions are chosen and combined in order to advance arguments about problems and solutions. In other fields similar and even identical distinctions are used differently – for example, in recent marketing literature about co-creation, where stakeholders, dialogue and mutuality are treated as dimensions of the market (e.g. Prahalad & Ramaswamy, 2004).

. . . and new realities

Public relations gains its specific identity from associating itself with the positive side of the distinction and marketing with the negative. That this fundamental distinction between PR and marketing is problematic has already been observed by Hutton (1999), who concluded that PR had an identity crisis. Critical and postmodern approaches, on the other hand, have questioned the positioning of public relations on the positive side of the distinctions. But they have not questioned the distinctions themselves. Rather they have used them as convenient vehicles for criticising the dominant paradigm. This has generated new reflections on the nature of PR and resulted in vivid debates that have established "the field's self-reflective institutionalization" (Christensen & Langer, 2009, 129).

However, the changing media landscape imposes a new reality for public relations and our empirical study of PR consultants' perception of this new reality points to how the distinction from marketing has become problematic. As a result, consultants' descriptions of their professional identity were at odds with the account they gave for their actual practice. When emphasising the uniqueness of PR consultancy they often compared themselves with marketing, leading to statements such as, "*We practise dialogue, they use a megaphone.*"

Establishing this distinction from marketing was a recurring theme in many interviews. It was accompanied by similar distinctions that all served to associate PR with the positive side of the distinction. The emphasis was on features such as symmetry, mutuality and transparency and projected a remarkable concordance with the core vocabulary of contemporary PR theories. However, when describing the challenges of their practice the distinction was not so clear. They would be heavily involved in online marketing, mainly because of the low costs and high synergetic potential in combined paid and 'earned' media space. They would also be more involved in market segmentation because of its convenience. The umbrella term for their activities appeared to be 'content management', a conveniently neutral term that does not indicate whether it is advertising or editorial content.

Reconstructing the public relations consultancy role

The PR consultancy role is primarily defined by and associated with expert skills in media and reputation management (Bernays, 1923; Schilling & Strannegård, 2010; Tyllström, 2013). This professional role has primarily gained its position and legitimacy in relation to the watchdog and gatekeeping function of the journalist and the traditional mass media (Nørgaard-Kristensen, 2003). However, digital and social media have made previously controlled communication processes available to a broader public participation, consequently undermining the gatekeeping function of traditional media institutions.

Reframing the PR consultant role

Professional roles are defined in relation to each other (Biddle, 1979), and the current development implies that public relations has lost an essential point of reference for its role and function. This raises questions concerning the professional expert role of PR consultancy and how it is being refashioned by the changes brought about by social media. This section deals with these questions. Based on critical management studies of consultancy work (e.g. Bouwmeester & van Werven, 2011; Fincham, 1999; Legge, 2002) and Goffman's notion of frames as a way of defining reality (Goffman, 1959, 1974), our main argument is that public relations consultancy is redefining its role as ethical guardians by appropriating values and functions formerly associated with the investigative journalist and traditional mass media. This shift is achieved by frames, claims and definitions pertaining to three areas: the societal and organisational context, required expert knowledge, and the professional values at the core of modern public relations consultancy.

Redefining the organisational scenery – And the problem

First and foremost consultants are involved in reframing the communicative situation, including the threats and promises it may hold for client organisations. The digital landscape is defined as one where traditional mass media and journalism have played out their role. The former threat of gatekeepers and scrutinising journalists is much diminished, and a radically new setting has emerged. Here, according to the consultants, it is the public, using social media, who carry the fate of the organisational reputation in their hands. They are powerful, strong and ultimately able to elevate the organisation to new heights, which is illustrated by one consultant:

> As for example Van Damme's epic splits for Scania. It was shared I don't know how many millions of times. It was so beautiful it made your eyes water.

However, the public can cause serious damage to trust and reputation, as in this example from another consultant:

> A shopkeeper poured a bucket of water over a beggar outside the store, but what he did not know was that someone recorded it with a phone. It spread like wildfire on the social media.

These changes in the media landscape constitute the primary frame created by consultants. Old fears and problems are replaced by new and maybe even more potent ones. In this setting, the organisation is also defined as more exposed to the public eye, and as more vulnerable. This situation and its seemingly inherent challenges demand a solution in terms of professional public relations expertise.

New knowledge and old expertise

Consequently, the second area in which consultants make substantial claims as part of their professional role construct concerns the framing of their expert knowledge and skills. Knowledge is the very essence of consultancy work, and these actors offer their clients a wide variety of services. On the one hand, there are technical, hands-on skills of how to manage social media in terms of tonality, manners, language and measurement. To a certain extent these skills are available to and managed by other actors and groups as well, including the clients themselves. However, in the social media landscape consultants frame this knowledge as pivotal to organisations, allowing them to act as vicarious publics or public representatives with a specific ability to explain social norms in social media, thus helping the client organisation to avoid public failure and image crises. On the other hand, their expert knowledge is framed as *"Knowing what really engages people and how to sincerely deserve their attention."* This knowledge is defined as a traded-down, fingertip, gut feeling, experiential, tacit and to be found only at the very core of successful consultancy work. In particular, this knowledge is unique. It differentiates public relations consultancy from other actors in the communication sector since it rests upon a set of distinctive values and norms.

Some values are (almost) forever

A third area of frames, then, constitutes the norms and values that are said to underpin this expert knowledge. In order to truly engage and deserve attention in the clutter and noise of social media, one cannot simply blurt out any kind of content in a large scale, one-way mode, as, for example, in advertising. Rather, the message and the idea it rests upon have to be authentic, open, democratic, true and essential. It has to get to the very centre of human values, expressed by one consultant as "*If communication ignores people, people will ignore communication.*"

Nevertheless, the role of the consultant is not only constructed as resting upon these socially accepted values. In a redefined social media society it is possible for these actors to make a crucial shift towards the role and professional values formerly claimed by journalists in terms of acting on behalf of the public good and safeguarding common interests. One consultant explains that

> *Social media changes our role because we constantly have to remind the client to review the whole process. If there is something rotten, sooner or later it will get out.*

With the narrative of powerful public and organisational transparency as a springboard, the consultants' professional role is thus increasingly crafted as the scrutiny of the ethical and moral aspects of their client's business. The logic of such claimed professional values is that organisations not only have to look good but also have to do good. Consultants see themselves as uniquely equipped to help client organisations to achieve this goal because their professional role is not primarily supported by commercial values or self-interest but rather by serving the public interest by critically examining the actual deeds of client organisations. We conclude that public relations consultancy is at the very frontline of adaptation, using a paradoxical professional role to adjust to a media landscape and society where firm boundaries, easily defined expertise and institutionalised professional roles and values are no longer valid.

Commodifying social media

In this section we stress how the *practice* of PR commodification simultaneously constructs consultancy commodities and client needs but thereby also contributes to a more or less well-grounded myth that the Internet brings about a strong public sphere. We use the concept of the double bind as our analytical framework. A double bind occurs when a person is exposed to paradoxical communications that create a situation where a person cannot win no matter what she does – of the type "do not do this or I will punish you" or "if you don't do this I will punish you" (Bateson *et al.*, 1956, p. 4). Applying the concept of the double bind to "how-to" books written by PR consultants, this section points out how consultancy discourses constantly create paradoxical messages that make it difficult to find an appropriate solution. Our argument includes a short analysis of how consultancy discourses commodify social media knowledge by creating urgency, imposing double binds and translating democratic ideals into strategic marketing resources.

Creating necessity and urgency

Engagement with social media is presented in the practitioner literature as inevitable because of forces lying beyond the agency of the actors, such as technological revolutions, digitalisation and globalisation. It is claimed that it is no longer a question of choice, as that level of argumentation was left behind long ago. Notwithstanding the matter-of-fact statements of a non-existent choice, it still seems important to create a sense of urgency and pressure in order to persuade actors to go out and communicate. Typically, this is done by creating tensions between threats and rewards.

Recurrent threats in the texts refer to asocial behaviour and backwardness. For instance, it regularly asserted that "people are talking about you on social media whether or not an organization is involved in social media; therefore, you must answer." Not answering the call, the explanation goes, is like turning your back on someone talking to you in real life, implying an unpleasant and antisocial behaviour.

Furthermore it is maintained that organisations not visible on social media will be perceived as "*odd as organizations with no presence in the telephone directory in the seventies or someone who refused to get a website in the beginning of 2000*" (Staktson, 2011, p. 82). Thus, a resistance to social media not only implies backwardness but also could endanger the organisation's very survival – being invisible on social media means being invisible in reality. The arguments draw on fear of lost opportunities and on the discourse of behavioural norms in social life. Proper behaviour is thus the opposite of asocial behaviour and backwardness, which is being communicative, visible, proactive, extroverted and willing to change – personal and organisational characteristics highly valued in Western society.

Imposing double binds on clients

PR consultants also use double binds to maintain clients' need for consultancy and solution. From the consultancy perspective the benefit of double binds is that no matter what, the client will end up with a problem and thus be in need of a solution.

The same arguments that are used to create necessity and urgency are used when establishing the first dimension of the double bind. In more abstract terms this can be summarised as, "You face a huge risk if you do not engage on social media."

This threat, however, is accompanied by pointing to various benefits of a social media presence. These rewarding themes revolve around the dominant discourse in PR: participation, dialogue, transparency, empowerment and civic engagement.

Social media works best when communication indicates mutuality, transparency, personality and engagement, the argument goes. Engagement is implied to be profitable as organisations can, for instance, involve themselves in dialogue and have a productive exchange with the public, disseminate information through networks of friends, and get ideas for new prospects.

Even though engagement may be profitable, it might also be dangerous. This is the second dimension of the double bind, which similarly can be summarised as, "You face a huge risk if you do engage on social media." Engagement implies an active audience. The audience is construed as active by giving accounts of the numerous users involved in social media. It is claimed, for instance, that Facebook has hundreds of millions of users, and when taking into account all those who use its "like" button or comment on different issues, the figure rises to billions, giving an impression of a highly active public. The public is not only active but also suspicious, with a scrutinising and critical gaze. The critical gaze is constructed by way of anecdotal evidence typically drawn from organisations' moral failures.

The public is thus rendered not only a productive source of innovation, creativity and ambassadorship but also a source of danger and pressure, creating the need for both guidelines on how to capture the opportunities by making relations productive and issue and risk management tools. The authors of how-to books portray themselves as the organisational guardians. They rely on an activated public in order to protect organisations from making the wrong choices, guiding them on their path through the new media landscape, created by digital naturals, offering them service when things go wrong. An "active" public enables PR consultants to turn their knowledge as experts in communication technologies into consultancy commodities. Thus, the need to construct an active public comes down to the issue of commodifying knowledge.

Digital public sphere or self-organising marketing network?

However, it would be wrong simply to reduce the construction of an active public to a matter of commodification. The idea of an active public resonates with the core ideals of public relations, which in turn resonate with Western democratic ideals. Thus, the construction of an active public serves to legitimise public relations as a positive force in establishing a fully functioning society, while at the same time creating needs for consultancy commodities.

These two interests correlate in terms of how 'engagement', 'dialogue' and 'friendship' are used in consultancy discourses. These terms draw on democratic ideals and thus create a strong ideological platform that resists any criticism. But when the terms are translated into strategic and tactical arguments, a discursive tension occurs between the interests of the client and the deliberative ideals of the public sphere.

In a concrete and goal-orientated context, the social interaction and communication enter as directly rewarding and productive. The discourse of friendship is typically transformed into that of an ambassador, while dialogue and engagement are transformed into the encouragement of ambassadors to share and disseminate information through networks of friends – in other words, free viral marketing.

Conclusions and future perspectives

In this chapter we have emphasised the importance of distinctions in creating identity for the field of PR, shaping practitioner roles and contextualising actual practice. We have chosen this focus because the advent and rapid diffusion of new media technologies change our social realities. New distinctions, such as online vs. offline, become meaningful points of orientation, while other distinctions lose their significance.

We have presented empirical findings that show how the pattern of distinctions that make up the PR identity has been destabilised – and how the PR consultants in our study have responded to that destabilisation. Our main finding is that the consultants' own accounts of their professional identity and professional practice result in a paradox: public relations is different from marketing, and yet it is the same as marketing.

But when they described their role they also needed to make distinctions that were paradoxical: the traditional PR role is defined in opposition to and symbiosis with the journalistic role and thus rests on a distinction between self-interest and common interest. However, the digital public spheres in social media have no binding force similar to the traditional public sphere that journalists operate in, and hence there is in effect no real difference between self-interest and common interest in social media. One can always choose another public sphere that fits one's self-interest better, with the result that digital public spheres become echo chambers.

When describing PR consultancy in terms of journalistic values and practices, the paradox occurs because this description is possible only when two conditions are met: (1) the distinction between self-interest and common interest is intact – without this distinction the journalist as representing the common interest makes no sense; and (2) the distinction between self-interest and common interest is not intact. The erosion of this distinction is a precondition for redefining PR as journalism because otherwise the journalists would occupy this space. Obviously the two conditions cannot be met, but because social changes do not happen overnight and rarely follow smooth linear sequences the traditional journalistic ethos is still strong, even if traditional journalism is dying.

Adhering to deliberative ideals and at the same time pursuing the commercial interests of their clients become unproblematic for consultants as they are in effect the same.

But engagement, dialogue and friendship on social media are far from unproblematic for their clients. Anecdotal evidence from recent flare-ups provides consultancies with convincing arguments that catch their clients in double binds. Such paradoxical messages ensure that clients end up with a problem no matter what they choose. The construction of an active public in this argument is presented as a Janus face: it is an asset and a liability at the same time.

We are currently witnessing how the hotchpotch of distinctions that is unique to the public relations identity is being reordered. This does not imply that the entire system of distinctions is falling apart. Public relations is indeed still capable of describing itself! But we have argued that some major distinctions have been destabilised. This situation is not entirely negative for PR. Yes, it comes with new threats but also with new possibilities. That said, new distinctions are needed in order to cope with new realities. By exposing some fundamental paradoxes in the PR identity, our study has shown that the principal distinction of marketing does not hold.

In terms of practice it is questionable if PR can maintain a competitive identity if it is based on outdated distinctions. Proclaiming that PR is all about dialogue, transparency and mutual understanding has the obvious shortcoming that PR is also about one-way communication, sugar-coating and one-sided persuasion. But in today's media landscape inhabited by digital naturals, there is an even more fundamental shortcoming. The set of distinctions that used to form the identity of PR is no longer unique. Long-term competitors, such as marketing, and newcomers, such as web developers, all claim to be engaged in dialogue with their audiences.

Under these conditions it is difficult to uphold a distinct identity for PR. On the other hand, this implies new possibilities for merging previously incompatible identities into new identities based on new distinctions.

In terms of future theoretical developments new distinctions will be needed, too. And perhaps, if the paradoxical nature of public relations is accepted as a starting point, these distinctions will be productive. If the problematic relationship between theory and practice is to improve, a good starting point would be to make a distinction at a higher order: a distinction between the distinctions that define practice and the distinctions that define theory. Ihlen and Verhoeven (2012) did just this when suggesting that PR should be studied like any other social activity. Much work is still needed, though, in terms of making distinctions that set apart PR research from sociology as the science of 'any other social activity' par excellence. The questions of what public relations theory is and what it should do still remain.

3 Exploring the language of social media in the discourse of public relations

Philip Young, W. Timothy Coombs and Sherry Holladay

By embracing technology, digital naturals have influenced PR practice in both overt and subtle ways. For instance, as customers began to embrace social media it forced practitioners to enter the realm of user-created content. The lure of monetizing social media channels was far too hard to resist. One subtle yet potentially profound effect is the way practitioners who are digital naturals have been shaping the discourse of PR. This discourse shift reflects PR's love affair with 'relationships'. What we term the discourse of the PR matters because it shapes both its practice and study. This chapter explores the way in which digital natural practitioners (and some academics) have been altering the discourse and considers the implications of that shift. The first section documents the shifting PR discourse both in practice and in academia. The second considers the problematic nature of the shift to relationship-centric language for PR and offers an alternative view through the lens of parasocial relationships.

The language of social media in PR

It is undeniable that the proliferation of online channels and platforms has brought many practical changes to the way the discipline of PR is executed. Some maintain that the changes are superficial, that the business and purpose of PR are unaltered; certainly a significant section of the academic community feels no need to radically realign theory to reflect the paradigm shift proclaimed by the 'digital evangelists'. These debates rumble on, but a strong case can be made that the emergence of what some term 'Web 2.0 technology' has been mirrored by a shift in the language of PR. The claim is that the discipline is increasingly articulating its purpose and culture through discourse associated with social media. Moreover, this shifting discourse is a result of digital naturals both populating the practice and being prime targets for PR activity.

Concepts such as *transparency*, *authenticity*, *conversation* and *engagement* are inextricably linked with the mainstreaming of social media practice; although their usage is not unique to social media (and predates the opening up of platforms and channels seen over the last two decades), the meanings of these terms have to a significant degree been negotiated across social media fora. In this process, many commentators who maintain blogs with a PR focus have developed a lexis that reinforces this progression. In 2012, the UK's Chartered Institute of PR chose to publish *Share This: The Social Media Handbook for PR Professionals*, in which some of the brightest names among the ever-growing band of digital specialists strive to bring the latest thinking to a mainstream market.

This chapter suggests the process by which practitioners have absorbed and utilised the terminology of social media is part of the evolution of the discipline itself. It does not seek to explore links between the texts of social media evangelists and changes in practice (see Chapter 2), as an investigation of the diffusion of ideas is well beyond its scope. It does, however, argue that there are links between the language of digital evangelism and the way that even PR's conservatives and sceptics conceptualise their discipline. It is not unreasonable to take this forward and argue that the change in language reveals a deeper change in the core nature of PR practice. The justification for this claim partly lies in the belief that PR agencies find it necessary to use the language of social media in their ongoing struggle with competing disciplines. The ability to engage in dialogue with stakeholders has been an important tool for those trying to claim space (and budget) for PR, not only from marketing and advertising but also from customer services and human resources, and it made a great deal of sense for PR to claim the language of conversation as its preserve.

Although it would be extremely difficult to trace and identify a robust connection between the work of commentators discussing the conceptual changes that are reflected in PR practice, it is hard not to acknowledge that the work of thinkers including Brian Solis and Steve Rubel has influenced thinking (not least in the approach of Rubel's employer, Edelman, which is positioned as one of the agencies with a higher degree of engagement with social media and an Internet-driven approach). Likewise, the tone of discussion has undoubtedly been influenced by *Naked Conversations* (Scoble & Israel, 2006) and *The Cluetrain Manifesto* (Levine *et al.*, 1999).

Brief analysis suggests ways how PR terminology and practice have been influenced by the discourse surrounding Internet-based communication. Digital naturals are a catalyst in this discourse shift because they are the ones initiating the new discourse. Our observations are rooted in English language discourse, and have a strong UK focus.

Context for the discourse shift: technological change

The term 'Web 2.0' was first used in January 1999 by Darcy DiNucci in an article entitled "Fragmented Future" and is most easily understood as the 'writable web'. Broader usage was encouraged by Tim O'Reilly, when O'Reilly Media and MediaLive hosted the first Web 2.0 conference in 2004. As well as handily describing the emergence of blogging platforms that allowed online publishing without technical skills (to be more fully realised by Facebook), the terminology was part description and part marketing device; the process of identifying emerging trends and articulating them with buzzwords is, of course, central to the commercial development of social media innovation.

The late twentieth century saw the beginnings of a significant change in the way people *receive* information, and from 2000 onwards, the emergence of these Web 2.0 platforms and social networks brought about a radical change in the way people *exchange* information; Phillips and Young (2009) refer to this as a 90-degree flip in the *vector of communication.*

The last two decades have also seen a radical change in the way people *find* information, with the emergence of search and, to a lesser extent, social bookmarking and peer recommendation. To an extent anyone who seeks to find information on the Internet is having their view of the world moulded by algorithms (and perhaps finding themselves trapped in a *filter bubble*; Pariser, 2011).

The proliferation of channels, and negligible cost of Internet-mediated transactions, has impacted significantly on a wide range of business models, from the music industry (iTunes) to the seismic contractions in newspaper sales across most Western countries. It is possible to argue that PR was slow to respond to opportunities of contracting news staffs (see Davies, *Flat Earth News*, 2008, for a critical exposition of PR-driven news production he demonises as *churnalism*) and also slow to exploit *brand journalism* – perhaps because years of bruising encounters had made some in PR fearful of claiming territory defined by the objectivity paradigm of traditional journalism.

Certainly, the fate of media relations is much discussed on PR blogs, from Tom Foremski's incendiary 2006 posting 'Die, Press Release Die! Die! Die!' to a considered analysis of the ways in which technology is killing the business model of (print) newspapers and magazines, and changes in engagement and access that are realigning notions of gatekeeping; that sports stars and celebrities can now communicate directly with fans is worth serious discussion.

Sharing is seen as good, but any historical reading will describe a discipline that found many elements of Web 2.0 profoundly disturbing, not least in its challenge to *command and control* gatekeeping. Blog commentary routinely contains acerbic assertions that, despite the claims of PR, organisations never did control their own messages. (In many cases this was a revelation apparent only in hindsight.)

The production of *user-generated content* and *co-creation* has been fuelled by the development of ever more accessible technologies, but the PR discipline has found this, too, to be a double-edged sword. Despite being considered by some evangelists to have a strong potential, *wikis* have not really moved into the mainstream (except, of course, Wikipedia); image sharing, on the other hand, certainly has gone mainstream, through Flickr and YouTube, and later Instagram and Pinterest. Note that Wikipedia entries, which form an important element of organizational reputation, can legitimately be regarded as conversations, certainly as negotiations – and are often ill-natured and decidedly unsocial. They are also examples of conversations taking place very much outside or around the organization itself, as there is a strong taboo against organizations participating directly in the conversation: We are talking about you, not to you! For a more detailed analysis of Wikipedia entries and corporations, see the research by Marcia DiStaso (DiStaso, 2012; DiStaso & Messner, 2010).

To sum up, any conceptual history has to have technological innovation as part of its spine, but the software innovations that produced sharing platforms, such as Facebook, YouTube and Instagram, were not inspired by the PR discipline.

Discourse change

The language of social media and social network is necessarily soft, and heavily influenced by the framing by Facebook of contacts as *friends* and approval ratings as *likes*.

Much language resonates with the notion of sociability, with an emphasis on sharing, comment and dialogue. Clearly there are business advantages to sharing, which promotes and encourages the continued and expanded use of network-based services, and can contribute to search engine optimisation. As well as being seen as a positive brand value, 'social' is promoted by some as an emerging business model.

There is a shift towards language that somehow conveys authenticity, and away from the language of organisations. Likes and comments are framed within the broad area of engagement, which is again a familiar organisational value, and have more personal implications than the more formal, less colloquial usages, such as 'feedback'. As communication advisers seek to steer organisations towards more social language, it is at least possible to see this in terms of a move from situational analysis of Grunigian application of systems theory to terminology that resonates more harmoniously with the lexis of interpersonal relationships.

The new vocabulary

On the back cover of the hardback first edition, *Share This* claims to be

> a practical handbook for the biggest changes in the media and its professions. It has been created by the Chartered Institute of PR (CIPR) Social Media Panel and was written in the cloud using many of the social techniques that it addresses.

The authors, or those involved in promoting the book, take it as read that the biggest changes involve social media, and are comfortable referring to 'the cloud', a concept that has only recently gained what popular currency it may enjoy.

Share This editor Stephen Waddington co-wrote *Brand Anarchy* with Steve Earl in 2012 and published *Brand Vandals* in 2013. Although not explicitly about social media, analysis of the text shows *Brand Vandals* contains 292 mentions of the term 'social' in its 123 pages, 199 of 'conversation', 39 of 'transparency', 73 of 'save', 73 of 'Facebook' and 93 of 'network'. Presciently, the groundbreaking first edition of *Online Public Relations*, by David Phillips (2001), includes 123 mentions of 'network', 75 of 'share', 68 of 'transparency', 38 of 'social', 25 of 'engagement' and 21 of 'conversation'. By examining the language in these books we can document the emergence of a new PR discourse that reflects the core idea of relationship.

How PR articulates its activities

A useful contribution to the literature of explanation is *What Is Social Media?*, an e-book by Anthony Mayfield (2006). The book noted social media is best understood as a group of new kinds of online media which share most or all of the following characteristics:

> Participation: social media encourage contributions and feedback from everyone who is interested. It blurs the line between the concept of media and audience.
> Openness: most social media services are open to feedback and participation. They encourage voting, feedback, comments and sharing of information. There are rarely any barriers to accessing and making use of content – password protected contented frowned on.
> Conversation: whereas traditional media is about "broadcasting", content transmitted or distributed to an audience, social media is better seen as conversational, two-way.
> Community: social media allow communities to form quickly and communicate effectively around common interests – be that of photography, a political issue or favourite TV show.
> Connectedness: most kinds of social media thrive on their connectedness, via links and combining different kinds of media in one place.
>
> (p. 5)

The point is the discourse in the PR practice has changed to a more relational focus, and this is a direct result of the influence of social media, via digital naturals, on the PR practice. As digital naturals promote the value of social media (and other digital media), they are altering the vocabulary and discourse of PR.

Academics: conferences and articles

One of the first academic conferences to focus specifically on PR and digital media was EUPRERA's EuroBlog Symposium, held in Stuttgart, Germany, in March 2006. The call for papers invited researchers to present empirical findings, theoretical insights or case studies that combine PR theory or communication/marketing theory and social software or focus on an international perspective:

> the Stuttgart symposium will bring together researchers from all over Europe to explore the challenges and chances of truly interactive technologies characterizing the 'Google world', including weblogs, podcasts, wiki, real simple syndication, folksonomies, social insights of EuroBlog 2006, a quantitative

survey on the usage of Weblogs by European PR professionals whose results will be published in early 2006.

This announcement appears to be one of the earliest uses of the term 'social software' in the academic discourse.

> Organisations are becoming more *transparent*, with more information widely available to a huge range of publics. Organisations are also becoming more *porous* or leaky, with any number of individuals or groups, external or internal, supplying their own information to those publics. The PR function cannot *control* the movement of information and opinion on this scale.
>
> (Fawkes & Gregory, 2000, p. 122)

In 2009, Phillips and Young suggested a number of terms to be employed by those seeking to understand online communications. The list includes *reach*, *timelessness*, *transparency*, *porosity*, *abundance* and *aggregation*. Their argument concerning the flip of the vector of communication has greater traction in practice, possibly because it can be translated into communities and conversation.

Drawing on Ye and Ki's (2012) article "The Status of Online PR Research: An Analysis of Published Articles in 1992–2009", Derek Hodge demonstrated a gradual increase in the number of scholarly papers addressing the topic of online PR, but also noted a worrying lack of rigour in their methodology. 'Dialogue' was a dominant term used in 116 articles, 'symmetry' in 47 and 'two-way' in 89.

It would also be useful to assess the content – or lack of content – referring to social media and online PR in practitioner handbooks or general academic texts. Typically, *The Public Relations Strategic Toolkit* by Theaker and Yaxley (2013) devotes just one chapter of 22 to digital PR. Note that Yaxley still warns that there are risks and benefits associated with early involvement with digital technologies. "Social media offer opportunities for two-way communications, including building virtual communities. However, this requires an approach which eschews a publicity model in favour of relationship building with publics, who are treated with respect" (Theaker & Yaxley, 2013, p. 233). Similarly, US introductory PR textbooks treat social media as more cursory than central to the practice of PR.

This review of the evidence indicates how digital naturals are changing the discourse in PR in both practice and academics. 'Relationship' is the core term in this shifting discourse. The relationship focus reflects the academic 'obsession' with the term that predates social media and the corresponding terms digital naturals have brought to PR. However, it is short-sighted to embrace the relationship discourse without reflecting on the problematic dimensions of this shift.

Problematic nature of the relationship discourse

While public relations researchers have been enamoured with applying the idea of relationship from interpersonal communication since 1984, there are those who have questioned the application (e.g. Coombs & Holladay, in press). One example is Thomlison (2000), who posited that 'relationship' serves as a core concept in interpersonal communication and public relations. Terms popularized in public relations via social media (the relationship discourse), such as 'conversation' and 'engagement', reinforce the idea of organizations and stakeholders being in relationships that are interpersonal in nature. Social media allow for the exchange of messages (two-way communication) that creates an appearance of a social relationship. However, any time a theory is taken from one domain and applied in another, there are likely to be problems and adaptations required (Hazleton, 2006).

There are two serious concerns with appropriating the interpersonal view of relationships (social relationships) into public relations. First, even with social media, stakeholders and organizations fit better with the notion of impersonal rather than interpersonal relationships (Miller & Steinbeg, 1975). Impersonal and interpersonal relationships differ in terms of markers for the closeness of the relationship. Examples of closeness markers would be the ability to make predictions about the other, the quality of the information shared, and the degree of trust. There are surface similarities, especially with trust, but the stakeholder-organization relationship appears to be more impersonal than interpersonal. As Coombs and Holladay (in press) noted, "If we pose a typically interpersonally-oriented relationship question like 'what are we to each other?' (e.g. friend, lover, sibling, work colleague), the relational label answers provided by organizations are unlikely to mirror the possible responses within close relationship contexts".

Second, the stakeholder-organization relations are more instrumental than consumatory. Consumatory relationships are valued for their own sake, while instrumental relationships are strategic in pursuit of some objectives. Admittedly there are some instrumental aspects to consumatory relationships. The problem is that stakeholder-organizational relationships are centred on the instrumental aspect of the relationship. Organizations do have the luxury of making friends just to have friends. Organizations monetize relationships with stakeholders because these relationships affect the success and failure of organizations designed to make a profit. We see the instrumental focus of the stakeholder-organization in the metrics used to assess public relations efforts in social media (Paine, 2011). Person-to-person relationships do not place so much weight on the monetizing of the relationship. Instead, the emphasis is on emotions. People do not have investors and employees who are concerned about their economic viability (Coombs & Holladay, in press). The conclusion is that interpersonal relationship is a poor model for the stakeholder-organization relationship, even if the relationship discourse of social media would suggest otherwise.

Parasocial relationships, not interpersonal relationships

If the interpersonal relationship model is not appropriate, how do we capture the stakeholder-organization relationship transpiring in social media? One alternative is to turn to the mass media literature and the idea of parasocial interaction and parasocial relations. Given that digital media do create mediated relations, parasocial relationships might be a much more appropriate and useful way to discussion the relationships that emerge between digital naturals and organizations in that milieu.

Horton and Wohl (1956) noticed a unique form of relationship between spectators and performers. Performers create an "illusion of intimacy" between themselves and spectators that mimics face-to-face relationships (Horton & Wohl, 1956, p. 217). The term 'parasocial' was used to describe this one-sided, non-dialectical relationship that is controlled by the performers. However, the spectators breed a limited sense of obligation for spectators, meaning they are free to withdraw from the relationship at any time (ibid.). A parasocial encounter occurs each time a spectator observes a performer. These encounters are parasocial interactions between the spectator and performer that can be referred to as a parasocial relationship (Ballantine & Martin, 2005).

People have been documented to have developed parasocial relationships with actors, musicians, fictional characters, athletes and websites (e.g. Derrick, Gabriel & Tippin, 2008; Hartmann, Stuke & Daschmann, 2008; Hoerner, 1999; Turner, 1993). The bulk of the research examines how viewers develop parasocial relationships with television characters and news presenters. Regardless of the target, the same dynamic holds true. The person (spectator) perceives that a relationship exists with the target and forms an attachment to the target (Schiappa, Allen & Gregg, 2007). Parasocial relationships are contrasted with interpersonal relationships (close social relationships). Typically, parasocial relationships are weaker and less salient than interpersonal relationships (Ballantine & Martin, 2005). These differences are logical given the one-sided and frequently mediated nature of parasocial relationships.

There is no doubt that stakeholders form some type of relationship with an organization in social media. Stakeholders are following and 'liking' organizational messages, so there is some connection emerging between the two entities. The notion of parasocial interaction (PSI) or relationship seems to capture accurately the stakeholder-organization relationships that emerge in digital media. Researchers have long hailed the interactive potential found in digital media, especially social media. People frequently are interactive with friends and family members in digital media. However, research examining websites, blogs, Twitter and Facebook find little interaction actually occurs between organizations (corporations and non-profits) and their stakeholders (e.g. Rybalko & Seltzer, 2010).

As is evident in many other chapters in this collection, the idea of digital media utilized for interactions is more potential than reality. Digital media are utilized similarly to traditional media because they foster parasocial relationships rather than social relationships. Organizations control the relationships characterized as being one-sided and non-dialectical. For instance, organizations are more likely to promote products and services on Twitter than to interact or to engage with stakeholders in that channel. One of the few instances where interaction occurs is when organizations respond to customer complaints online (Jansen *et al.*, 2009). Organizations are not really part of the conversation; rather, organizations articulate a number of short monologues. Digital media provide an environment where stakeholders can connection with their messages. Instead of being a fertile ground for two-way communication and interaction, the digital media commonly are a barren area, providing one-way communication dominated by the organization.

In physics there is a concept known as exotic matter. Exotic matter is particles that have yet to be discovered but are within the realm of possibility, according to mainstream physics. Exotic matter is hypothetical and can violate known laws of physics. Even with the interactive nature of digital media, true interaction between stakeholders and organizations remains more exotic matter than documented occurrences. While cloaked in the language of interaction and interpersonal relationships, digital media rarely are an actual manifestation of this language. More commonly, digital media provide one-way communication that, at best, cultivates parasocial relationships between stakeholders and organizations.

Interestingly, even in an environment rife with digital naturals on both sides, stakeholders and organizations seem happy with establishing parasocial relationships. Both sides appear willing to satisfice. Stakeholders do not always want close relationships with organizations featuring regular interaction. Most stakeholders simply want certain information that might be useful to them. Organizations do not want to invest the time and money required to create actual interactions (social relationships) with stakeholders. It is easier and cheaper to facilitate parasocial relationships. Perhaps simple connections are the dominant and preferred method for the stakeholder-organization relationship, making parasocial relationships valued by both sides.

Conclusion

This chapter attempts to capture the way the thinking and practices of digital naturals are influencing the discourse of PR. There has been a noticeable shift in the discourse of PR with the emergence of social media. This new PR discourse builds around the core idea of relationships. PR researchers and practitioners were mesmerized with the idea of relationships long before social media, but now the interest has intensified. The focus on relationships tends to treat the stakeholder-organization relationship as a form of interpersonal relationship.

We reviewed the problems with treating the stakeholder-organization relationship as an interpersonal relationship. The idea of an interpersonal (close) relationship translates poorly to stakeholders and organizations. Instead, we argued that the stakeholder-organization relationship is more productively treated as a parasocial relationship. Even in social media, the stakeholder-organization relationship is mediated and dominated by the organization. The relationship is not about interaction but about posting and finding information. We should be careful about overindulging the idea of interpersonal relationships in public relations. Even in an environment populated by digital naturals, the relationships between stakeholders and organization are more parasocial than interpersonal (social). Discourse can be deceiving. PR may talk about interaction with stakeholders, but the reality does not reflect a widespread move to interaction in the stakeholder-organization relationship occurring in digital media.

4 Rotation curation on Instagram

A cultural practice perspective on participation

Cecilia Cassinger and Åsa Thelander

Visual social media offers new possibilities in public relations. Social media is seen as materialising the shift of communication perspective from a transmission view towards a co-creational perspective according to which users create and share their views. While a number of studies have examined public relations and text-based social media (e.g. Wright & Hinson, 2008), less is known about the role played by *visuals* and visual social media. Visuals are becoming increasingly important in social media, partly because they allow people to communicate quickly and succinctly. Visual channels such as Instagram, Flickr and Tumblr currently belong to the fastest-growing social media for young people and commercial actors (*Global*, 2014). Today, social media content is primarily visual and is created, shared, reproduced and disseminated at a higher speed than previously, by both professionals and amateurs, and for strategic and non-strategic purposes (Manovich, 2001; Mirzoeff, 1998; Murray, 2008). Overlaps between the professional and amateur production of images, the strategic and the everyday, raise questions about what kind of vision social media produces and what role this vision plays in democratic processes.

Including everyday practices in communication activities is believed to contribute positively to civic society and engagement. Dahlgren (2006), for instance, argues that civic competencies cannot be understood only within the context of political theory, but must also be analysed from the viewpoint of everyday life, as these competencies are part of the development of the subject. Dahlgren maintains that we need to look beyond the public sphere into the experiential domain of everyday life and its sensemaking processes if we are to understand the origins of civic competence. Thus, he advocates a cultural turn in citizenship studies, which could illuminate the microdynamics of democracy. Social media makes public participation less distinct from everyday activities like consumption, entertainment and leisure. Everyday practices in social media therefore challenge the conventional view of the public sphere as focused on civic rights and responsibilities and as separated from the cultural sphere (cf. Burgess, Foth & Klaebe, 2006). Social media merges the private realm – where people experience and make sense of the public – with the political.

The popularity of the concept of deliberative democracy during the two past decades has underscored the important role played by mundane communication in democratic processes. Deliberative democracy builds on "communicative processes of opinion and will formation that precede voting" (Delli Carpini, Cook & Jacobs, 2004, p. 317), and is discursive talk-centric (as opposed to a voting-centric) (Chambers, 2003). Even though deliberative democracy recognises the key role of communication, it neglects the cultural dimensions of civic engagement and citizenship. The neglect of culture is problematic given that participation in democratic societies is often defined as having the right to contribute to the collective formation of meaning and to be able to access various systems and structures of communication through which needs and desires can be articulated (Deetz, 1992). The ability to contribute in communicative processes is not shaped in formal political settings, but is very much tied to competencies and different kinds of capital (cf. Hermes, 2000).

Approaching democracy from a cultural practice perspective is more apt, we argue, to understand how digital naturals, a group characterised by specific forms of competencies required in social media (see Chapter 1), relate to democratic practice. This group is described as social media–literate and viewed as less concerned with the conventional distinctions between private and public, and political and personal, which become blurred in social media. Work is intimately linked to one's private activities and vice versa.

In recent years, visual social media has been integrated into city branding strategies with the aim of involving citizens in co-creating the image of the city to attract tourists, new residents and capital. This chapter aims to examine the democratic potential of a place-branding strategy where visual social media is used to engage citizens in co-creating images of the mid-sized Swedish city Landskrona. The focus is on the experiences of citizens participating in *rotation curation*, and not on the place-branding strategies *per se*. Rotation curation means that the content creator for a social media account is changed regularly; each week a different person curates the account. This approach has become popular, in particular, in the promotion of places. The best-known campaign is perhaps the Curators of Sweden, which handed Sweden's official Twitter account to selected citizens to market their country to an overseas audience (curatorsofsweden.com). The campaign received much attention and inspired several similar initiatives across the world, but attracted a great deal of criticism after one of the curators made a series of racist tweets. Critics advocated a higher level of control over curators' tweets. The questions we raise in the current study concern the kind of participation that rotation curation in visual social media creates, for whom, and the conditions of participating. Studying how citizens partake in various communication strategies in visual new media is important, we believe, to better understand how everyday culture is mobilised in strategies used for engaging citizens, and what the consequences for democratic processes may be. The study sheds light on the social conventions that underpin the everyday practices of visual social media and their implications for citizen engagement.

The chapter is organised as follows. We first account for the theoretical underpinning of the study departing from a practice-based approach to the production of visual content in social media. Second, we present the empirical case that informs our argument, consisting of citizens' experiences of taking part in the imaging of a city via the online photo-sharing and social networking platform Instagram. We then outline three analytical categories through which the characteristics of visual practices may be better understood in relation to digital naturals. We conclude by returning to the relation between everyday life and deliberative democracy and discussing the implications of the study.

Visual social media in everyday practice

The need to widen the concept of the public sphere to include the realm of everyday life has in part been warranted by the popularity of the notion of deliberative democracy, which underscores the importance of everyday life in democratic processes (Chambers, 2003; Dahlgren, 2006). Dahlgren (2006) argues that deliberative democracy is too restrictive in that it misses forms of speech that unintentionally reach the political sphere. It also neglects communicative strategies such as narrative, irony, visibility and aesthetic interventions, which may disrupt and increase the complexities of dialogue in the public sphere, and in so doing challenges the Habermasian rational view of speech. Cultural perspectives could help us to understand how alternative communicative strategies for example mobilise identities and meanings that become political. The cultural perspective on democracy can also highlight asymmetries and inequalities in communicative processes. Whose voice is heard? Who has the ability to use communicative strategies? The ability to speak in public often correlates with cultural capital and power. In order to apply a cultural perspective lens to communication and citizen engagement, we have adopted a practice-based approach (Reckwitz, 2002; Schatzki, 1996, 2001; Warde, 2005) to studying experiences of participating in a place brand project concerned with curating representations of the city in visual social media. Here, the study is concerned with the practices of producing vision (Bal, 2003), and not the visual representation of the city. Practice theory is not a coherent field of research but an approach based on grand theories (e.g. Bourdieu, Foucault, Latour, Giddens), which focus on social action. Here, the study is concerned with the practices of producing vision (Bal, 2003), rather than the visual representation of the city. The focus on practice, however, means that the researcher accepts a set of basic assumptions, such as that social life is performative, that practices are collectively organised and coordinated by shared understandings, procedures and engagements, and that practices are relational and change over time. Practices are also viewed as combinations of mental frames, artefacts, technology, discourse, values and symbols (Orlikowski, 2007; Schatzki, 1996). A particular combination of these different building blocks constitutes practice, which for example can be "routinized ways in which bodies are moved, objects are handled, subjects are treated, things are described and the world is understood" (Reckwitz, 2002, p. 250). Thus far, there are few studies in which practice theory is applied to amateur photography *per se*, though scholars have argued for an expanded definition of photography practice. Pink (2011) for instance emphasises the role of photographic practice rather than representation. She argues that the definition of photography practices should be expanded to include the experience of being involved in projects and activities where photographs or other visual content is produced. Practice theory acknowledges the role of technique as well as social conventions and personal competence (Larsen, 2005), so amateur photography can be understood as an activity based in everyday practice, conventions and technologies (Schatzki, 1996). Following Pink's use of practice theory in a study of the experience of photography we focus on how "personal trajectories and uses of technology interface with how people experience, imagine and create representations of their urban environments that are related to collective activist projects" (Pink, 2011, p. 95).

Amateur photography

To understand the micro-practice of amateur photography we turned to a classical study of how private family photo albums are produced (Chalfen, 1987, 1998). Chalfen (1987) argues that photographs are embedded in a communication process that includes five events which must be taken into consideration when analysing photography. Hence, it is a communicative perspective on practices of picturing. First is *the planning event*, which concerns when photographs should be made, who makes them, what kind of equipment is used and what kind of preparation in terms of knowledge is needed for taking photographs. Second, *on camera shooting* includes camera technique. Third, *behind the camera shooting* considers who is included or excluded from a photograph and the kinds of settings, environments, activities, events, systematic arrangements, posing, social relationships and verbal instructions, in order to get a feeling of managed presentations. Fourth is *the editing event*, if and how images are arranged or rearranged, and finally, *the exhibition event* is how it is socially organised, who initiates it, promotes or restricts it and when it takes place. The components can be used to describe the operation and how an impression and event are formed into a visual code – the photograph.

Previous research, particularly on tourist photography, pays attention to the role of social convention. Urry (1990) formulated the *tourist gaze* to describe the learned ability of how to see things, which is a collective and culturally shared ability. Ways of seeing and representing places are also mediated, and Urry (2002, p. 151) suggests the *mediatised gaze*, which means that the media make places famous and tourists raise their expectations in accordance with the mediations. Theories about gaze have been criticised for their focus on seeing and vision, not least from a performance perspective. In a study of travel photography, Larsen (2005) outlines an approach to performance which accommodates Urry's (1990, 2002) notion of the tourist gaze in order to acknowledge the social aspect of tourist photography. Hence, practice is guided by social conventions. "When stepping into particular stages, pre-existing discursive, practical, embodied norms and concrete guides and signs usually choreograph tourists" (Edensor, 2001, p. 71).

Traditionally amateur photography has been about creating images as one wishes to see them – that is idealised images. Through choices of what to photograph, how to frame the photographs and what is shared and saved, people construct images of their life and identity. Special events, such as holidays, trips, anniversaries and birthdays, are often photographed. Children tend to be photographed to capture their development (Sarvas & Frohlich, 2011). The function of photography is to document and save for remembrance. Photographs are also used for communicating the present. Photographs are given to friends and relatives to show a current situation. Characteristically, amateur photography focuses on private events and emotions and therefore can appear banal and visually uninteresting to an outsider. Incorrectly, this type of photography has been accused of being insignificant (ibid.). However, from a personal perspective they are important and trigger memory as well as emotions.

Digitalisation has altered the role and function of amateur photography. Cameras are more accessible, and new means to distribute images have emerged. Van House (2011) concludes that prior planning is reduced and photographs are taken more spontaneously, particularly when smartphones are used. As everyday life situations are being photographed to a greater extent, the range of subjects regarded as photo-worthy is extended. Recent research claims that the function of private photography has changed from remembrance to identity formation. We "use digital cameras for live communication instead of storing pictures of life" (Van Dijck, 2008, p. 58). In an empirical study Van House categorised personal photography into four social users – namely personal and group memory, relationship creating and maintenance, self-representation and self-expression. Hence, photographs are taken and shared for self-presentation, affirmation of bonds, mediation of everyday life and sharing of experiences.

Researchers tend to overemphasise the changes due to new technology, claiming that new functions and behaviours have replaced old ones. However, recent empirical studies of photography (Pink, 2011; Van Dijk, 2008) suggest that "old" ideas, practices and technique are integrated or exist parallel to the new ones. Shove and Pantzar (2007) believe that practices of digital and analogue photography are interrelated. In sum, new technology has not replaced practice that was based on previous or "old" technology; rather the different types of practices are intertwined.

Imaging the city on Instagram

The theoretical argument unfolded in this chapter is based on a case study of an initiative to market and brand a city involving Instagram implemented by Landskrona, in southern Sweden. Landskrona seems to be among the first to have embraced the strategy of rotation curation on Instagram, and one can expect other cities to emulate the strategy. Hence, this is an example of a *deviant case* (Patton, 1990), a case in the forefront where knowledge can be expected to be interesting for others. The initiative was launched to counter negative media attention focusing on assaults and honour crimes. Each week different citizens control the municipality's official Instagram account and publish his or her photographs from the city. From the perspective of the city administration, sharing the official account with citizens is believed to increase participation in civic life among local actors and create a sense of belonging, ultimately promoting a more positive image of the city. Participants are recruited from volunteers who register their interest on the municipal website. The official requirement is that participants should have a personal Instagram account. Since Instagram is an application, participants also need a smartphone. Instructions for the participants are few but have been developed as the project has progressed. The account had about 800 followers at the time our data was collected.

In order to learn about amateur photography practice, personal experiences of participating in the place-branding initiative were captured through qualitative photo-elicitation interviews (Burt, Johansson & Thelander, 2007; Clark-Ibanez, 2004; Collier & Collier, 1967/1999; Harper, 1998, 2002). The interviews were conducted in July and August 2013. By then 30 citizens had been responsible for the account, and half were selected for the photo-elicitation interview. The rationale for selection was to find participants who reflected as many different experiences as possible. Male and female participants of different ages were selected. Those who had received the most likes or comments were chosen on the rationale that their photographs must have evoked feelings and must be meaningful for visitors. Participants engaged in different phases of the project were also selected. Instagram photographs taken by respondents were used to let them develop ideas of their own photographs and the conditions for producing them.

Experiences of participation

The lack of instructions from the project manager on how to image the city led to participants interpreting the task in various ways. To make the task meaningful, the participants activated knowledges and competencies. To use Dahlgren's terms, different everyday competencies were activated based on previous experience and knowledge, which in turn had consequences for how the task was performed. Three ideal types of Instagram photographers were identified: the *tourist*, the *strategist* and the *professional*. Ideal types originate in the work of Weber (1978), who defines them as an abstract analytical construct that will never be discovered in this specific form (see e.g. Aronovitch, 2012). The researcher constructs ideal types based on selected characteristics, so consequently they are about differences. In the typology ahead, characteristics of the ideal types of users are presented.

In the following text we focus on the ideal type of the strategist, which we identify as the digital natural. This type of participant activates knowledge from social media to perform the task. The task is easily integrated in their everyday use of social media. They are skilled in using different social media services, and their use of the account appears to be strategic and professional compared to the other groups. Social media and Instagram conventions, however, guide strategists' practice.

Planning – Sharing personal moments

Social media is a special thing since it is not possible to separate – at least not for me who is so involved and works so much with it, work and leisure. That is the way it is. Work and leisure merge. I may well use my job account to post photos of a weekend activity.

(Lisa)

The photo task is easily integrated into the strategists' everyday use of social media. They take and publish photographs on a regular basis, so this task merely encourages them do so more frequently. According to this group it is necessary to publish one photograph per day during "their" week. They publish less frequently on their private and professional accounts.

Participants claim that they want to counterbalance the negative image of the city. Compared to the other ideal types, the strategists focus on photographing activities and people rather than buildings and picturesque views of the city. In the interviews the strategists dissociate themselves from the postcard view of the city. Instead they want to inform others about ongoing projects and events, and they publish photographs of work-related activities, like meetings, workshops and seminars.

I did not think that I would gain anything from it personally, but that it was a good way of marketing the Fire and Rescue Service a bit. (. . .) I mean we want to reach out to people. Amongst other we have problems with stone throwing and, well, people shoot rockets at us and point green laser at us, and all that. I thought that Instagram is a media which the kids use and that they might be more influenced by images here than in some magazine.

(Benjamin)

The engagement with mundane work life distinguishes the strategist from the other types of users. They see activities that they are involved in themselves as photo-worthy, so they share them with others. The function of photography is to share a moment based on what the photographer perceives as interesting. However, the focus on mundane events and personal experiences makes the photographs uninteresting and insignificant for participants in the other ideal types. The tourists and professionals often did not recognise the contexts and people photographed by the strategists. Moreover, they viewed posting personal aspects of work life as attempts at personal branding and thus a misuse of the account.

The strategists emphasise the importance of the instant character of Instagram, where photographs should be spontaneous and reflect a moment. In contrast to the tourists who plan activities and places to visit, this group does not schedule or plan anything particular during the week they are responsible for the account. They seem to be confident that "interesting aspects" will occur spontaneously.

The strategists have an imagined audience for their photographs. They speak about audiences in terms of followers of the account. Their idea of audience is related to users of Instagram, which means that they are not necessarily geographically bound to the city. Although they may have a clear idea of who follows their own personal accounts, they are less certain about the identity or location of followers of this account.

Photo shooting – To be instant

It is enough to use a smartphone camera. It is called Instagram because it is instant. I mean it is supposed to be spontaneous and capture the moment.

(Lisa)

Participants used their own smartphones to take the photographs. Hence, the device is familiar and easy to use. Moreover, it is in line with their ideal of instant photography, so they are not restricted by any technical limitations the camera may have. Likewise, they apply the same reasoning to photographic technique. "Instagram photographs should not be technically perfect." The instant character is more important, and it is the value of using Instagram. It is essential that the photographs appear spontaneous.

Although digital capture makes it easy to take many photographs, and then review and choose the best, participants do not seem to take full advantage of the possibility. They take few photographs, select and apply a filter to improve the image and then publish it instantly. Professionally trained photographers struggle with the instant ideal. It goes against their professional instincts to publish imperfect photographs.

Behind photo shooting – To be authentic

First I planned to take black and white photographs and focus on architecture but it turned out differently. I thought that I have to be more general and show what I think is beautiful and it has to be spontaneous.

(Cara)

In line with the importance placed on the instant character of the photographs, this group does not want their photographs to appear staged or arranged. Spontaneous, natural, relaxed and real are words they use to describe what they want to achieve.

It is unthinkable to publish non-contemporaneous photographs, and they are upset when other users have published obviously "old" photographs. In this case they criticised participants who published photographs clearly taken in the summer during a week in winter.

Instagram conventions guide their planning, choice of motifs and way of photographing. In the quote earlier, a women talks about how her original idea does not fit the Instagram conventions. Colours are important, and you should appeal to a broad group of followers.

Editing – Filtered expressions

Instagram filters are used to improve photographs. Enhancements include creating better photographs (contrasts and colours). The strategists used filters but reflected on their use, and criticised other users for inappropriate use of filters. They themselves published photographs without filters and hashtagged them "#no filter". In contrast to the other groups the strategists had the technical understanding needed to download and utilise third-party filters. Hence, they were not restricted by the affordances of Instagram and could employ their social media knowledge to expand their creativity.

Possibilities for editing are greater than ever. The large range of filters provided by Instagram makes it possible to retouch photographs. At the same time filters mean that nothing new is produced – only altered. Technologically mediated reality is displayed. The use of filters underscores temporal orientations, in particular the past orientation. Instagram offers many different vintage filters that make an event look old, while being shot in a modern context. For the strategists, a filter was a way of expressing mood and atmosphere; sometimes the decision not to use filters was itself expressive.

Display – Strive for "likes"

The strategists have the self-imposed objective of increasing the number of followers for the account during their week. Drawing on their experience of Instagram and other social media they apply strategies for increasing follower numbers, including using hashtags and geotags.

The strategists are particular about likes as this is a way to increase interest in the account. They have well-developed ideas about which types of photographs generate likes, and two stand out. First, well-known and picturesque views of the city are known to generate likes. The popularity of the overly simplistic postcard view, however, annoys them. Second, they think that photographs of well-known people generate likes. Followers like photographs of people they know.

> In my view this photo says less than this one with the visit of the equality minister. It's strange that in terms of likes, that this photo of the cinnamon buns received double as many likes as the one of the minister.
>
> (Christina)

The strategists expect photographs to generate likes, and regularly check the account. During their week, they visited the account several times a day. Likes represent immediate feedback on their photographs. On the one hand, likes are stimulating for themselves, and on the other hand they are seen as a reward for followers. "You should publish photographs that your followers appreciate," as one strategist expresses it (Amy). The goal of achieving many likes guides their selection of photographs to publish. Consequently, in order to please both themselves and their followers they also post postcard views of the city. It seems contradictory that they, on the one hand, want to photograph interesting and different aspects of the city, and on the other hand seek likes, which are based on familiar and well-established aspects. Instead of pursuing their ideal of presenting interesting and personal images of the city, they chase likes by publishing photographs that they suspect are attractive to a broad audience.

Another type of feedback is comments. To reply to comments within a reasonable time is expected behaviour on Instagram, according to the strategists.

Controversial photographs, comments and replies are avoided; the tone of voice is polite. In one of the comments, for instance, a strategist's posts are criticised for focusing on work life and meetings. In her reply the participant politely explained her point of view, choosing not to start a quarrel, which would be her normal reaction, as it was not "the right place". Hence, the official status of the account means that the strategists do not want to make it a subject for debate. This group explicitly states that they do not want to publish too many photographs during the week they are responsible for the account as it disturbs the flow at Instagram. One photograph per day seems to be their goal, but they usually end up with around three. Therefore, they also criticise participants who publish too many photographs.

> Some participants publish 50 photographs. They do not think in terms of quality of a photograph. They just want to show a moment. . . . I think they spam. They occupy the stream. If I have 50 followers and one of them publishes 50 photographs I will not be able to see photographs of anyone else.
>
> (Tim)

The strategists are especially particular about social norms of what constitutes a correct and accepted post. For example they are careful about maintaining the distinction between the private and public life and have explicit strategies for what to publish on different accounts. The borders between their private Instagram account, their professional account and the official city account were important to them. They were reluctant to display their private life and did not want to feature their friends and family, or reveal details about their private life in what they posted on the city account. Hence, they presented a personal, but not private, image of the city.

Conclusions

In this chapter we have applied a cultural analytical lens to experiences of participating in a project of imaging the city in new visual media. The aim of the research was to examine the democratic potential for a city's branding strategy where social media is used to engage citizens in rotation curation. The initial questions concerned the kind of participation that such strategic initiatives create, for whom, and the conditions of participating in them. Our findings show that adopting a communication strategy based on visual social media is dependent on citizens' competencies and capital and is embedded in everyday life. In particular we observed that participants took on three major roles, which we labelled tourist, strategist and professional. The different roles were tied to the use of different social conventions in photography. Digital naturals produce what can be called an Instagram gaze that guided their practice and had consequences for the photographs taken and published. The Instagram gaze makes us see events – in our case the city – through a social media lens where actions are staged in order to be experienced in a particular way. Posts are often produced to amuse, entertain or please other followers. Hence, integrating Instagram into a communication strategy does not necessarily mean that novel images are generated, but that they are choreographed according to the conditions of Instagram as a medium. It is suggested that the Instagram gaze involves a more complex relationship between the dichotomies of private and public, and personal and political. From our observations, the Instagram images which received the most likes were characterised by the portrayal of people and the use of innovative filters. Participants made use of everyday culture to make sense of citizenship and their relation to the city. On the platform of Instagram the overlap between the public and the private sphere is a necessary and an important characteristic of the medium. Another key feature of Instagram as medium is the focus on the "here" and "now", the "instant". The consequence of this time frame is that posts become short-sighted and very much focussed on the needs of the present (often tied to the number of "likes" that might be attracted). The search for likes means that little time is left for reflection of past, future or alternative imaginings of the city. Likes are dependent on followers immediately recognising an image and finding it attractive. To be easily recognised, the image must follow certain conventions and be encoded in a particular way.

What, then, does this say about citizen participation and democracy? According to Crang (1997) the failure to collectively imagine different pasts and futures in the present makes a message apolitical. Another way of understanding this is to say that time and space are compressed in visual social media and it is not possible to imagine anything but what is right here and now in front of the participants. The vision of the city constructed through Instagram leads to disorientation and disruption in the experience of time and space, which smooth over potential conflicts on the media platform. Hence, within the confinements of visual social media, public participation becomes apolitical. Time-space compression leads to a fairly homogenised view of what the city and citizenship mean; it could have been a city located anywhere because the photography follows certain conventions of photographic practice that are not limited to a particular time and space. In view of this finding it is uncertain what the political implications for the city are. We may wonder what is created through strategically organised forms of participation and what it does to the city and those living there. As a final concluding note, visual social media involves a high degree of interaction but little interactivity. The lack of interactivity may indicate an overly strong belief in previous research on what can be accomplished in political terms through co-creating meanings and images in social media.

To minimise any reputational risk associated with losing control of the official account, the city administration seems to have entrusted it to "safe hands", in this case local celebrities, city employees and politicians. The selection of participants raises questions of asymmetries in power and who can participate in the project. Social inclusion is the ambition of the project, but in contrast to social justice participation takes place on terms set by the municipality and social conventions. Our study clearly shows that the ability to participate in defining the city is tied to high levels of social and cultural capital. To deliver social justice an agenda for achieving equality must be developed. At the same time this controlling approach leads to a homogenised and even stereotyped vision. It is likely that a bolder selection of participants would have led to more diverse expressions.

5 Social intranets and internal communication

Dreaming of democracy in organisations

Mats Heide

By the time I defended my dissertation in December 2002, intranets had become a naturalised media that was widely used in both private corporations and public organisations (Heide, 2002a). But when I started my doctoral studies in the mid-1990s, intranets were still in their infancy and not yet widely employed by organisations. The intranet was then regarded as the hottest and coolest media for internal communication, and communicational professionals were greatly excited to have a new medium in their toolbox. They wished strongly that intranets would improve communication professionals' status and internal legitimacy. The intranet was a "new media" and believed to have great potential for improving internal communication. As so often before, expectations were high – it seems that whenever a new media has been introduced, it has been accompanied by unrealistic expectations (Marvin, 1988). Typically, these might include improved relations between people in different countries, regions, organisations or departments, democratisation, the reduction of time and space and more efficient learning processes. In an organisational context the introduction of new media is often related to expectations of changes in the organisation structure and production, such as a flatter hierarchy, increased productivity and more cooperation between co-workers (Orlikowski *et al.*, 1999).

The swift implementation of new information and communication technology (ICT) media in organisations during the 1990s can be explained by the computerisation movement – that is the strong, general discourse that depicts computers as universal tools for improvements of various kinds (Iacono & Kling, 2001). A global report by McKinsey (2013) shows that 89% of companies use at least one type of social media – an increase of 17% since the previous year. According to the report, social media was most often (83%) used for internal communication. Even if most large organisations have some form of intranet with tools for social interactions, there are few examples in the research literature of successful social intranets. One challenge is that different consultant reports on organisational communication show that the larger part of a communication departments' budget is allocated for covering the costs of running, updating and managing the intranet. Paradoxically, the intranet is often the media least appreciated by the co-workers. This is a surprising result given the prevalence in the workplace of digital naturals who readily embrace similar media in their non-work lives.

This paradox is certainly frustrating for communication professionals who still believe in and have large expectations for the social intranet. Another challenge is the fear of democratisation. Many organisational leaders believe that transparency, increased access to information and boosted communication among organisational members will challenge existing power structures, since information and knowledge are power (cf. Foucault, 1980). Nonetheless, the real concern should be that an increased information and communication flow never appears in many organisations, as usage is too low (cf. Friberg, 2011).

This chapter discusses the use of social media, and more specifically the social intranet, in internal organisational communication and identifies what is needed to improve democratisation processes in organisations. I discuss what we mean by a social intranet, and then briefly present earlier intranet research, followed by a discussion of dreams that arise with the introduction of new media. The final section examines the value of informal communication in organisations.

On defining social intranet

An intranet can be defined as an internal Internet protected from encroachment by users outside an organisation with the aid of firewalls, which aims to improve internal communication, to facilitate access to and exchange of information, and to function as an interactive working tool (Heide, 2002a). Implementing an intranet challenges the traditional publisher-push model of communication and encourages a pull model, where organisational members are expected to be active and keep themselves informed by taking part in published information (Telleen, 1997b). This change was a paradigm shift in internal communication and initially caused great problems in many organisations, especially when it was decided that all internal information should be published on the intranet. Old media, such as house magazines and minutes, were transferred into digital form. This was particularly problematic for co-workers who did not have individual access to a computer, perhaps having to share a terminal with several others during lunch breaks, and so they did not get as much information as before. Another effect was to give co-workers new possibilities for publishing information themselves. Consequently, co-workers had to acquire several communication roles – users, authors, publishers and information providers. In my dissertation I discerned two intranet arenas – an information arena and a communication arena (Heide, 2002a). Hence, by the mid-1990s the interactive and social function of an intranet was already highlighted and seen as its most important aspect.

At the time when social media, such as Facebook and Twitter, had become commonplace, there evolved a discourse on *intranet 2.0*, which emphasised the social functions of the media. Intranet 2.0 was gradually replaced by the concept of a *social intranet*, which today is the most common term. Kaplan and Haenlein's (2010, p. 61) frequently used definition of social media is "a group of internet-based applications that build on the ideological foundation of Web 2.0 and that allow the creation and exchange of user-generated content". Social media can, in a more straightforward way, be defined as a "media for interaction" (Mangold &

Faulds, 2009). The social aspect of an intranet is the opportunity to both create content and distribute it to other users in the network. Social media has several characteristics that are highly valued in internal communication – interaction, co-creation, discussion, user-generated content, multi-model communication and dialogue, all characteristics are supposed to result in increased communication quality and in "improvements in operational efficiency, team collaboration, innovation, and cultural transformation" (Young & Hinesly, 2014, p. 427). Simply put, a social intranet can be defined as "an intranet which contains several different social functions where coworkers can easily contact, communicate and share knowledge with each other" (Lundgren, Strandh & Johansson, 2012, p. 11).

We can only speculate why the word "social" was added. The term "social intranet" could be interpreted as a statement that intranets have developed from connecting people to information to connecting people to people. However, in some sense it is a "shop window arrangement," signifying no real or fundamental change. In other words, "social intranet" sounds better and more comprehensive and may increase the status of the media. And social intranet tends to suggest new possibilities among users, not least among communication professionals, who once again seem to hold such expectations for the medium. In some way social intranet is an oxymoron since the social aspect, such as interaction, cooperation and dialogue, has always been an important element. Intranets usually develop through three stages, the last one being cross-functional communication (Bark & Heide, 2002). This stage is reached when organisational members are using an intranet's social networking and discussion group tool. Already in the mid-1990s (Bark, 1997) the reasoning was that the real value of an intranet shows when dialogue functions are used on a wide basis in an organisation. However, almost 20 years later these social aspects are not widely used. Several reports show low adoption of social media in organisations (e.g. Bradley & McDonald, 2011), which is often explained by suggesting that organisational members lack digital literacy or are hesitant about new technology (Young & Hinesly, 2014). Another explanation is that there must be a "critical mass" of users for social media to be a success in an organisation and a leadership that facilitates a collaborative organisational culture (ibid.). However, it is interesting to note that none of these explanations are new. In 1997 it was underlined that a collaborative culture is fundamental to a successful intranet (Bark, 1997).

Research on social intranets

Social media has received considerable attention from scholars across different disciplines. In fields such as strategic communication and public relations, social media has been studied as a vital part of an organisation's core communication strategy (Khang, Ki & Ye, 2012; Weinberg & Pehlivan, 2011). The potentials include user interaction, which in best cases produces more involvement (Kaplan & Haenlein, 2010), and co-creation (Gustafsson, Kristensson & Witell, 2012). According to research, social media offers organisations new possibilities for communicating and relating to different external stakeholders or groups, thereby building and maintaining better relationships. There is a strong general belief that social media campaigns will produce a synergetic effect, where users share, discuss and diffuse a company's marketing message in their personal networks, which in turn can have a large influence on sales, reputation and, in the long run, the organisation's existence (Kietzmann *et al.*, 2011). This outcome has been studied when it comes to relationships with customers (e.g. Malthouse *et al.*, 2013), but relationship building with organisational members through social media remains a neglected research area.

A search in the EBSCO database on the term "social intranet" rendered only one record – Lüders (2013). This research examined the adoption process of a social intranet in an international ICT company. The one conclusion from the study is that there are two archetypical users – the contributor and the reluctant user. The latter uses an intranet only as an information channel and not for dialogue or interaction. Lüders also concludes that the reluctant user will hardly ever transform into a contributor.

An extended database search on the combination "social media" and "internal communication" resulted in merely three articles in the scientific journals *Business Horizons* and *Public Relations Review*. In the first article, Omilion-Hodges and Baker (2014) propose that internal stakeholders have received little attention from scholars compared to external ones. They underline that managers pay more attention to external stakeholders when it comes to organisation branding and organisation identity. The conclusion is that everyday talk in organisations produces organisational identities and has a strong influence on external perception. Members act as important ambassadors when they speak about their organisations in both professional and private contexts (Heide & Simonsson, 2011). They incarnate the organisational values – *live the brand* – so there is then a high probability that they both enjoy work and do well. If these ambassadors are digital naturals, their use of social media may well lead to them sharing and spreading their understanding and positive attitudes towards the organisation to a wider audience.

At the same time, it is fairly common for organisations to develop virtual communication strategies which state how to produce and maintain good relations with different external groups (Kelleher, 2006). Internal communication firms rarely have any strategic plan for communication with internal "stakeholders" – that is co-workers – and they misjudge the value of co-workers as ambassadors of the organisation (Omilion-Hodges & Baker, 2014).

The second article, by Ruck and Welch (2012, p. 301), is a review of internal communication effectiveness assessments, and one conclusion is that "internal communication theory and assessment has not caught up with the impact of social networks and media within organizations." And finally, Verčič and Verčič (2013) argue that the use of social media in universities tends to level the power distance between professors and students. In other words, very few articles have been published on social media and internal communication. Some texts refer to research on social media use within an organisation, but this appears mainly in conference proceedings and has not yet reached traditional research journals. This is somewhat strange as practitioners rank both social media and internal communication as very important issues in surveys, including the European Communication Monitor (ECM) and equivalent studies. I share the opinion of Ruck and Welch (2012) that research is still missing in organisations when it comes to internal social media. Scholars in strategic communication and public relations mainly pay attention to external communication, and those within organisational communication who do focus on internal communication seem not to be much interested in social media as a phenomenon. The latter is confirmed by a search in *Management Communication Quarterly*, a highly ranked and prestigious research journal that mainly publishes in the field of organisational communication. A search of its database for January 2003–October 2014 on the term "social intranet" returned no records at all, while "intranet" returned only two: Vaast's (2004) "O brother, where are thou? From communities to networks of practice through intranet use" and Child and Shumate's (2007) "The impact of communal knowledge repositories and people-based knowledge management on perceptions of team effectiveness". Both concern organisational learning and knowledge management through the use of an intranet. Vaast (2004) reports that *communities of practice* can use an intranet to expand the identification and experiences of common practices with remote colleagues beyond the local level. Communities of practices are highly situated and develop through mutual interaction and face-to-face communication when co-workers work together (Lave & Wenger, 1991; Wenger, 1998). As an effect of the collaboration they develop common work practices and an identity – for example teacher, hairdresser and communication professional. Wenger, McDermott and Snyder (2002) claim that local communities of practice can expand through the use of ICT and develop *networks of practice*. These networks do not share the same social work context, do not interact directly and could never be as strong as communities of practices. However, they can produce a sense of common professional membership and share practices (Vaast, 2004). According to Vaast, the use of the intranet by communities of practice produces an emergent complementary relationship between the local and network level. Child and Shumate (2007) have tested which of the two knowledge management (KM) strategies work best: intranet as an information/knowledge repository or a people-based knowledge management approach (cf. Hansen, Nohria & Tierney, 1999). The first KM strategy aims to collect knowledge (i.e. information) in a database accessible from an intranet, and the second connects organisational members with others with certain experience and expertise. Intranet as a knowledge repository is an expression of and belief in *technical determinism*, where it is taken for granted that access to information *per se* can "give" users new knowledge. The people-based KM strategy is founded in a sociocultural understanding, where communication and sense making are seen as vital for the production of new knowledge (Vygotsky, 1978). Earlier research has shown that a people-based KM strategy is more effective in practice when it comes to complex problems and situations (cf. Heide, 2002a). Child and Shumate (2007) recommend that managers offer communication training, emphasise relationship building and support the development of communities of practice.

In the latest handbook of organisational communication (Putnam & Mumby, 2014) we find one chapter that discusses a related research area – namely ICT in organisations. Equivalent chapters also appear in earlier handbooks (see Jablin & Putnam, 2001; Jablin *et al.*, 1987). ICT in organisations is a broad field that emerged at the end of the 1950s and early 1960s, as scholars in communication, informatics and management began to focus on this phenomenon. There are two distinct streams within this research area. The first focuses on the use of technology and how it influences the informal and formal organisational structures; the second pays attention to the relationship between ICT and how organisational members communicate with each other. According to Rice and Leonardi (2014), the two streams have merged, since both handle aspects such as influences, implementation, use and outcomes. Their review of research on ICT and organisations shows the adoption and use of ICT are not solely an individual decision but influenced by individual, social and institutional contexts. Factors such as intra-organisational norms and agendas, emotions towards a certain ICT, power and organisational culture can each influence use. As with many other research fields in organisation studies there has been a development from understanding ICT in a technologically deterministic way to a social constructionist pole (cf. Falkheimer & Heide, in press). Today the use of ICT is understood as a product of social negotiations and influence (DeSanctis & Fulk, 1999; Fulk, Schmitz & Steinfield, 1990).

Radick (2011) claims that in most cases intranets are more frustrating than supportive and helpful to organisation members. For Radick a fundamental problem is that the technology rules, not co-workers' needs for certain functions. To the frustration of communication professionals many intranet functions and tools are used either improperly or never at all. Nielsen (2013) pinpoints that social tools are often kept separate from the broader intranet, which might make it a social stack and another silo of information. Too often social tools are not integrated into the intranet. Members prefer to use e-mail and personal networks for information distribution and for knowledge exchange and production (Heide, 2002a). Surprisingly, this situation seems still to be true in many organisations – co-workers prefer to use e-mail (cf. Radick, 2011). Scholars have also reasoned that digital naturals, those who are comfortable with social media, also prefer to use these media in a professional context. Nevertheless, research shows this is not necessarily always the case (Friedl & Verčič, 2011).

New research by Young and Hinesly (2014) summarises factors that are believed to make social media more optimal for internal communication compared to traditional media. They list four factors: (1) communication among organisational members in an international organisation independent of space and time, (2) synchronous and asynchronous communication, (3) easier storage and retrieval of information compared to traditional media, such as e-mail and written documents, and (4) the formation of virtual groups for team projects. Virtual groups can also be used as a tool for improving management communication – from CEO to employees – by using video streaming. The social aspect here could be posting comments and voting. In other words, such communication is an example of democracy in organisations.

In sum, research on social intranets is very limited. At the same time there are floods of journal articles, websites and white papers produced by and aimed at practitioners. The abiding impression is that most are written by IT and organisational consultants who wish to sell more products and services by encouraging grand dreams of more efficient communication and democratic dialogues.

Wishful dreams of new media

As mentioned earlier, technological determinism still prevails and people in the Western world are often fundamentally positive towards new technology, as exemplified by a quote from a professional technical journal:

> Social media opens new possibilities to make individual coworkers and their competences visible. Such things are hard to measure in money but the investigations that we have conducted show great profit in the long run.
>
> (Åsblom, 2012, p. 14)

This is a typical view and expectation of what social media can accomplish. There is also a strong belief that social media platforms offer an open arena where people can discuss different political standpoints, which in the best cases increases organisational democracy with more involvement and participation in decision making. Further, there are many dreams that social media can reduce power distances between managers and co-workers (Verčič & Verčič, 2013). However, Hampton *et al.* (2014) report that people in general are reluctant to reveal their political opinions and speak out about policy issues in social media. This tendency is explained by the *spiral of silence*, a classical theory by Noelle-Neumann (1974), which states that individuals prefer to suppress their opinions if they know or assume their audience will not share their beliefs. An effect of this is that only the opinion of the majority will be present in public debate, and in an organisation co-workers tend to be hesitant to express their views that differ from the colleagues' or managers'. Hampton *et al.* (2014) conclude that the Internet reflects the offline world, and the belief in social media as a free, democratic communication arena is nothing but a chimera.

Back in the mid-1990s when ICT was slowly being introduced into organisations, there were hopes that it could improve cross-lateral communication and learning in large organisations. In 1997 I noted people were generally over-optimistic about the potentials for new media to tear down barriers and flatten organisational hierarchies (see Heide, 1997). However, a new media could not *per se* change communication patterns or structures in an organisation (Heide, 2002b).

Whenever a new medium is implemented in an organisation it is profoundly influenced by managerial procedures and practices, and reflects power hierarchies (cf. Eriksson-Zetterquist, Lindberg & Styhre, 2009). An intranet facilitates distributed leadership, where organisational members participate in decisions, what Telleen (1997a, 1998) terms a distributed organising model. In most cases it requires changes in the organisational culture, and a willingness among managers to change communication patterns and structures. A problem in almost every organisation is that new learning and knowledge stay where they are produced and are not shared with other organisational units. In other words, learning tends to function rather well within a smaller unit, but aggregated learning is more problematic. Bradley and McDonald (2011) claim virtual communities can improve cross-lateral communication, and thereby also organisational learning. Leistner (2012) delivers the same reasoning, claiming that bridged silos will lead to improved efficiency and decline in redundancy. One way to reach a bridging is to increase collaboration between co-workers in different units by teamwork. According to O'Leary (2012) social media enables collecting and sharing information and knowledge from various sources. However, a large challenge for all managers and communication professionals who want to improve internal communication and make an organisation more democratic is that most people need an a priori communication relationship before they approach other organisational members (cf. Yuan *et al.*, 2009).

In sum, a more critical and reflexive approach to the dreams of what the use of social media in organisations could achieve and change is missing. I would like to propose more research on the value of everyday talk or informal communication in organisations, and how internal social media (i.e. social intranets) could facilitate this form of communication and improve organisational democracy.

The value of everyday talk

In the early 1900s the value of everyday talk in organisations was emphasised by Chester I. Barnard (1938/1968) in his bestseller *The Functions of the Executive*. Communication scholars and others have increasingly emphasised that everyday talk is vital and fundamental for human understanding and sense making (Weick, 1969), the building and maintaining of relationships (Tracey, 2002), learning (Vygotsky, 1978) and the ongoing identity construction process (Alvesson & Empson, 2008). However, organisational leaders have not embraced word of mouth to any larger extent. On the contrary, informal communication has too often been understood as negative and deleterious, related to gossip and incorrect information that deceive organisational members. Many managers today still have a rather low understanding of the value of everyday talk.

Past research showed that e-mail was the most used and valued media among co-workers at Ericsson Mobile Communication in Lund (Heide, 2002a). More than a decade later, e-mail still seems to dominate internal communication, even when managers state that social enterprise system should be the primary media (Young & Hinesly, 2014). The employees I interviewed at Ericsson underlined that they preferred to use the more informal e-mail, because they were afraid of the publicity in discussion groups, which hindered their participation. They did not want to "make fools" of themselves by asking "stupid" questions that all employees could read. Further, they were hindered by the knowledge that their conversations were stored and searchable. Other aspects mentioned were the absence of incentives to participate in virtual discussion groups, and that high specialisation made knowledge sharing difficult. Ericsson employees had their own solutions, using e-mail distribution groups and local servers, to share experience and expert knowledge.

This grassroots solution seemed to work well since the members shared similar experience and education when working on the same project. Employees also felt they had better control over who participated in discussions and who had access to the information. Once again we can conclude that information and knowledge sharing tends to function well on a local level but is more problematic on an overall organisational level. My findings still appear to be valid, and new research confirms workgroups use "new ICT to share knowledge with each other when they perceive that it enhances their professional reputations, when they have experience to share, and when they are structurally embedded in a network" (Rice & Leonardi, 2014, p. 434). The same tendency is evident when it comes to sharing negative upward communication (cf. Heide & Simonsson, in press; Tourish & Robson, 2003). Negative information is essential for decision making; without it, there is a large risk that decisions are based only on information with a positive bias. For Harige and Tourish (2004, p. 204) an organisation without upward communication is like "a bird with one wing". The problem is that middle managers often hinder the information flow and prevent negative information from co-workers from flowing upward to top management (Tourish, 2005; Tourish & Robson, 2006).

Conclusion

There is a general and strongly held belief that the fast development and implementation of new (social) media will be reflected with an equivalent fast development in communication practices. This belief is reinforced and spread by the popular media and pop-management literature describing dramatic and revolutionary organisational changes produced by social media (cf. Rice & Leonardi, 2014). Sometimes this story is reproduced in research articles – for example Young and Hinesly (2014). But while technology changes fast, human behaviour, habits and practices in organisations tend to develop much more slowly. Returning to my old research field, I can verify that not much has changed in communication practices and patterns in organisations as an effect of social media. Certainly that is what my literature review shows.

We still know too little about what wider use of social media in organisational communication, with an increased visibility of co-workers' communication and "transparency", might bring. As digitals naturals populate the workplace, there is a solid base of employees to utilise the social intranet. There is also a clear ironic paradox here. As the new millennium began Starck and Kruckeberg (2001, p. 52) stated, "Through communication/transportation technology, new communities can and are being formed, yet anomie and societal fragmentation exist perhaps as never before." Even when we have new and advanced ICT at our disposal, traditional power structures and communication practices do not change by themselves. If we want to know how social media could support and facilitate more democratic organisations, scholars in strategic communication must conduct more qualitative case studies which include aspects such as culture, structure, management practices and power in their analysis. The lesson that we have to learn from history is that we should always be vigilant towards all forms of technical determinism, and ask what factors other than a new medium are needed to change practices in an organisation.

6 Digital naturals and crisis communication

Significant shifts of focus

W. Timothy Coombs and Sherry Holladay

As digital media made its entry into strategic communication, many practitioners tried to leverage that development into a business. Some consultants rang alarm bells about the revolution that had occurred. Crisis communication is one of the areas of strategic communication where consultants were alarmist. Crisis management involves the management of information and meaning through the pre-crisis, crisis response and post-crisis phases of crisis management (Coombs, 2010a). Managers were told that everything they had known about crisis communication was worthless. For a price, these insightful practitioners would help them to navigate this new digital environment. Financial self-interest aside, the effects of digital media on crisis communication have been evolutionary rather than revolutionary. Digital media, or more precisely the willingness of stakeholders to use digital media, has changed crisis communication in many ways.

The stakeholder use of digital media embodies the digital natural's comfort in using these channels. Moreover, stakeholders communicating using digital media are reshaping crisis communication in a myriad of ways. Yet the changes reflect the need to modify existing practices more than rendering existing knowledge and practices obsolete. This chapter identifies the various ways digital naturals have helped to transform crisis communication. The chapter structure follows the three-phase model of crises by examining the influence of digital media on the pre-crisis, crisis response and post-crisis phases of crisis management and communication.

Pre-crisis phase: changes to mitigation and preparation

The pre-crisis phase is composed of mitigation and preparation. Mitigation seeks to reduce or even eliminate crisis risks. Preparation involves the actions organisations take to be ready when they must actually face a crisis. Digital naturals' proclivity for digital media requires crisis managers to adapt their traditional mitigation and prevention efforts.

Mitigation involves efforts to identify and to scan for crisis risks. The increased use of digital media by stakeholders (digital naturals) is causing new crisis risks. Comments in online channels can damage reputations and precipitate a crisis. Such comments might involve a perceived problem with a product or displeasure with the sources an organisation contracts with in its supply chain. Traditionally, mitigation efforts focus on crisis risks related to operational concerns. Crisis managers must scan new sources of information for crisis risks and develop new categories and analytic tools for the new reputational risks. We will return to this point in the discussion of paracrises.

Crisis preparation centres on developing the crisis management plan and training the crisis management team. The crisis management plan might include pre-drafted messages that can be released immediately after a crisis occurs (Coombs, 2015). Pre-drafted messages originally included news releases and some web page information. With today's digitally savvy stakeholders, the pre-drafted messages should include tweets, Facebook posts and other social media texts. Crisis teams need to include the social media manager to ensure consistency in the crisis messaging. Furthermore, crisis team training needs scenarios involving reputational risks that transpire online. It is problematic if the social media messaging does not recognise that a crisis exists or places messages online that are incongruent with the crisis messaging.

Employees are a unique stakeholder during a crisis. They can be victims of a crisis and always have a stake in the crisis because of the way crises can harm their employer. The research on internal crisis communication has found that employees are often under-informed during a crisis (Mazzei & Ravazzani, 2011). Social media tools, including internal social media, can be used to update employees. Employees can be ambassadors during a crisis by representing the organisation to their friends and families (Frandsen & Johansen, 2011). Informed employees make for more effective crisis ambassadors. Crisis plans must include the employees. Moreover, if employees are digital naturals, they may post to their social media accounts about the crisis. Organisations should embrace rather than attempt to stifle employee crisis-related communication during a crisis. Employee social media posts can be beneficial to the organisation if the employees are informed about the crisis. Employees can be encouraged to report only verified information provided by the organisation but be free to express that information in their own voices.

The shifting nature of crisis and the emergence of the paracrisis

Crisis management and communication developed in the 1980s primarily to address crises that disrupted or threatened to disrupt organisational operations, what can be called operational crises. Over the last five years, organisations have seen an increase in reputational crises. Reputational crises can be defined as "the loss of the common estimation of the good name attributed to an organization" (Booth, 2000, p. 197). Sohn and Lariscy (2014) refined the definition of reputational crisis following Fischer and Reuber's (2007, p. 25) idea that "an organization has a reputation for something". They defined reputational crisis as "a major event that has the potential to threaten collective perceptions and estimations held by all relevant stakeholders of an organization and its relevant attributions" (Sohn & Lariscy, 2014, p. 24). Moreover, Sohn and Lariscy drew a distinction between corporate ability (CA) and corporate social responsibility (CSR) reputational crises.

CSR becomes a critical factor in reputational crises. Corporate reputations are accepted as valuable, intangible asset for corporations (e.g. Deephouse, 2000; Turban & Cable, 2003). Currently, over 40% of the corporate reputation is derived from stakeholder perceptions of CSR, making CSR a critical element of reputations (Fombrun, 2005; Smith, 2012). CSR can become a crisis risk. If stakeholders perceive an organisation to be acting irresponsibly, the corporate reputation is damaged (Bebbington, Larrinaga & Moneva, 2008; Eisenegger & Schranz, 2011). Managers must be concerned about CSR-related reputational crises. A CSR reputational crisis "is conceptualized as a major event that poses a threat to reputation associated with norms and values cherished by society and socially expected obligation" (Sohn & Lariscy, 2014, p. 25). One way in which a CSR reputational crisis emerges is when stakeholders attempt to redefine current organisational practices as irresponsible (Coombs, 2010b; Coombs & Holladay, 2012b).

The crisis management literature has a category of crises known as challenge crises. In a challenge crisis, stakeholders claim an organisation is operating in an immoral or irresponsible manner (Coombs, 2015; Lerbinger, 1997). For instance, Greenpeace has claimed that H&M was irresponsible because it used certain toxic chemicals in its supply chain (Coombs, 2014). In essence, the challenge is a risk rather than an actual crisis. If more stakeholders accept the challenge, the challenge has the potential to damage the organisation's reputation. However, if handled effectively, the risk is mitigated and the reputation remains largely intact. CSR-based challenges are really paracrises. A paracrisis appears similar to a crisis but is actually a situation in which an organisation is forced to manage a crisis risk publicly (Coombs & Holladay, 2012c). It is important to note that the number of paracrises is on the rise (King, 2011).

Digital media have become the favoured tools for creating paracrises (Coombs & Holladay, 2012b, 2012c). The challengers seem to be digital naturals who are comfortable using various online communication channels in their efforts to redefine corporate practices as irresponsible. Digital naturals are a driving force in the rising number of paracrises. Paracrises are creating a significant shift in crisis communication. In the past, most crisis risk management transpired in private. Paracrises move crisis risk management into full view of stakeholders. In turn, crisis managers need to make communicative decisions about how best to respond to the attempts to redefine their current practices as irresponsible.

The response options for a paracrisis differ somewhat from the basic crisis response strategies because risks are not the same as an actual crisis. The basic response options for paracrises are: (1) refusal, (2) refutation, (3) repression, (4) recognition/reception, (5) revision and (6) reform. Refusal is when managers choose to ignore the CSR-based challenge. Some challenges pose no real threat to an organisation and can be dismissed. Refutation is when managers counter argue. There are times when managers must defend their current practices and claim what they are doing is right. Repression involves efforts to prevent the challengers from disseminating their messages. This is a dangerous strategy because it can lead to charges that the organisation is violating a group's right to express themselves. Recognition/reception occurs when managers acknowledge a problem but take no action. Revision is when managers make some changes to their practices but do not make all the changes desired by the challengers. Reform occurs when management makes the demanded changes and even notes the challenger's role in facilitating the change process (Coombs, in press).

Crisis response phase: new channels and tracking

The crisis phase focuses on the immediate response to the crisis and guiding the organisation and stakeholders through the disruptive period that a crisis can create. Digital media use is altering the channels used during a crisis and how organisations can track reactions to crisis communication. Moreover, digital naturals as stakeholders are increasingly becoming part of the rhetorical arena, adding their voices to crisis communication efforts (Frandsen & Johansen, 2010a, 2010b).

The most obvious way digital media influences crisis response is that there are now more channels available to an organisation when responding to a crisis. Among the core beliefs in crisis communication is the need for a quick and consistent response. Digital media has a role to play in both. The beauty and curse of digital media are that it allows for a fast response. Managers can quickly post messages to digital media outlets, such as Twitter and Facebook. The curse is that stakeholders come to expect very fast responses. During a crisis, managers must still deliberate over decisions as well as seeking and verifying information. The need for careful, deliberative action can translate into what is often perceived as a "slow response." Speed is relative, and digital media has created rather unrealistic expectations about how quickly an organisation can and should respond. The pre-drafted messages discussed in the pre-crisis section are one way of increasing the speed of the crisis response. At least the organisation can be quick to release an initial holding statement.

There is a school of thought in crisis communication that social media channels have a unique effect. The belief is that there is a channel effect that causes stakeholders to react differently to a message depending on whether it is delivered via a social media channel or a traditional media channel (Schultz, Utz & Göritz, 2011; Utz, Schultz & Glocka, 2013). However, the data from the studies can also be interpreted as a stealing thunder effect. Stealing thunder occurs when an organisation suffers less damage from a crisis when the organisation itself is the first source of information about the crisis. An organisation does less damage if stakeholders first hear about the crisis from the organisation than if they hear about it from another source, such as a news story (Arpan & Pompper, 2003; Claeys & Cauberghe, 2010). A recent study indicates that social media use in a crisis is more likely to have a stealing thunder effect than a channel effect (Coombs, Claeys & Holladay, in press). However, an argument can still be made for a channel effect. Regardless of the interpretive framework, there are some distinct advantages to utilising social media channels as part of an organisation's crisis communication response.

Consistency helps to maintain the credibility of crisis messaging. It appears odd when an organisation's social media messages show no relationship to its crisis messages, a point raised in the pre-crisis communication section. For example if the organisation's website has crisis information but its Facebook page does not mention the crisis and instead is promoting the latest marketing effort, critics will notice the inconsistency and discuss such inconsistency in social and/or traditional media. The social media manager should be on the crisis management team to help ensure consistency between the organisation's crisis messaging and social media messaging. Social media channels do not have to become the organisation's crisis broadcasting system, but there needs to be some connection to and recognition of the crisis.

As noted earlier, researchers in internal crisis communication wisely have argued that employees can become ambassadors to external stakeholders during a crisis (Frandsen & Johansen, 2011). In essence, employees are a very credible channel of communication for reaching the family and friends of employees. When employees are digital naturals, they can use digital media to echo the organisation's crisis messages. There is always the risk that employees will present a different message from the organisation. However, if employees are kept well informed and encouraged to share the crisis information, the odds are good that the vast majority of the employee posts will reflect the interests of the organisation that employs them. Most employees want the organisation to perform well in a crisis because it serves their interests as well.

Stakeholders who are digital naturals are willing to post comments about the organisation's efforts to manage a crisis. Researchers have shown crisis managers can track stakeholder reactions very easily through blogs, comments on news articles and social media posts (Coombs & Holladay, 2012a, 2014; Valentini & Romenti, 2011). While not a representative sample of stakeholder reactions, digital media messages do offer a rough real-time evaluation of how people are reacting to crisis responses. Their reactions indicate whether an organisation needs to adjust its crisis messages – whether the crisis messages are being accepted or rejected.

As digital naturals post messages about the crisis and the organisation's crisis management efforts, they become part of what Frandsen and Johansen (2010a, 2010b) call the rhetorical arena. A rhetorical arena is the space that opens before, during or after a crisis and is created by the voices of the actors talking about the crisis. Besides the organisation in crisis, the rhetorical arena can include other voices, such as political actors, the media, consumers, activists and community members. The rhetorical arena is the first true multi-vocal approach to crisis communication. Most crisis communication research and theory are univocal – they centre on the voice of the organisation in crisis. Crisis communication comprises multiple speakers and listeners. The rhetorical arena model has a macro and micro level. The macro level involves mapping the voices that emerge in the rhetorical arena. The micro level is composed of four parameters: genre, context, media and text. The four parameters serve as filters that affect all mediated strategies. The macro level is the most salient aspect of the model for this chapter because digital naturals are inclined to add their voices to the rhetorical arena via digital media.

The rhetorical arena is a revelation in its argument for the need to consider a variety of voices communicating about the crisis (Frandsen & Johansen, 2010a, 2010b). The "other" crisis voices can be important contextual factors that limit or enhance the organisation's crisis communication efforts. If an organisation is lauding its crisis communication efforts while customers are posting comments about how ill-informed they are and how callous the organisation appears to be, who are other stakeholders likely to believe?

Digital naturals are willing to populate the rhetorical arena, and crisis managers must recognise the potential influences of the "other" voices in the rhetorical arena. The mapping of the various voices in the rhetorical arena is more than simply monitoring stakeholder reactions to a crisis. The stakeholder messages may have nothing to do with the organisation's response to the crisis but still affect how people react to the crisis and the organisation in crisis. Considering how other crisis voices shape the crisis context is a larger concern than simply examining reactions to the organisation's crisis communication efforts.

Post-crisis communication: evaluation and communication concerns

The post-crisis phase is when an organisation is returning to regular operations or "business as usual". The idea is that the urgency of the crisis has passed but there are still crisis-related factors that the organisation must address. Some of these factors are internal, and some are external. The internal factors involve evaluation of the crisis management effort, while the external factors involve the continuing need for crisis communication.

Internal factors: evaluation

There are two elements of crisis communication evaluation: (1) performance and (2) effectiveness. Performance involves the evaluation of the effectiveness of the crisis team and the crisis management plan during the crisis response. The team performance as a unit and individually is examined for strengths and weakness. This knowledge is used in efforts to improve team performance and to enhance the value of the crisis management plan. Effectiveness means to what extent the crisis communication effort achieved its goals. Common goals in crisis communication include decreasing the amount of negative media coverage about a crisis, the ability to place the organisation's message in the crisis media coverage, and the accuracy of the crisis media coverage. Given the importance of digital media, evaluation of crisis effectiveness needs to consider both traditional and social media sources (Coombs, 2015). It is not enough to assess the common crisis communication goals only in traditional news media. Social media sources can be important venues during a crisis and their content can be evaluated as well (Coombs & Holladay, 2014).

External: continuing crisis communication needs

The fact that the urgency of the crisis has passed does not mean the need to communicate about the crisis ends. Stakeholders often make inquiries during a crisis. The crisis team may not have the necessary information and may promise to send that information when they have collected it. In fact, one element of the crisis management plan is to track stakeholder inquiries (Barton, 2001). Post-crisis is the time to review those requests and to ensure the information requests are fulfilled as promised. Following up on information requests builds credibility and trust with stakeholders. The amount of requests and variety of stakeholders requesting crisis-related information have expanded due to digital media use. News media representatives are not the only stakeholders making informational requests that need to be taken seriously. For instance, influential bloggers, activists or community groups might use digital media to make information requests that require an organisational response.

The main effects of the crisis might be over, but that does not mean all the effects from the crisis have passed. The organisation might need to provide updates to stakeholders about how the crisis has affected its operations. Examples would be airlines updating passengers on the effects of a severe snowstorm on flight disruptions through Facebook, or Boeing using Twitter to update interested parties on the progress of company efforts to resolve the battery problems on its new Dreamliner. Social media channels are ideal for posting updates about information. The updates should include progress and results of any investigations into the crisis event.

A significant aspect of any crisis response is adjusting information – communication designed to help stakeholders cope psychologically with a crisis (Holladay, 2009; Sturges, 1994). Digital naturals often turn to digital media to help cope with the trauma from a crisis. For example stakeholders often create digital memorials to honour the victims and to commemorate the event as a means of facilitating healing (Coombs, 2015). Digital memorials are a form of adjusting information – messages designed to help people to cope psychologically with a crisis. Organisations must decide how they will relate to digital memorials. The initial question is "Should the organisation create a digital memorial?" A more important question might be "If a digital memorial emerges, how should the organisation relate to the memorial?" When stakeholders create the memorial, organisations must consult the creators of the material. If the creators do not want the organisation involved, those wishes must be honoured. When the organisation is the cause of a crisis, victims and those close to them may not want the organisation involved. However, the organisation should recognise the existence of the memorial in its crisis messages as a sign of respect.

The discussion of memorials and healing raises an interesting point about crisis evaluation. Crisis evaluation is about the organisation, not the stakeholders. This does make sense because it is the organisation in crisis that is conducting the evaluation. However, given the new digital platforms for communication and stakeholder willingness to use them, we may need to rethink evaluation to include stakeholders. We will elaborate on this point by considering the potential problem of the organisation-centric view of crisis communication.

The organisation-centric view of crisis communication

From its origins in corporate apologia, crisis communication has considered the organisation's reputation as a dominant outcome variable (Hearit, 1995, 2006). Consider how image repair/restoration theory (Benoit, 1995) and situational crisis communication theory (SCCT) (Coombs, 1995; Coombs & Holladay, 2002), the two dominant theories in crisis communication research (Avery *et al.*, 2010), centre on reputation. The emphasis on organisational reputation as the primary outcome variable reveals the strong organisation-centric focus of crisis communication theory and research. By far the dominant concern in crisis communication is the effect of the crisis on the organisation. However, there is some research that focuses more on the crisis effects on stakeholders, including work on instructing and adjusting information (Holladay, 2009; Sturges, 1994) and the discourse of renewal (Ulmer, Seeger & Sellnow, 2007). Kent (2010) is one of the researchers who have argued for a need to focus even more on stakeholders during a crisis. As documented in this chapter, digital naturals have shifted crisis communication thinking and practice. One final influence of digital naturals on crisis communication might be a shift towards a more stakeholder-centric view of crisis communication.

The discussion of reputation as the outcome variable for crisis communication indicates how researchers and practitioners are defining effective crisis communication. Defining effective crisis communication as protecting the organisational reputation is a specific reflection of the organisation-centric focus of crisis communication. Changing to a stakeholder-centric view of crisis communication would require a dramatic shift in the measures of crisis communication effectiveness. Crisis communication effectiveness from a stakeholder perspective should involve providing timely warnings, stakeholders engaging in behaviours that protect them physically, and taking action to help stakeholders cope psychologically. Note how these effectiveness measures are derived from instructing (tell people how to protect themselves physically from a crisis) and adjusting information (Holladay, 2009; Sturges, 1994). It should be noted that focusing on the victims (stakeholders) yields reputational benefits for an organisation in crisis as well. However, the measures of effectiveness would be based on the stakeholders and not determined entirely by the effects on the organisational reputation, purchase intention, share price or some other organisational variable.

Crisis communication researchers and practitioners rarely examine instructing and adjusting information or utilise them as outcome variables. As a consequence, we know little about what makes for effective or ineffective instructing and adjusting information, nor do we have precise tools for assessing the effectiveness of these messages from the perspectives of stakeholders. As noted in this chapter, there is a growing need to consider stakeholders during a crisis throughout the entire crisis process, from scanning to reactions to crisis messages. Again, this need to consider stakeholders is driven by their increasing use of digital media, and that, in turn, increases their salience in the crisis management process. It is logical to include a shift in evaluation to stakeholder crisis concerns. After all, if stakeholder needs are poorly addressed during a crisis, the displeased stakeholders are likely to discuss these issues in social media. We have seen such discussions about poor treatment of "victims" during the Costa Concordia sinking and crisis communication efforts. Digital media and the willingness of stakeholders to use it (a digital natural mentality) should result in a greater consideration of stakeholder effects when evaluating crisis communication efforts, thereby eroding the heavy organisation-centric bias in crisis evaluation.

Conclusion

Digital naturals are comfortable in the online environment. Their attitude towards and use of digital media are being felt in the developing field of crisis communication. In this chapter, we have outlined the various ways the increased presence of digital media is changing crisis communication. The commonly used three-phase model of crisis management was utilised to highlight the many ways digital media has resulted in adaptations to existing crisis communication practices and thinking. Digital media has touched every facet of crisis communication, from prevention and preparation to response and follow-up communication. Crisis managers who have not adapted to digital media will find their crisis communication less effective than those who have embraced the changes.

This is another instance where digital naturals are a driving force in changes to strategic communication practice. Crisis managers cannot ignore how crises warning signs appear due to stakeholder use of digital media or the role digital media can play when communicating crisis communication messages to stakeholders. Digital naturals are creating a more complex environment for crisis managers. Ashby's (1956) law of requisite variety holds that the repertoire of response to a problem must be as diverse as the problems the responses address. The idea of requisite variety has had a strong influence on organisational theory. Strategic communication and crisis communication have ties to organisational theory, making the law of requisite variety applicable to them as well. As outlined in this chapter, crisis managers must respond to the complexity added by digital media by incorporating digital media into all relevant facets of crisis communication. To address the new challenges created by digital naturals, crisis managers must adopt the mindset of the digital naturals.

Part II
Modern democracy

7   The dream of enlightenment within digital reach?

Concepts of modern democracy

Howard Nothhaft

In the very last paragraph of his three-volume series on the Information Age (*The Rise of the Network Society*, 1996; *The Power of Identity*, 1997; *End of Millennium*, 1998) Spanish-born Manuel Castells, one of the world's foremost communication sociologists, arrives at a fairly optimistic conclusion. On the eve of the twentieth century, Castells contended in *End of Millennium*, human society might well stand on the doorstep of a bright future: "The dream of Enlightenment, that reason and science would solve the problems of humankind, is within reach" (1998, p. 359). Far from being naively utopian, Castells makes it clear, however, that he considers the door closed at present, even blocked. For the human to enjoy sustainable material well-being, reconciliation with nature and even reinvigoration of spirituality, far-reaching changes have to take place:

> Our economy, society and culture are built on interests, values, institutions and systems of representation that, by and large, limit collective creativity, confiscate the harvest of information technology, and deviate our energy into self-destructive confrontation. This state of affairs must not be.
>
> (Ibid.)

The core question of the NEMO project asks what consequences the emerging new media have had, have now and may have for 'modern' democracies and community engagement. The questions to answer are (1) *whether*, (2) *for what reasons* and (3) *under which conditions* Western citizens can expect a more democratic, more modern democratic or simply 'better' society to emerge from the advent of ICT (information and communication technology) and social media – in every case understood not only as technologies but also as cultures. The issue under scrutiny, in other words, is whether 'digital democracy' comprises the 'institutions and systems of representation' Castells had in mind.

It is of course naive to expect a clear-cut answer. When scholarly authors address complex matters, answers come bundled with their own questions. In order to discuss the various and differing answers seriously, it must be made clear, therefore, *what concept of democracy* the respective author assumes. For that reason, this chapter disentangles the different concepts of democracy which are tacitly and implicitly assumed when authors argue for or against new media's potential for a better society. It is based on a loose, synoptic literature review which draws on earlier work by Lincoln Dahlberg. The review takes some liberties in order to facilitate understanding,[1] but begins and ends with an attempt to systematically map the positions.

Mapping the territory

In order to systematically map the positions, let us begin with the assumption, to be discarded later, that we have at least a working conception of democracy – that is we know what going in the right or wrong direction means. With a working conception in mind, we can map the utopian and dystopian extremes. The utopian extreme is, of course, that the brave new media world will inevitably, due to the frequently postulated inherent democratic nature of communication technology, not only be factually more democratic but also be perceived as more democratic. In addition, the more democratic society will also be more functional – for example provide a better material life for its citizens on a sustainable basis. The dystopian opposite would be that social media democracy will inevitably, again due to some inherent quality of social media and not because of other factors, be less democratic, and also be perceived as less democratic. Moreover, the brave new media society will become dysfunctional – for example unsustainable and simply a bad place to live in.

Then there are utopian and dystopian variations. Maybe the most prominent dystopian variation is illustrated by society becoming less and less democratic without people noticing. On the contrary, they are delighted to live in a 'free' world where they can *buy* anything with just a click of the mouse. In its care about the consumer of old, the dystopian picture is reminiscent of the position of the Frankfurt School, and as such favoured by left-wing, anti-consumerist intellectuals like Zygmunt Bauman. It is taken up, however, by critics of the recently revamped cyber-libertarian movement, scholars such as Dahlberg. Dahlberg (2010) points out that the producer-consumer (prosumer), the 'DIY-citizen' of a 'Web 2.0-democracy', deludes him- or herself in an even worse way: not only consuming and paying for content but also *producing* content, *unpaid*, for capitalist site owners, while engaging in a cyberspectacle of ultimately pacifying character, similar to drug use. The experience of freedom, once again, is what 'ensnares' us: "the passivity of the cyberspectacle is induced through the very interactivity celebrated by cyberlibertarians and other digital democrats" (ibid., p. 341).

The alternative right-wing horror scenario is a deterioration of society's *functionality*. Because of more and more 'democratic' squabbling, because *everything* is under scrutiny, because previously sacrosanct authorities are subject to ridicule in silly YouTube videos, and secret documents delivered into the hands of the public by the likes of Julian Assange, nothing gets done anymore: the nation grows weak and falls prey to its adversaries internal or external.

The term 'conservative' already suggests that conservative intellectuals are less concerned with the introduction of *new* democratic institutions, and more concerned with the status quo's *functionality*. That is why conservative democratic theory does not figure prominently in this chapter. It is always there, however, in the form of nagging questions: What about order? What about prosperity? What about things *working*? What about our *enemies*? David Graeber, one of the most prominent anarchist theorists, arrives at the same conclusion. He argues that right-wing and left-wing political conceptions are fundamentally different insofar as they are rooted in different conceptions of the 'realities' of power. The right-wing argumentation, Graeber points out, is rooted in ontologies of *violence*: to be realistic means that *destructive forces* have to be reckoned with. In contrast, left-wing theory almost always is a variation on the ontology of *imagination*: the realities-in-waiting are the ones that count: new and hitherto supressed forces of creativity and productivity (Graeber, 2012, p. 73).

In that line of thought, maybe the most prominent advocate of looking towards democracy's functionality *as a state* – with the first and foremost task to guarantee *order* – is the US political scientist Samuel Huntington (1927–2008). Huntington is best known for his 1996 book *The Clash of Civilizations*, but his political legacy lies in his role as advisor for the governments of Brazil and South Africa in 1970s and 1980s respectively. Huntington advised the governments of both countries in accordance with the core argument outlined in his 1968 treatise *Political Order in Changing Societies:*

> The most important political distinction among countries concerns not their *form* of government but their *degree* of government. The differences between democracy and dictatorship are less than the differences between those countries whose politics embodies consensus, community, legitimacy, organization, effectiveness, stability, and those countries whose politics is deficient in these qualities.
>
> (1968, p. 1; italics mine)

"Men may, of course, have order without liberty. But they cannot have liberty without order. Authority has to exist before it can be limited," Huntington writes in another passage (1968, p. 7).

Caught up with liberal right- and liberal left-wing dystopias, it is easy to forget that there is a third alternative: *that nothing happens.* It is admittedly hard to imagine that major socio-technological innovations, such as Facebook, smartphones and cloud computing, do not effect any change at all. It is not hard to imagine, though, that the consequences *for democracy*, on balance, might just remain limited. And that would be the case, in particular, were we to give up the idea of a stable conception of democracy. In reality, the concept of democracy is by no means a fixed category, but subject to reinterpretations – that is erosion or reinvigoration itself. Every generation grows up in their own world. So 'nothing happens' might mean that the changes are quite dramatic when viewed from a synchronic, historic perspective, but the *discrepancy* perceived by the people between the *ideal* of democracy and what they see on the streets and in the media *here and now* is not altered dramatically because *both*, ideal and reality, drift in the same direction.

Finally, there is a fourth pathway. The development here is that there is factually more democracy or at least not less when measured against the old ideal. Measured against its own political rhetoric of engagement and participation, the actual practice of the new ideal begins to fall short of its promises, however: there is less *perceived* democracy. This results in people's disenchantment with politics, which, in turn, lowers the functionality of society. The scenario seems far-fetched at first, but in her analysis of democratic discourse and practice in municipal politics, Åkerström (2010) traces exactly that: the curious development of 'cosmetic democracy', where politicians enthusiastically embrace or at least pay lip-service to grand ideas of participatory politics, but then are worn down by exactly that: the people's participation itself as well as the constant need to communicate, inform and include. The need to stage politics makes it increasingly hard to actually 'do' politics. As the term 'cosmetic democracy' expresses, the problem lies not in the veiling and cloaking of something that is repulsive but in the creation of expectations, or the pressure to conform to expectations created by someone else, which then cannot be fulfilled.

Conceptualisations of democracy

The introduction should have made clear that a discussion of different ideals of democracy underlying argumentations for a newer, more modern democracy is vital. It is curious, therefore, that many scholars writing in the field tend to avoid the question. Dahlberg (2011), who has immersed himself in the discourse and practice of digital democracy advocates, only recently remarked,

> For well over a decade there has been widespread enthusiasm about the possibility of digital media technology advancing and enhancing democratic communication. This enthusiasm comes from a surprisingly diverse array of political interests, ranging from government officials to anti-government libertarians. As a result there are very different understandings of the form of democracy that digital media may promote, with associated differences in digital democracy rhetoric and practice. Despite this diversity, digital democracy (or e-democracy) is often talked about as though there was a general consensus about what it is.
>
> (Dahlberg, 2011, p. 855)

While many authors seem to regard the concept of the *public sphere* as the natural lynchpin connecting media and communication to democracy and devote considerable space to it, a shared understanding of democracy, curiously, is taken for granted. There is no doubt, however, that the question "What kind of democracy?" re-emerges when it comes to the controversial concept of *public interest*, which, in turn, lies at the very centre of many definitions of the public sphere. The following section therefore offers a typology of five 'modes' of democracy. The typology is indebted to a similar one suggested by Dahlberg (2011), to which we return, but introduces some new elements.

- Aggregative democracy (vote)
- Deliberative democracy (talk)

- Synthetic democracy (post-politics, post-democracy)
- Pluralistic democracy (agonistic democracy)
- Material democracy (autonomist democracy).

Aggregative democracy

There are many different forms of democracy, of course. In his classic study, Held (1987, 2006) discusses ten paradigmatic historic models, among them the democracy of the Athenian polis, Republicanism, liberal democracy, direct democracy, deliberative democracy, pluralism and competitive elitism. Observers of the political landscape, such as Belgian political philosopher Chantal Mouffe (1943–), draw attention to the fact, however, that deep down the standard concept implicitly and explicitly underlying democratic systems, and particularly democratic *practice*, in the Western world is the *aggregative model*. The key theorist of aggregative democracy in Mouffe's eyes is political economist Joseph Schumpeter (1883–1950); she explains the core proposition of aggregative democracy with reference to him as follows:

> [W]ith the development of mass democracy, popular sovereignty as understood by the classical model of democracy, had become inadequate. A new understanding of democracy was needed, putting the emphasis on aggregation of preferences, taking place through political parties for which people would have the capacity to vote at regular intervals. Hence Schumpeter's proposal to define democracy as the system in which people have the opportunity of accepting or rejecting their leaders thanks to a competitive electoral process.
>
> (Mouffe, 2000a, p. 1)

The point of aggregative democracy, thus, is that politics is not about 'common good', 'general will' or 'public interest', although these terms might be employed in political rhetoric. Mass democracy is about *parties* offering *leaders* bundled with a *package* of courses of action which are *engineered* to satisfy a large number of individuals with individual interests and preferences so that they, on balance, aggregate around the respective party. The key benefit of aggregative democracy lies in its capacity to produce *compromises* and by that a certain minimum degree of *stability* or *order*: not the least because the caste of professional politicians consists of *reasonable* people with *considered* opinions (as opposed to easily swayed popular opinion of the 'masses'). There is a price, however. Again summarising the aggregative standpoint, Mouffe emphasises a side effect which theorists freely admit, but which seldom makes its way into party manifestos:

> Popular participation in the taking of decisions should rather be discouraged since it could only have dysfunctional consequences for the working of the system. Stability and order were more likely to result from compromise among interests than from mobilizing people towards an illusory consensus on the common good.
>
> (Mouffe, 2000a, p. 2)

One of the theorists, who freely admit that there might be 'excess democracy', is Huntington. In his section in the report to the Trilateral Commission on the Governability of Democracies (*The Crisis of Democracy*, 1975), a document prepared for the worried political elites in the United States, Europe and Japan, Huntington puts Mouffe's point more bluntly: "The effective operation of a democratic political system usually requires some measure of apathy and noninvolvement on the part of some individuals and groups" (Crozier, Huntington & Watanuki, 1975, p. 114). Twenty-first-century critics would add, maybe, that if the wrong people and groups start to become conscious, they need to be shocked and stunned into apathy (Klein, 2007) and frightened into non-involvement by a constant state of war (Graeber, 2013; Hardt & Negri, 2012).

Mouffe, of course, diagnoses the aggregative model with its reliance on political parties and professional politicians, and its inherent exclusion of marginal groups, as the very reason for the growing disaffection with political institutions and processes in the Western democracies. Since the aggregative view effectively reduced democracy to "procedures for the treatment of interest-groups pluralism" (Mouffe, 2000a, p. 2), it is hardly surprising that the people either are weary of politics or drift towards the extreme fringes, which, in contrast, do not offer compromises but *populism*. The discussion about alternative approaches which are democratic and liberal, but not *aggregative*, has been ongoing, in Mouffe's account, since at least the 1970s. The two problems to solve are: How can we arrive at courses of actions which are not only pragmatic compromises engineered by a class of political professionals whose primary interest is re-election, but also *genuine* expressions of a 'general will', a 'public interest' – that is consensuses oriented towards a 'common good'? And how do we then pursue our courses of action, which are bound to be far more consequent and drastic than what we are used to, *without* breaking the will of those who happen to disagree, without violating liberal values, such as freedom of conscience, the protection of property, the rule of law – in short, without transgressing into what is the individual's *private sphere*? (It must be remembered, here, that non-democratic or just illiberal democratic systems are faced with neither problem in the full sense: in communist regimes for example the party 'knows' what the common good is and individual freedom is by definition subjected to the public interest. The mainstream answer given to the two questions and later rejected by Mouffe in favour of her own leads us deeper into our subject and straight to the public sphere.)

Deliberative democracy

The term 'deliberative democracy' was coined by political philosopher Joseph Bessette (1994), but the theoreticians first and foremost associated with deliberative democracy arguably are German philosopher and sociologist Jürgen Habermas and US political philosopher John Rawls (1921–2002). The core idea marks nothing but a return to the roots of democracy in the Athenian polis of the sixth century BCE with the public debate in the *agora* at its centre, however. Put very simply, it is that *deliberation* – that is arguing about matters – has a power of its own. By engaging in *genuine* deliberation it is possible for citizens to arrive at *consensus* – as opposed to systems of compromises – about the common good concerning specific issues. The agreements are *rational* and as such, by force of the better argument, *just* or *legitimate*. In the best of worlds, no breaking of wills and no violation of values are necessary because the involved parties quite simply 'see the light' because of "exchange of arguments among reasonable persons guided by the principle of impartiality" (Mouffe, 2000a, p. 4).

One cannot overemphasise the importance of the principle of impartiality here. Rawls devised the philosophical 'tool' of the 'veil of ignorance' in order to illustrate what impartiality means (*A Theory of Justice*, 1971); Habermas, on the other hand, developed an elaborate theory of what a *genuine* – that is power-free – *deliberation* ('Diskurs') means as opposed to discussion (*Theory of Communicative Action*, 1984). Both authors agree in their diagnosis that it is the *absence* of genuine, impartial deliberation on important matters of public interest which perpetuates injustice and repression, for if debates of such quality *would* take place – and take place publicly, for all to see – that is not in *secret* – good-willed actors would 'see' the unfairness of their demands, or be publicly exposed as not good-willed. This conception is, of course, very different from aggregative democracy, because it is geared to arrive at *one* solution. In aggregative democracy, on the other hand, it is common practice that concessions to one group have to be paid, politically, by behind-the-back concessions to another group – not because the second concession is fair, but only because the second group has the power to block the first concession.

Even though the criticism of Habermasian thought is well documented, his ideas remain the first and foremost answer to the question of how media and communication contribute to democracy: via deliberation in the public sphere. Iosifidis explains (2011, p. 621): "Although the historical status of Habermas's theory may be questionable, he nevertheless pioneered in pointing out that the public sphere – a conceptual rather than physical place – and democracy – expressed through engagement in rational discussion – are closely connected."

It is not difficult to see why then the concepts of deliberative democracy and the public sphere appealed to the early theorists of Internet democracy (for the following, see Dahlberg, 2011, p. 859). The first argument was that, due to the Internet's interactive character, the *masses* presupposed by Schumpeter no longer existed. The second was that Habermas's ideas might have been idealistic in the physical world, with its time-space restraints and its power-topography, but in the flat and egalitarian cyberspace, the ideal of the public sphere, the dream could just come true. "The first wave of enthusiasm for internet-based visions of digital democracy was largely predicated upon the desire to produce virtual public spheres," wrote Loader and Mercea (2011, p. 757).

James Fishkin (1991) has shown that deliberative democracy *can* work under certain circumstances, not only producing evidence-based decisions of superior quality but also leading to raised levels of public spiritedness and social cohesion (for a concise research overview, see Dahlgren, 2009, pp. 98–99). Despite this fact, scholars nowadays are by and large in agreement that digital democracy 1.0, virtual public spheres in the service of a democracy more deliberative and inclusive than the aggregative specimen, has never developed on a large scale and very seldom progressed past the stage of the experimental. Multiple reasons have been identified (Loader & Mercea, 2011, p. 758, for the following arguments): (1) the Internet never was power-free; digital deliberation was plagued by the same problems as deliberation face-to-face; and (2) scholars from cultural studies and feminism pointed out that the style of rational debate envisioned by Habermas and Rawls was that of factually privileged, wealthy, white males.

Interlude: so from where do we depart?

The high hopes placed on a digital deliberative democracy 1.0 with virtual public spheres were definitely disappointed, but there is widespread agreement that Web 2.0 is indeed qualitatively different. Nevertheless, probably due to the fact that many of the authors who had already accompanied digital democracy 1.0 are still around now, 10–15 years later, the "fanfares of transformative rhetorics" (Loader & Mercea, 2011) are now being sounded with rather less enthusiasm by academics. But again there are hopes. One reason is, first, that there is a wealth of empirical proof attesting that certain forms and modes of political activity and civic engagement have been made possible, easier and more effective by social media technologies, especially decentralised, spontaneous, disruptive action of a *resistance* or *guerrilla* character (see Schölzel, 2013). There is a lot going on in the Internet, and it does not hold anymore to simply discount this as apolitical. Second, it is beyond doubt that the first and second generations of digital technology *did* play a part in the mobilisation of the masses for large-scale, popular reform *even in the face of repressive, anti-democratic regimes*, and continue to do so – the events commonly dubbed the 'Arab Spring' are the prime example here. Third, it has been more or less proven, quasi-experimentally, that second-generation socio-technical digital 'tools' *can* enhance deliberative procedures (Dahlberg, 2011, p. 860).

From a purely technological point of view, it remains unquestioned that new media provide *the potential* for more or better democracy. Norén summarises the democratic affordances of the technology as follows (for the following Norén, 2008, p. 32).

- Integration of horizontal and vertical communication patterns in one medium
- Circumvention of intermediaries, such as the news media, locating more power with the citizens or the political system
- Boundary-crossing and time-space-independent forms of communication and interaction that facilitate the circulation of ideas and opinions throughout society
- Decentralisation and democratisation of common communication resources
- Increased access to large bodies of politically relevant information.

Norén emphasises, of course, that potentials materialise only in conducive contexts: there is no guarantee that potential actually translates into democratic discourses or practices of a higher quality (ibid.); the opposite might happen.

The first and foremost reason why deliberative democracy does not always work might be, then, that people have been *socialised* into the repressive patterns of prevailing aggregative democracy. This, of course, is a rerun of Adorno's argument against Popper concerning the holism of societal issues: new forms of democracy can be toyed with, but they cannot be comprehensively tested because that demands a radical departure from the old ideas: a burning of the ships. It is worth noting, however, that the argument can be turned against utopians: the fact that direct democracy, anarchism or communism works in some occupied factory in Paraguay does not mean that you can build a global society on it.

It could be the case, of course, that grand-scale deliberative, direct democracy works only if tried without alternatives. Or it could be the case that everything beyond aggregative democracy is a pipe dream due to some fundamental human flaw, and the exceptions prove the rule. What separates analysis from rhetoric, however, is to keep what *is* apart from what *should* and what *could* be. And it is here, then, that three very different understandings of how new media can contribute to modern democracy part ways. The following section therefore discusses synthetic and agonistic democracy in conjunction. In the section after that we then turn to the only concept offering an alternative to the current understanding of democracy as a political principle: material democracy.

Synthetic vs. agonistic democracy: post-politics/post-democracy

Post-political and post-democratic thinkers argue that the ideal of democracy, or at least a proper notion of politics, has been lost. It is a line of argumentation associated with thinkers such as Chantal Mouffe and Slavoj Žižek (post-politics) and Colin Crouch (post-democracy). Here, post-political thought might be best understood as a radicalisation of Mouffe's argumentation against aggregative democracy. The core lies in the diagnosis that after the fall of communism in the 1990s, liberal democracies have ceased to be 'democratic' in a *genuinely political* sense: politics has deteriorated into social administration of capitalist market economies to which no alternative is thinkable; power in polycentric societies rests neither with the people nor with political parties who make *decisions* but largely with experts and technocrats who do what is seemingly *necessary* – that is presented without alternatives – to manage *risks*, especially of an environmental kind. Crouch argued, in a similar vein, that modern democracies are evolving into elite aristocracies with a democratic façade (2004).

The most prominent figure attacked by post-political thinkers is British sociologist Anthony Giddens (1938–). Giddens's enduring political legacy is his association with the 'Third Way', 'centrism' or 'radical centre' in politics (*Beyond Left and Right: The Future of Radical Politics*, 1994). The Third Way, as exemplified by Tony Blair's New Labour in Britain, is characterised by attempting a *synthesis* of traditional left-wing social policy – that is state interventionism – and right-wing economic policy – that is laissez-faire capitalism. The core idea, put very simply, is that *the state* should strive for greater equality and justice in society, yes – not by *redistribution* of wealth, however, but by *empowerment* of people.

It is the central role of the *individual* or 'the Self' engaging in fluid and dynamic constellations – for example engagement in social movements or protest networks – which distinguishes Giddens's concept of late modern societies from traditional political approaches. Giddens's political ideas are not naively action-theoretical, however. They are founded upon a conception of the individual which does not contrapose, as is done in traditional sociology, the macro level of structure with the micro level of individual agency. In *The Constitution of Society* (1984) Giddens envisions a dynamic process of *structuration* instead: societal structures are not just 'there' but are *created* in the first place and then continuously *re-created* by individuals who are by and large *competent* actors in their social environments (as opposed to clueless prisoners of the system entangled in false consciousness); structures not only constrain human agency but also enable it.

Against the backdrop of the theory of structuration, Giddens then analyses the condition of the individual in late modernity as characterised by reflexivity and disembeddedness (*The Consequences of Modernity*, 1990). With reflexivity Giddens not only emphasises that late modern societies are post-traditional and require individuals to choose how to live and who to be. Reflexivity begins where insights about society *immediately* flow back into society. Reflexive modernity, thus, is continuously reforming *in opposition to itself*, while classical modernity was a grand reform defined, statically, in opposition to traditionalism. The same holds true for the identities of individuals, which are fluid and continuously created in the light of what one learns and how one has lived so far, the key challenge being to uphold an authentic narration, a 'story' of one's Self (*Modernity and Self-Identity*, 1991). With the concept of disembeddedness, Giddens draws attention to the fact that individuals in late modernity do not live their lives in their physical surroundings exclusively (1990).

Norén (2008, p. 31) holds that research on ICT and democracy can be broadly grouped into two strands. The *formal political strand*, commonly associated with the slightly old-fashioned term 'e-governance', is concerned with how *government institutions* could and should make use of new technologies to enhance democratic procedures – for example decision making, voting, petitioning, and so on. The *civil society strand*, in contrast, is concerned with the 'democratic potential' of collectives and individuals using new media technologies *for all kinds of things*, including, of course, public activism and campaigning. It is here, at the crossroads of the 'dutiful citizen' (Loader & Mercea, 2011) engaging in politics by participating in rational public deliberation, where Habermas and Giddens part ways. Interestingly, it is also identified as the paradigm shift distinguishing the elusive e-governance 1.0 from social media democracy 2.0:

> The distinctiveness of this second generation of internet democracy is the displacement of the public sphere model with that of a networked citizen-centred perspective providing opportunities to connect the private sphere of autonomous political identity to a multitude of chosen political spaces
>
> (Loader & Mercea, 2011, p. 758)

The net result of Giddens's ideas, then, is a conception of democracy which goes far beyond the concept of the properly political and concerns itself with *civil society* – that is a much wider scope of individuals' lives, which are viewed as at least not un-political. It may be no exaggeration to say that Giddens identifies *self-actualisation* of individuals expressed in *identity politics* as the new major driving force. Here, the assertion of the homosexual way of life for example is not seen as a by-product of abstract political notions of equality but is due to the fact that gays concretely asserted their right to live the way they want publicly, often in creative, provocative and entertaining ways. For Giddens and other thinkers of reflexive modernity, *political action* in the narrow sense of the word is only *one* solution among many for a problem in society. Much more is expected from social movements, private-public partnerships, technological innovations and, for that reason, forms of deliberative democracy leading to smart solutions and active trust. The 'fancy, formal deliberative suit' of high and earnest politics is not always required, however, as Dahlgren (2009, p. 98) points out: "A chattering society is more likely to lead to participation than a tight-lipped one."

Giddens's ideas about of disembeddedness in time and space, dis-embedding/re-embedding mechanisms and reflexivity have inspired scholars such as Jan Van Dijk (cf. 1999, p. 20–21) to approach early twenty-first-century societies with the concept of the 'network society'. It is also clear that Giddens arrives at very similar conclusions as Castells when it comes to identifying *the locus of power* and/or the source of identity in post-industrialist, polycentric societies: they do not rest with the state, the masses in general or certain castes or classes in the traditional sense of the word anymore, but with *networks* consisting of individuals but not reducible to individuals.

While some are enthusiastic about networks as a more 'natural' form of organisation when compared to hierarchies, others point to the democratic deficits. Anthropologist Janine Wedel (*Shadow Elite*, 2009) has traced how 'flex nets', such as the neoconservative network around Richard Perle, Paul Wolfowitz and Douglas Feith, formed an unaccountable 'shadow elite' from the beginning of the Nixon years to the end of the George W. Bush era. 'Flexians' wield immense power just out of reach of any democratic control because they are organised in networks of individuals, flexnets, which do not 'stand up' in public. The flexnets 'colonise' the traditional institutions of power, such as the US Department of Defense in the instance of the neocons, without ever buying the ideal the institutions officially stand for, without ever transferring their loyalties away.

The most important critique of the Third Way is that its assumptions are factually false: our societies are *not* post-scarcity societies where redistribution ceases to be the core problem; there are no 'neutral' experts; the emphasis on the individual is not driven by a humanistic vista towards self-actualisation but by a more or less covert neo-liberal agenda of governance-beyond-the-state. Third Way politics constitutes the systematic attempt to undercut the *antagonism* (or agonism, in Mouffe's terminology) necessarily inherent in everything that is properly political. The result is a political landscape and intellectual climate where disagreement with the hegemonic beliefs and assumptions not only constitutes a political position but also betrays a *moral failure*. In the environmental sphere for example the Third Way is characterised by a dedication to ideas such as *sustainability*, with which it is impossible to sensibly disagree with – because they are formulated in such a way as to hurt nobody, and therefore are void in the political sense. According to critics such as Slavoj Žižek (2006), this shortcoming is hidden, however, by rhetoric that claims the very opposite. The 'new way' posed as radical for suggesting to go along with smart ideas that work without ideological prejudice. What was not said, however, is that this formula necessarily upholds the general way that things work *at present*. In Žižek's words,

> To say that good ideas are 'ideas that work" means that one accepts in advance the (global capitalist) constellation that determines what works (if, for example, one spends too much money on education or healthcare, that 'doesn't work', since it infringes too much on the conditions of capitalist profitability).
>
> (2006, p. 1)

It could be said, therefore, that the Third Way has achieved aggregative democracy par excellence through the masterful use of strategic communication. The result, according to the harshest critics, is that politics or democracy in the ideal sense is dead. This is evidenced, one might add, by the prominent positions of spin doctors, such as Alastair Campbell, in the apparatus of Third-Way democracies. Healthy, vibrant politics *are* communication in their own right; thus, the introduction of the term 'political communication' as opposed to genuine politics can be interpreted only as a symptom of hollowing-out, of decay. The term 'synthetic democracy', with its double meaning, captures this.

Post-political and post-democratic thinkers criticise deliberative democracy in the sense of Habermas and Rawls in a narrower circle. But they also criticise synthetic democracy, which contains deliberative elements as one ingredient, in a wider circle. The critique of synthesis democracy, once again, is that it dresses up politics in ethical and technical clothes and dissolves the public sphere by equating it with 'life'. The critique of classical deliberative democracy targets its fixation on achieving *consensus* by means of rational deliberation. Dissent, authors like Mouffe contend, is in fact the lifeblood of democracy. An "agonistic" approach, which Mouffe argues for, "acknowledges the real nature of its frontiers and the forms of exclusion that they entail, instead of trying to disguise them under the veil of rationality or morality" (Mouffe, 2000a, p. 17).

This critique, however, is the point where synthetic democracies could *also* claim their superiority over aggregative democracies. The party-oriented type of professional politics may have left some room for tensions and passion, but could not cope with provocation and disruption, fun, humour, irony, sexiness and satire, with the whole spectrum of human expression beyond rational argumentation. A conception of 'life politics' where the self does not seek safety in institutions but embraces the reflexive management of risks opens up 'politics' for these modes of expression. Yet again, that is exactly what post-political thinkers criticise *in turn*, because they wish, by and large, to hold on to the idea of a sphere which is properly political.

What Dahlberg (2011) identifies as the *counter-public position*, in turn, depends on what it is contrasted against. The idea that the Internet makes it possible to articulate excluded voices – to associate, to campaign, to contest, to form groups, to identify, to organise, to protest, to resist – can be appreciated only against the backdrop of what exclusion *means*. In depoliticised democracies – that is synthetic democracies – exclusion means something very different from repression in totalitarian regimes. In repressive regimes counter-public activity means debating what is forbidden to debate under threat of dire consequences, working against the state. It is not so clear what the term encompasses in 'free' or at least 'freer' systems. It does happen, of course, that outspoken proponents for whatever are subjected to hate campaigns by Internet trolls who make terrorising public figures their hobby. But it is not the *apparatus of the state* that is turned against the views in question. In synthetic democracies 'critical' or even 'radical' counterpositions are toyed with, are embraced as 'interesting'. They become an integral and stabilising part of the hegemonic *discourse* which contains its own counterarguments in a demonstration of openness. Agonistic pluralism as it is proposed by Mouffe must be understood against the backdrop of the *synthetic* conception of politics, otherwise it would not amount to much more than a reformulation of classical antiquity. The strategies by which synthetic democracies embrace their own antitheses are the reason why authors such as Mouffe insist on the reinvigoration of the properly political. Dissenting voices should not only be toyed with but also be *heard* – that is *taken for serious.*

Proponents of synthetic democracies, which do not describe themselves as such, believe it should be the people, not politicians and intellectuals, who decide what is to be taken for serious. Power should not, as in the mono-centric, aggregative model, be held by politico-economic elites alone. It should be 'held', if that is the right term, by networks which are open and meritocratic in principle, so that a poly-centric society arises. What critics denounce as de-politicisation, the 'foreclosure' of politics proper, to synthetic democracy it is just the acknowledgement of life politics. The majority of the people do want normality, order. They don't want to be ruled by a small elite that thinks only of itself, but they do want to be governed, in their interest, so that they can get on with their lives. They want that things come together: peace and prosperity, a sustainable future for themselves and their children, a humane society and so forth. This is not likely to be brought about *en passant* by ideological debate. On the contrary, 'smart' steps based on broad consent about the 'right' direction are required. That the consent sometimes has to be engineered by clever communication is not per se undemocratic, as long as the engineering is done in the interest of the people.

Material democracy

Material democracy, a neologism introduced here in the same way as synthetic democracy, must be appreciated against the backdrop of our contemporary welfare societies with the majority of the population living under conditions of wage labour or as salaried professionals. Material democracy is, in contrast to the other four models, not overly concerned with communication. 'Say' does not count much when you have to work or commute two thirds of the day and are in arrears with your mortgage payments and loaded down with credit card debts. The Occupy movement did and does not occupy public places to merely demand a *say* for the 99% (for a recent insider account of Occupy Wall Street, see Graeber, 2013). What was demanded was an effective redistribution of *material wealth* away from the 1% who controlled 38% of the country's wealth in the United States in 2001. What counts, in true Marxist tradition, are the *material means of production*. The emphasis in the expression 'networked self' would be clearly on *work*.

There are, of course, reasons why the term 'material democracy' is preferred to autonomist-Marxist democracy here. The primary reason is that I wanted to use a generic term in order to group a variety of approaches by different theorists. The spectrum is quite broad. On the moderate end it begins with demands for constitutionally guaranteed, sufficient citizens' income paid out unconditionally and independent of other means to everybody from cradle to grave. At the radical end, there are communist and anarchist demands for a complete abolition of the state. The moderate ideas are propagated not only by radical left-wing activists but also by highly successful capitalist entrepreneurs (e.g. Dirk Rossmann in Germany), and even have been toyed with, in modified forms, by liberal economists, such as Milton Friedman or Friedrich von Hayek. But even the more radical ideas, such as redistribution of wealth, global debt relief and abolition of the international finance and investment system (Wall Street, IMF, etc.), which only one or two decades ago were the domain of hard-core activists, have become increasingly acceptable objectives to 'normal' citizens.

A secondary reason for the semantic shift is that a concept labelled 'Marxist' is unlikely to get a fair hearing since the socialist-communist experiment has been universally declared a failure at terrible cost. It is worth mentioning, however, that the universal failure proposition is not universally accepted: Graeber (2012, p. 15), himself an anarchist and alter-globalisation activist, points out that the Soviet Union existed for nearly 70 years, during which time agrarian Russia was transformed into a technologically advanced global superpower competing with the United States in the space race. But even those who concede the failure of socialist experiments – and the economic collapse of the Eastern Bloc and the failure of North Korea as a state cannot be seriously denied – point out a crucial twist: that self-declared socialist states, such as the German Democratic Republic, never turned out as material democracies. It was simply not the case that *everybody* took ownership in the means of production. On the contrary, the means of production were administered and controlled by ideologically driven, elite-controlled *party apparatuses*. But this argument, in turn, provokes an even stronger counterargument by the critics. If it is true that no states organised along the lines of material democracy ever existed or exist, then why is *that* so? The self-supplied answer is: *because it became clear, in the process, that the whole idea is just a theoretical pipe dream.* The answer given by the proponents of the pipe dream is very different, in turn: earlier attempts, they hold, did not fail but were *made* to fail, because imperialist capitalist regimes were terrified at the prospect of the huddled masses awakening to the possibilities of a better life, and aggressively undermined and continue to undermine every attempt of material democracy to unfold.

It is at this junction that the work of contemporary theorists of material democracy sets in, and where social media innovations are supposed to make a difference in practice – that is open up modes of collaborating, cooperating, distributing, exchanging, giving, networking, participating and sharing which were not available 25 years ago. It is here, furthermore, where the concepts of agonistic democracy and material democracy touch but do not blend.

The problem of explaining, discussing or even advocating material democracy is that conceptualisations struggle uphill against concerted efforts to brand them as impossible, as 'not working'. Graeber (2012) diagnoses that the heart and core of twenty-first-century neo-liberal capitalism are a war against the fantasy of the people. It is due to gigantic efforts of global capitalism, he maintains, that ordinary people shaken by the financial crises of 2008 and onwards find themselves in a grotesque situation: on the one hand it becomes increasingly clear that neo-liberal capitalism does not work (anymore, either), and on the other hand almost no one seems to be capable of envisioning a viable alternative (see Graeber, 2012).

In true critical tradition, *theorists* of material democracy try to uncover, then, which firmly entrenched concepts, terms and myths mask alternatives. What goes on at the same time, however, are *practical* experiments with alternative forms of life/production/economy, which collapse or transcend the concept of politics proper. The hopes placed on digital media by proponents of material democracy are twofold, therefore: to prevail against concerted efforts to be ignored, silenced and discredited on the one hand, and to prove that material democracy works on the other. In the first effort, material democrats constitute a counter-public which *contests* the hegemonic beliefs. In the second effort, however, material democrats wish to extricate themselves from what pluralistic agonists see, in contrast, as the very battlefield for the struggle: the political proper. They want to become autonomous of the benefits politics might or might not bestow. This, after all, is the root of the term *autonomy*: to live in society, but by your own rule. Whereas proponents of world democracy, like George Monbiot (2003), want to expand or re-expand the spectrum of what can be seriously discussed and seriously influenced, and that might or might not include alternatives to capitalism, material democracy's impetus is, furthermore, to reduce the spectrum of what *needs* to be discussed. If you constitutionally guarantee people a basic income amply sufficient to live, a discussion about who has the leisure to blog about politics becomes irrelevant.

The key theorists and activists of material democracy do not simply reiterate Marxist dogma. Scholars such as Antonio Negri, Michael Hardt, David Graeber or Judith Butler have developed figures of thought which fundamentally challenge the existing paradigm. In his bestselling anthropological analysis of debt in human history (*Debt: The First 5,000 Years*, 2011), Graeber fundamentally challenges the concepts of market, economy and money for example. Graeber begins by the examining the narration offered by one of the founding fathers of liberal capitalism, Adam Smith (1723–1790). Smith argues that money was invented because of the human propensity to trade and exchange goods, and the impracticalities of the barter economy. It is a version of history which is repeated in introduction to economics until today, even in textbooks by *Keynesian* Nobel laureates in economics (i.e. Joseph Stiglitz and John Driffill's *Economics*, 2000). The problem with Smith's narration, which seems to have been copied in a distorted way from medieval Persian philosopher Ghazali anyway (cf. Graeber, 2011, KL 5891–5895), is that it is not supported by a single shred of anthropological evidence. "The problem is there's no evidence that it ever happened, and an enormous amount of evidence suggesting that it did not," Graeber writes (Graeber, 2011, KL 588).

What Adam Smith makes up, Graeber convincingly shows (for the following argumentation cf. Graeber, 2011, ch. 2), is plain fiction as far as everyday village life is concerned. A barter economy, where furs are traded for cloths, only ever existed in trade *with strangers*. Among one's own community, affairs were handled differently, either in a gift economy or with credit. The often-told story that Europe reverted to a barter economy after the fall of the Roman Empire is true insofar as *coin* disappeared, but that did not mean a return to universal bartering. Anthropological evidence shows that people kept track of *credit* by using the old Roman system. The twist is that Adam Smith's story places the emphasis on money's *natural* emergence. For Adam Smith and the liberal science of economics, which he practically founded, money was not *created* but naturally emerged, as a convenience, because of the human's propensity to engage in economic transaction, egoistically, but ultimately for mutual benefit. Graeber's argumentation, in contrast, emphasises that the separation of the *market*, with its *market forces* on the one hand and a *sociopolitical* or *civic space* on the other, is an artificial separation: the founding myth of laissez-faire capitalism. The separation is made possible by the medium of *impersonal money*, backed by the force of the state, which allows us, theoretically, to treat even our neighbours as if they were *strangers*. And that, as Naomi Klein points out, is exactly the world imagined by the archpriest of late twentieth- and early twenty-first-century free-market capitalism, Milton Friedman: "In his view, the state's sole functions were 'to protect our freedom both from the enemies outside our gates and from our fellow-citizens: to preserve law and order, to enforce private contracts, to foster competitive markets'" (Klein, 2007, p. 6).

The idea that humans engage in *rational market transactions* in one world and live, love, hate, mistrust, doubt, foster, nurture, encourage and so forth in another, quite separate world has become entrenched in our thinking. What we are recently experiencing as a rise in importance of *communications* might be sensibly reframed, then, as attempts to overcome the artificial separation: companies want to not only sell goods and services but also engage with people in their respective lifeworlds. What critical scholars react to is that the bringing together of worlds does not mean a return to the good old days where the baker was your neighbour. On the contrary, what we experience is a re-entry of non-commercial values, but on commercial terms. Habermas's (1984) phrase the 'colonisation of the lifeworld' still captures the phenomenon.

The separation of business vs. life has severe democratic implications, which, in turn, explain why social media is considered a key factor in overcoming the separation. The neo-liberal contention that the market should be left alone, or to experts exclusively, *is* foreclosure of politics *par excellence* in the sense diagnosed by the thinkers of post-politics. An area which is political to its core, the creation of money, is kept beyond the reach of the citizens. But radical material democracy's greatest ambition is not to reconquer the institutions which create money, credit, debt, currency, banking, and so forth in order to pursue *other* politics here. The greatest ambition lies in breaking the stranglehold the international financial system has on everyone's life by showing that it is only needed in a much reduced form.

Graeber's account corresponds with the ideas proposed by Antonio Negri and Michael Hardt (*Empire*, 2000; *Multitude*, 2004; *Commonwealth*, 2009; *Declaration*, 2012). The argumentation of Hardt and Negri revolves around the idea that in the beginning of the twenty-first century, *the multitude* is finally in a position to claim *the commons*, and therefore to overcome capitalist world order – that is the *empire*. With the concept of the multitude, Negri and Hardt depart from traditional concepts of 'class' or the 'masses', emphasising instead a multitude of 'singularities': an aggregation of individuals who are irreducibly different but have interests which overlap with other individuals' interests – a concept obviously not unrelated to the concept of *swarm intelligence*. The essence of material democracy, then, is that the *multitude* frees itself from dependence on capitalists owning the means of production, and takes collective ownership of the *commons* – that is everything produced independently of capital. In his discussion of Negri's ideas, Dahlberg (2011) recounts instances of materially democratic, virtual productive cooperatives, such as Linux, Wikipedia, Freecycle.org or IndyMedia. The core project of material democracy, thus, is not a new *ideology* but a new practice of living and 'doing business' and 'making politics'.

Strategic communication re-enters

Let us return to Castells and our opening question: (1) *Whether*, (2) *for what reasons* and (3) *under which conditions* Western citizens can expect a more democratic, more modern democratic or simply 'better' society because of the advent of new media?

After reviewing five different conceptualisations of democracy and mapping the territory, a picture is emerging of how new media can come into play as 'democratic factors', always viewed, of course, against a certain conception of democracy. Indeed, there seem to be three paradigms.

The first understanding, the *optimisation paradigm*, is that democracy has been realised already. What we have to do now is to carefully and sensibly integrate new media into the existing democratic framework and to adapt our institutions, structures, discourses and practices – which are sound in principle and the guarantors of harmonious, prosperous lives for the majority of the people. The greatest hope is that the technology-culture nexus emerging due to social media *invigorates* the people's interest and faith in what remains, in principle, *aggregative democracy*. The hopes are for a democracy that is more inclusive, more humane, more sustainable – that is all in all 'smarter' than the forms and modes we are familiar with. What new media takes to a new level, then, is *synthetic democracy* which is reflexive – that is continuously self-improving.

The second understanding is that the *ideal* of democracy, what democracy *really* is, has been lost and is in dire need of recovery. Digital media, *in the catalytic paradigm*, offer the forms to expose and outmanoeuvre false forms of democracy. This may happen by forms of *deliberative democracy* or by *resistance* and *counter-public activity* contesting the aggregative or synthetic mainstream, the hegemony. The greatest hope is that the position of the pretenders and seducers, liars and propagandists, becomes untenable. For some thinkers the next step, then, is a return to the optimisation paradigm, but with a better deal: once a 'real' democracy – that is a form of government that deserves the name – has been established, it is time to return to 'normality'. Others, in contrast, are extremely wary of 'normality', which is seen as a particularly devious form of repression. They are willing to accept a constant state of contestation, embracing it as the essence of political life: real democracy, they argue, is necessarily *agonistic democracy*.

The third understanding is that a new age has dawned. The current disaffection with politics is due to a fundamental lack of *fit between contemporary society and the established democratic practice*. What is going on now might or might not be in accordance with some old-fashioned ideal of democracy, but that is not the point anymore. The greatest hope is not to reclaim some elusive lost paradise, for some say in affairs for the 99%. The great hope is to find the way to an entirely new, as yet unthought of future that was not possible without the technology at hand. This, of course, is the *revolutionary* paradigm which aims at *material democracy*.

Note

1 One liberty is that I group authors together who, in my opinion, postulate by and large the same generic argument – although they themselves might emphasise the differences. Thus, Chantal Mouffe, Jacques Rancière and Slavoj Žižek come in the same box; you buy Jürgen Habermas and get John Rawls for free; the spectrum of material democracy begins with an unconditional citizens' income and ends with abolition of state authority. Another liberty I take is that I sometimes paraphrase the jargon: Rancière's concept of *la police*, in opposition to *le politique* (politics proper), becomes simply 'order' or 'normality'. The third and most far-reaching liberty I take, however, is to sometimes create an artificial voice – as is the custom in philosophical debates. The artificial voice *aggregates* the writings of several authors of one school or tradition. It constitutes my attempt to go beyond the jargon, to bring forward what I consider the logical, generic argument in everyday language. As will be seen, the voices then are employed rhetorically to engage with other artificial voices representing other schools or traditions.

8 What do digital naturals demand from democracy?

Marja Åkerström and Philip Young

From the moment they discovered the Internet, evangelists and idealists began to proclaim grand visions of its potential to transform democracy. Often, these visions sprang from an optimistic championing of the empowerment they believed, or wanted to believe, the online world would bring.

By the 1990s, in Sweden, as in America and the rest of Europe, high expectations were spreading quickly among researchers. At the same time, governments and civic authorities were setting great store on the Internet's potential for revitalising democracy, and for strengthening the possibilities of dialogue, especially between citizens and civic authorities.

Two decades on, many people continue to believe the Internet to have great potential to deliver new and better possibilities for democratic engagement and participation (even though the online landscape is evolving rapidly, and surveillance and privacy issues are eroding trust and creating new discomforts). Already, a generation has grown up with online technologies, in a "participatory culture" (Fuchs, 2014) facilitated by "spreadable media" (Jenkins, 2013); across the world, societies are beginning to experience democracy in forms negotiated by digital naturals.

As researchers who also teach strategic communication at one of Scandinavia's leading universities to students who could be expected to very much display the qualities ascribed to digital naturals, we wanted to know how they think and act about "democratic practice". Very broadly, we asked ourselves, how do digital naturals understand the terms and meaning of democracy, political engagement and strategic communication in today's media landscape?

We wanted to know whether digital naturals are developing alternative strategies for democratic understanding, engagement and expression. Are there, for instance, alternative ways of handling responsibility and accountability? What is common sense for digital naturals? What is political communication in the online environment (and what isn't)? How does their experience reflect this assertion by Manuel Castells (2013, p. 413): "The greater the autonomy of the communicating subjects vis-a-vis the controllers of societal communication, the higher the chances for the introduction of messages challenging dominant values and interests in communication networks."

Earlier research within political communication (e.g. Strömbäck, 2010), political science (e.g. Dahl, 1999; Nord, 2008; Petersson, 1991, 2005) and media and communication studies (e.g. Hadenius & Weibull, 2008) puts significant emphasis on the interplay between the main actors of political communication at a societal level – that is citizens, media and authorities (politicians and employees) – but does not extensively address other possible relationships. Can new patterns of the opinion making process be identified by digital naturals? What characterises the activities, collective meaning making, negotiation and participation processes and actions performed online by digital naturals? This study used focus group interviews (seen as miniatures of a "thinking society") to try to go beyond these directed patterns of thoughts on democracy and capture other ways of thinking.

Although our study sample was age-restricted, we would strenuously avoid imposing a calendar-derived starting point for digital competence. We are uncomfortable with framings that suggest certain individuals are somehow born with native rights, and that those born outside some notional boundaries are without those rights, and accorded the status of immigrants. Immigration can be linked to concepts such as assimilation, integration and *othering*.

With these points in mind, it may well be that people in a certain age group have differing notions of, say, personal privacy or approaches to storing and retrieving information that have been influenced by online experience, and which may also impact approaches to civic engagement, but the contention is that so many other factors are in play that a division based on birthdate and circumstances is of little value.

From the literature it would be reasonable to conclude that the digital naturals in our sample would be "smartphone cyborgs" (see Chapter 1) – namely that their mobile device would be used throughout the day, and would be their primary source of information on many topics. They would expect to be able to look up information on any subject at any time, and to an extent this would replace the need for memorising or recording facts.

They would consider it natural to communicate with friends in any part of the world, and would expect to receive news as it happens (they would not be bound by the geographical and temporal restrictions of, say, the postal service or daily newspaper routines).

Their experience with social networks, such as Facebook and Instagram, coupled with commercial services, such as Amazon or TripAdvisor, has accustomed them to commenting, reviewing and ranking, and to expect response to their comments. This access to information and routine engagement is accompanied by an expectation of transparency, both in commercial or civic processes and by (crowdsourced) fact checking.

Their engagement with news services would not involve single-source, chronological narration: if they find an event interesting, they will gather information from a range of sources, collating a personally curated narrative that will combine real-time commentary with historical artefacts.

Very broadly our respondents reflected these assumptions. What they did not do was show any great enthusiasm for the aspirations of those who see digital as having the potential to transform participatory democracy.

Although they accepted as a given that they had access to information and to engage in the public sphere in a way not possible before the advent of digital and online technologies, and privileged responsiveness, accountability and direct participation, there was little indication that they felt smartphones increased or enhanced political participation.

The study

The research questions that guided the study were:

RQ1 How do digital naturals define democracy, strategic political communication and political engagement on a national and international level respectively?

RQ2 How do digital naturals perceive their own capabilities and possibilities to engage in and affect democracy and society through new and social media?

RQ3 What does it take to strategically communicate politics through social media channels today and how can the channels and scenes of information and political communication be described and understood?

RQ4 What are the relations between the publicly communicated ambitions of a revitalised civic sphere online and the perceived possibilities and practices of social media, and how can this be understood?

Methodology

As the study aimed to go beyond 'common' ways of studying political communication and to broaden definitions of democracy, politics and political communication, it has been guided by abductive (and to a certain extent inductive) theory. Empirical results from the focus group interviews have been correlated to and analysed in relation to theories and results from earlier research and theory. The inductive perspective has been used by asking questions like *What is this an example of?* This means that qualitative studies were used, in this case by lending the characteristics of the case study method. The case study method, as it has been used here (according to Merriam, 2006), accentuates the *descriptive* (thick description), *heuristic* (collecting data step-by-step), *inductive* and *particularistic* (the particular study can give knowledge on a general problem) nature of a phenomenon. The case study method in this sense also means *interpretation in context*, and it specially considers *phenomenon in constant change* (ibid.). This applies well to the explorative aim of the study and to the rapidly changing environment and architecture of the Internet. Definitions of main conceptions (e.g. democracy and politics) and the descriptions of the discourse of new media were thereby delegated for discussion by the digital naturals themselves.

Collection method and selection criteria

The study started with collecting data from five moderated and semi-structured focus groups which facilitated dynamic interaction between three to five persons (or 6–8 persons, depending on the grade of structuration on the moderators' part). Focus group interviews were useful as the respondents negotiated and discussed the meaning of online interaction and engagement. The method is advantageous as it puts less attention on individual meanings in favour of the collective meaning-making process (Wibeck, 2010). Focus groups are in this case seen as miniatures of a "thinking society" (ibid.) where discursive characteristics can be identified and analysed with for example Foucauldian tools (strategies in interactions).

We began by identifying three groups of engaged and experienced women and men. Each group included members selected in order to get a "prismatic" input of personalities and a diversified output of opinions. The first group was identified by one of our strategic communication students whose network we felt reflected a rich array of opinions, contradictory positions and perspectives that promised dynamic discussion and various standpoints. The selection of subsequent groups followed on from the results of the preceding group. Three groups were interviewed during 2013 and the other two during 2014. Most were studying on an international joint master's programme in strategic communication at Lund University, and this interested us as we could hear opinions and ideas from for example Belgian, Icelandic, French, Dutch and Swedish perspectives. From the outset, we recognised that most participants were taking courses which the investigators teach and assess, and thus many had some level of awareness of our research interests and propensities.

The focus groups

Each focus group lasted for approximately two hours and was recorded. The conversations were moderated in English by the authors. Using two moderators meant one could lead the discussions while the other analysed the answers and posed complementary questions. The interviews were transcribed by two master's students who did not attend the focus groups. The results have been compiled and analysed by the authors. In total 20 respondents (distributed into these five focus groups) were interviewed.

Each session opened with a moderator reading an extract from the opening chapter of Nick Harkaway's *The Blind Giant* (2013). In the introduction, Harkaway visualises a digital dream world, where everything that could possibly go well has:

> Shining healthy people move through a sunlit space filled with birds, plants and slick technology . . . in groups, they discuss politics, ethics, science and literature. They are voracious, interested in everything.

Many administrative and commercial decisions are managed from moment to moment – and very few companies or government departments are ever unavailable, at any hour of the day or night – but even now it's easier to have a degree of scheduling so everyone has a shared sense of time – it helps social cohesion.

So midway through each afternoon, the whole society pauses in what it is doing to vote in a series of plebiscites, each individual drawing on his her own expertise or experience to answer today's pressing questions: a perfect, ongoing participant democracy in which reason prevails, moderated by compassion and goodwill, and the strong measured centre holds sway.

Anyone doing something too engrossing to participate – be it surgery or scuba – need not vote, but frequent abstention is considered odd. No one has to vote on everything, but it is generally accepted practice to vote on issues in which you are disinterested as well as those that directly affect you because the network of connection and consequence is such that nothing takes place in isolation.

With access to all the information in the world, both curated and raw data, people are well able to make informed choices and, through their combined intelligence, solve problems which seemed intractable to the old style of government which relied on notionally expert leaders. No one goes hungry, no one is alone, no one is unheard.

This is the happy valley, the high plateau of technological culture.

(p. 9)

After the reading participants were asked to give their understanding and opinions of some of the key themes of the digital dream – namely:

- Citizens' *right to engage* in politics, to *be heard* and to make their *own* decisions
- Every actor's *possibility of full* participation and *power* in *political issues*
- Equal and full *availability of information and knowledge*
- *Technology's ability* to build collective intelligence
- Technology's ability to provide *anonymity* and thereby equality.

These themes were used as analytical standpoints as they have been extensively discussed in earlier research and theories of political communication.

Limitations of methodology

In one sense, the respondents were drawn from a limited and homogenous population: all are well informed and educated in communication, and therefore cannot be presented as representative of the wider population. That said, our aim was to interview information-rich respondents who could give thoughtful and conversant opinions. A strength of the qualitative study is that it closely takes account of every argument given, even if it has been advanced by only one respondent. Our results are therefore not allocated to predetermined categories but are diversified and prismatic in order to fulfil our aim – namely to discover new ways of thinking about democracy in the new media landscape.

Results and analysis

The results are presented in three conceptual sections: what democracy *is* (how to define and talk about it), what democracy *does* (how to act/perform/not act) and what democracy *can* be (how to think about achievements).

What democracy is – Conventional thinking on definitions and unconventional practice

The first theme discussed in the focus groups concerned the definition of democracy itself. A notable result from this part of the sessions was that digital naturals define democracy as being limited strictly to formal procedures and IGOs (ingovernmental organisations), and consider the content to be discussed and managed – that is politics – to be something boring, detached from ordinary life and ordinary people. Additionally, some respondents didn't see their own actions and communication on social media as *political*. They put little weight on their own contributions and had little confidence in their own capability to influence and change societal issues. Nevertheless, when speaking with them about their actual online performances, the opposite was displayed. The answers of one respondent can serve as an example. Regina, a 21-year-old female communication student, whose humour blog (*Egoina*) is top-ranked on some blog lists (e.g. www.bloggportalen.se), doesn't perceive herself as political even though she writes about equality and gender issues that can easily be defined as political matters. In her view politics is not about everyday practice:

I: Do you feel that people listen to you because of your blog?
E: Yes, I do. But I don't write about political stuff.
I: You write about equality, people read it! Do you have any feeling that it is making a difference then?
E: Yes, but . . . I don't see that as a political thing. I see it like everyday . . . practice . . .

So Egoina has more than 120,000 unique visits every week, but Regina still doesn't consider herself influential or her communication political. Nevertheless, her way of using humour related to societal issues concerning equality matters can certainly be seen as a strategically communicative tool for gaining attention and influencing followers. In this way *humour* seems to be a successful tool for strategic communication. Considering the number of visitors her blog attracts, it is reasonable to assume that many visit on a weekly or even daily basis. This means that her communication must be perceived as not only *entertaining* but also *rewarding* and as *meaningful progress* for her followers as they probably *do* go back to listen to a new story (and embedded argument). One could even argue that this example captures some ingredients that perceptually and theoretically seem to be absent in conventional definitions of political strategic communication.

Target groups for strategic political communication – Objects of change

As previously described, earlier research within political communication tended to focus on the interplay and strategies between the main actors on a societal and local level (citizens, media and authorities), thereby measuring trust towards media, politicians and employees and trying to find cause and effects for lack of engagement in elections and so forth. This is not hard to understand as the formal procedures in a representational democracy are structured around these relationships and procedures. However, when this theme was introduced in the focus groups they didn't solely mention these three actors. Instead they gave their own examples of how they were being influenced and of whom they themselves sought to influence. The prime target group often mentioned was *other citizens* and not *directly* the politicians, even though they did comment on this (see the section on availability and accountability ahead):

I: Are the people who matter hearing your voice?
DN: Yes
I: Formal politicians, are they hearing your voice?
DN: No, but I think the people that matter are the young girls, young people who are reading the things I want them to.

This suggests the respondent is directing her communication towards peers and other citizens by trying to change not how politicians think but how peers think:

DN: The thing is, for the last couple of years Sweden Democrats have risen in Sweden. I think all the immigrants see this as a problem . . . immigrants aren't bad for Sweden, as Sweden democrats say. So I want to change the view of the Swedish people . . .

Early in the history of the Internet, when prominent politicians around the world replied to e-mail from citizens, it was seen as illustrating how digital media could enhance successful political communication. In Sweden former foreign minister Carl Bildt is often cited as an example of how this new democratic potential can be expressed. In contrast to this conventional discourse and way of thinking, the objects of change and influence for the respondents were other people. One conclusion is that communicative actions might be more strategically successful when they are horizontally performed on the Internet, through blogs and similar platforms as digital naturals tend to direct their communicative actions towards peers.

Availability and accountability

As we have described, digital naturals do politics in their own way. They tweet, retweet, blog and comment in order to engage their peers, whom they consider to be their primary target group for communicative actions. But if and when they contact politicians *directly*, they believe they are able to discern whether that communication is genuine or "fake". They believe they know how to identify and sense if the answers given online are trustworthy or if replies are automated or ghosted. In other words, they consider themselves to be media-literate insofar as they are sensitive to the way messages or communication acts are conducted and handled online. They are fully aware that politicians, especially those with high positions, often don't have the time to reply and communicate personally and that "ghostwriters" may answer, but the digital naturals don't care as long as they perceive the answers to be reliable so that they can count on the answers and arguments given to them.

DN1:   I know big bloggers who have employees who run their Facebook pages and stuff. Do you know Jens Stoltenberg, the Norwegian . . . I follow him on Facebook and he is really good. He posts like every day.

DN2:   But he has got a ghostwriter . . . for what I know.

DN1:   But it feels like him, so it doesn't really matter.

I: It feels like him, so it doesn't really matter?

DN1:   Yeah, it's a little personal touch.

DN3:   If they can be accountable for what they say, then it's probably . . . it works for me.

* I = interviewer; DN1, 2, 3 = different digital naturals

Digital naturals see *availability* as very important and something that must be guaranteed by everyone who communicates online; if it is not the addressed person who communicates with them, this does not matter as long as it *feels* genuine and as long as the politician can be held *accountable* for the answers given. Some political as well as business organisations have already realised this; those who still use auto-replies are not taken seriously by our sample group.

Reasoned action and what democracy can be

The results of our fourth and final research question, concerning relations between publicly communicated ambitions of a revitalised civic sphere and the *perceived* possibilities of social media (as described briefly earlier), show a discrepancy between ambitions and reality. Digital naturals consider much online communication to be very far away from the idea of the "rational man". According to our sample, rational discussion as described by the Habermasian theory of reasoned action is rare (e.g. Habermas, 1996). The majority principle states that if enough people act in a certain direction online, this will make a difference. According to the digital naturals the majority principle is close to what they refer to as "clicktivism", where people have opinions and repost facts despite having no grounds on which to judge their veracity. This is seen as problematic as the majority principle outweighs rational discussion. The digital dream can easily turn into a nightmare! The DNs could give plentiful examples (e.g. "Kony 2012") which underlined the result described earlier.

DNs mostly retweet and repost comments and information from their peers, but they don't check the facts and don't search for alternative sources, rather confining discourse to sources identified by their friends. They seldom read newspapers or other traditional media channels, but *when* they do, they are satisfied by the channels they themselves are familiar with, or by those recommended by their friends.

I: Has social media made any difference to your engagement with politics?
DN: Yeah, I follow Barack Obama on Instagram. Yeah, and it's also on Facebook people share like articles from *Aftonbladet* [high-circulation Swedish newspaper] about political stuff and that's why I read it, because my friend reposted it.

This suggests that the gatekeeping functions which were once held by chief editors of old media channels now are partially replaced by the digital naturals themselves.

DN: I agree with you, I tend to look at the information on Facebook instead of going to the actual websites of the newspapers, which actually is problematic, I think, because then there is another person or other people that decide not frame, but choose for me . . .
I: Gatekeeping function?
DN: Yeah, they are gatekeepers. For the information, and I let them to be the gatekeeper, so that's why I am kind of passive, and I know I should go on the news sites myself.

In the long run this means that individual DNs can live in parallel worlds and can stick to different "truths". They do see it as problematic but explain it as a discourse of contemporary life where source control is considered to be too time-consuming. These results show a tendency that might increase in the future where different people are differently informed and where the common ground for facts, truth and knowledge tends to be stripped down and fragmented. This extreme relativism, which is nurtured by different online communities where "anything goes," might to a certain extent even explain why some contemporary conflicts tend to be stigmatised today (see Chapter 11). Additionally, this means that the ambition of collectively coming closer to truth, or as O'Reilly (2005) talked about, collective truth, as a specific quality for Web 2.0 is valid only within a certain community.

Democracy is not indispensable for digital naturals who know how to play the game

One of the most striking results from this study was the suggestion that democracy was not seen as indispensable for some of the DNs. They talked about strategic ways to sidestep the formal procedures of democracy and how to adapt to less transparent informal rules in order to reach individualistic goals. Democracy was often portrayed as a nice utopia.

DN: I came from another culture where democracy didn't exist . . . I think democracy is about equal rights. But I know you don't have to have democracy to get well educated or to succeed in life. That's what my parents told me, the thoughts they had, that impacted me . . . So I like the thought of democracy and I think Sweden is a country (which) is very open to all cultures and stuff. And I think that is why Sweden is such a good country. So democracy works here, but it doesn't work everywhere . . .

Furthermore, when they described how to achieve these goals, they often used the terminology of *game playing*.

DN1:   I think that once you accept that it is only a game, you join the game, but it's . . . I don't know, very individual. Actually it's not very democratic.

DN2:   So I feel that not from like saying that democracy is bad or something, I just see it as a thing . . . people are not aware of it, some people are aware of it, that people with power can influence, but it's not spoken transparently, but one needs to be aware of it. It's a game in the end.

DN1:   Yeah, but then again it's about who has the power to set the rules.

Here DN1 and DN2 highlight a salient element of the broader focus group discussions: *an individualistic approach to democracy* by which everyone has to find her or his strategies and ways in order to succeed. In these cases democracy was seen not as a collective project of building a society for the common good but as a playing field where everyone is required to be well informed and media-literate in order to succeed. Social media and the Internet were seen as helpful tools in order to achieve personal goals that might be held by other individuals as well and therefore managed and performed all together in a pseudo-collective way.

According to the DNs the crucial challenge was *knowing how to play the game*. Yes, some felt well informed but still powerless, and considered that *others* (media literates, digital elites and lobbyists) could impact democracy in ways that they themselves could not; we also saw another grouping which expressed the view that they did feel *satisfied and well informed* and believed this to be good enough. Those who claimed they knew how to play the game (media literates) suggested that digital technologies meant it was now easier than before for them to influence and cause change. Again, others thought information overload meant it was harder to influence and change because it is harder to get attention.

The digital naturals discussed the higher transparency on the Internet as it increases visibility of politicians' actions. The higher visibility was seen as an advantage for media literates as it was seen as a strategic tool to put pressure on politicians to act and to be accountable. They also claimed that this transparency on the Internet demanded to be handled in different and new ways.

DN1: To be strategic is to have the right feeling for transparency on the Net and to know how to handle transparency . . . You can't be strategic if you have no boundaries between private, business and politics . . . again, this is from a strategic perspective, the private life is the private life, you have the social media that is one life, and then the political sphere belongs in political sphere. But if you are . . . completely open on all these spheres, then how can you be strategic? Then how to make strategic choices? You can't because then you have exposed, I'm not saying that you are going to do bad things, but you still have exposed information which can contradict if you're in a . . . to minimise the risks . . . that is to basically minimise the risk for not being exposed to things that you cannot control any longer . . . it would damage your reputation . . .

So while in one sense digital naturals no longer seem to distinguish between online and offline (they reject *digital dualism*), the distinctions between the "front stage" and the "back stage" on the Internet have become more important to handle, and indeed play a critical role as some state that they actually live their lives more online than in the material world.

DN: . . . with the digital media today that's what you need to be aware of. And that's what I talk about, being aware of what you are doing in the cyberspace. We live more in cyberspace than we actually live in the outside . . .

At the same time as experiencing digital communication that diluted their sense of place and time, and gave them access to conversations and discourse that were little concerned with distance, they could be said to tend towards *homophily*, used by sociologists to mean "love of the same". Certainly, our respondents recognised information-gathering behaviours that seemed to resonate with Eli Pariser's conception of the *filter bubble*, where algorithm and constricted networks can also limit exposure to new ideas.

Conclusion

Our study looked at the experience of a group of individuals of similar age and situation; all had propensities that accorded reasonably closely with those expected of digital naturals.

On the first research question it can be stated that definitions of what democracy is tend to be limited to formal procedures, even though digital naturals actually do politics in new and influential ways by directing their opinions to peers, which are described as their primary target group for communicative actions. On the second research question, about how they perceive their own capabilities, results suggest that some of them describe themselves as media literates, and when they try to direct their communication efforts to politicians they are aware of the fact that politicians may use ghostwriters, but this is not seen as problematic (provided accountability can be guaranteed). Some feel themselves to be well informed, but others show low self-esteem, as they don't consider themselves to be media literates and, as a consequence, feel powerless. When they examine what it takes to strategically communicate through social media today, they describe different strategies for handling transparency and they also use the terminology of game playing.

Finally, when they describe the relations between publicly communicated ambitions of a revitalised civic sphere and the perceived possibilities of social media they identify a discrepancy between ambition and reality. Digital naturals consider much of the online communication to be very far away from the idea of the "rational man" and state that clicktivism outweighs rational discussion. Although they consider it problematic that they don't check facts and sources themselves, they will often repost information which they cannot verify.

Furthermore, they don't privilege democracy as being indispensable, nor do they recognise themselves as a part of a collective project of building a society for the common good. It appears that the digital naturals we spoke to see modern democracy as a playing field, and each individual must understand the rules and know how to play in order to gain personal influence and power in society.

9 Social media and parliamentary infighting

Digital naturals in the Swedish Riksdag

Nils Gustafsson

In May 2014 I met an American scholar who was doing research into the social media strategies of members of the US House of Representatives. She had heard me presenting an earlier version of this text and wanted to discuss a comparative approach. I wanted to explain the ways in which Swedish parliamentarians had very different social media strategies than members of the US Congress, so we flipped open our laptops to make things visual. On her screen was the Facebook page of a representative in her sample, and on mine was the Facebook profile of a member of the Riksdag. The contrast was illustrative to the extent that it made us smile. The American's Facebook page was filled of picture after picture of him with veterans, with local politicians, with celebrities, in meetings with various types of interest organisations and so on. The Swedish politician's timeline was topped by a picture of plastic soda bottles and a couple of bowls full of potato crisps. The caption told us that she was excited about watching the Eurovision Song Contest with her children. Other pictures gave evidence of her support for a football club and interest in running and cycling, with a couple of campaign events mixed in. Both were senior politicians and were heading into election campaigns (the European Parliament election in May and the Swedish general election in September, and the US midterm elections in November, respectively). A first impression might be that the American's Facebook strategy was more profession-alised and business-like, whereas the Swedish parliamentarian gave a more inti-mate and personal, perhaps even private appearance. Which approach is the most rational? That is not so easily determined. A point this chapter wants to make is that we cannot judge and analyse the Facebook behaviour of political actors from a global perspective without taking into account the very different structures these political actors encounter and which shape their strategies.

Studying the way politicians use social media is important in several ways. One obvious reason is that more and more communication is produced, channelled and transformed through social media in what Andrew Chadwick (2013) has called the media system. Another reason is that whereas the overwhelming majority of previous studies focus on the political use of social media during election campaigns, the period between elections can actually be more important to understanding how social media is changing internal power structures in the political system.

One could easily get the impression that political actors make decisions on strategy based on the notion that various Internet tools and social media are either useful or not useful. Papers studying 'adoption' or 'non-adoption' of Internet tools and social media seem to rest on this underlying assumption (e.g. Gulati & Williams, 2013; Jackson & Lilleker, 2009). But politicians "use specific tools for specific purposes with specific implications" (Nielsen, 2011, p. 756).

Academic papers often limit their empirical data to content analyses of politicians' social media profiles or notice their use of different platforms (Facebook, Twitter, Instagram), their number of posts, the number of followers and the volume of interaction (e.g. Bruns & Highfield, 2013; Vaccari & Nielsen, 2012). In order to gauge the underlying reasoning behind this, interviews and other qualitative methods are valuable complements to quantitative content analyses (not least because privacy settings in some platforms – e.g. Facebook – make it difficult to gather data from profiles; cf. Larsson, 2014, p. 16). Most often, there is also a temporal focus on the election campaign and the interaction between politicians and voters/journalists/activists (e.g. Enli & Skogerbø, 2013; Nielsen, 2011; Strandberg, 2013). However, the focus on elections disguises the importance of political communication in intra-party competition. Especially in party-centred systems, internal competition is vital to understand which candidates get elected to parliament and appointed to high office, and how policy is formulated.

Another problem is the research often treats parties as monolithic units rather than as organisations made up of individuals in networks (Katz & Mair, 2009, pp. 761f.). Often, only communication at the top, central level is studied (i.e. party leadership/communications units), whereas the everyday political communication of individual politicians, below the party leadership and outside of election campaigns, goes largely unnoticed.

Lastly, research should be sensitive to the very different opportunity structures that result from different election systems (cf. Black, 1972). Candidate-centred democracies (USA, UK) should produce different strategies to party-centred democracies (most European countries) (Enli & Skogerbø, 2013, p. 771). The work environment of the individual parliamentarians will also matter, as politicians who can outsource social media updates to campaign staff or regular staff (cf. Nielsen, 2011) should be more strategic and mainstreamed in their use than politicians who do all the updates themselves.

This chapter uses in-depth interviews with 37 parliamentarians from seven parties of the Swedish Riksdag to study individual politicians as players entangled in an intricate game for power and influence over the entire election cycle. It examines both intra-party and extra-party relationships, and the strategies affected by politicians' individual dispositions as well as demographics and seniority, and the political opportunity structure of the Swedish election system and the communication norms of their parties.[1] *How do parliamentarians use social media to further their strategic goals in an intra-party setting?* The perspective is explorative. In doing this, the aim is to provide the literature on strategic political communication with an understanding of the political uses of social media and other digital tools that takes into account the conflicting goals in different arenas of democratically elected politicians.

Intra-party competition: the Swedish case

Politicians want to achieve things. Their parties want to gain votes, form governments and legislate. While individual politicians work to fulfil these goals, they also have personal goals in their political careers.

For parliamentarians, politics has become a full-time job. Original reasons for engaging in politics might vary: when you have made your way into the central national political system, maximising personal influence is an important goal for staying in the system (Black, 1972; cf. Sieberer, 2006, p. 152). Maximising influence might mean working in different arenas with slightly differing objectives, but everything will serve the central goal of building and maintaining a strong platform from which to carry out the parliamentary work. In order to achieve this, a number of strategies are utilised where different categories of people are to be influenced. For instance getting elected in a party-centred system with proportional votes in multi-member districts means building support among members of the party district responsible for nominating candidates for the ballots. Since most voters vote for the list of ranked candidates the party has decided on rather than for individual candidates, the nomination process is more important than the actual election campaign (Depauw & Martin, 2008, pp. 105f.). Building local support usually includes travelling around local party chapters. Gaining a position within parliament once elected, however, necessitates a favourable standing with the party leadership, and – to a lesser extent – among fellow parliamentarians (Sieberer, 2006).

Parliamentarians with career ambitions must be able to handle conflicting demands: on the one hand, they have to build a strong individual position in their parties (in competition with other parliamentarians), yet on the other hand, they have to be loyal to the party (in cooperation with other parliamentarians). At the same time, they must operate within party-specific opportunity structures. Group norms determine what behaviour is desirable under certain circumstances and how far an individual parliamentarian can go in distinguishing him-/ herself from the parliamentary party group (PPG). These norms help to strengthen coordination and group identification. Barrling Hermansson (2004) uses the term *party culture*. Party culture is essentially the social meaning that actions carry for the group. Studying party culture is studying the signs that this culture manifests and how party members see themselves as a group (ibid., p. 22). The party culture is the language with which a party defines itself. The norms of communication in a political party are the elements of party culture which determine how members should behave when communicating internally and externally. For instance the party cultures in the Swedish Riksdag can be categorised in terms of collectivism and individualism. The Social Democrats and Moderates are thus characterised as collectivist parties, whereas the Green and Liberal parties are characterised as individualist, with other parties falling in between (Barrling Hermansson, 2004).

Political parties in flux: structural change and social media

Political parties and their internal opportunity structures are not static. Katz and Mair (1995, 2009) claim that political parties in the late modern era of Western societies have undergone a change from mass and catch-all parties to cartel parties, which as a result of organisational logic, globalisation, the end of the Cold War and other societal changes grow together with the state, engage more in depoliticised inter-party collusion and grow financially dependent on state subsidies, thereby becoming more independent of party members and supporters (Katz & Mair, 2009, p. 755). Election campaigns become less dependent on activists and more "capital-intensive, professionalized and centralized" (ibid.). Campaign strategies and tools will become increasingly similar across parties (ibid., p. 756). This hints at individual behaviour of candidates becoming less important as campaigns and communication strategies are mainstreamed.

On a more general level, political parties evolve as a result of changes in alliances among organisational actors and as a result of environmental pressure (Panebianco, 1988, pp. 240, 243). Among types of environmental changes that affect political parties we find for example changes to electoral legislation, new technology, changes to the media system and so on. On a societal level, cultural shifts will also affect organisations. These changes affect both the formal and the informal structures (i.e. party culture) of a party. However, organisations are also a product of their past and are marred by institutional inertia (ibid., p. 261).

Two major trends in politics in recent decades that have been studied by researchers are mediatisation and personalisation (Strömbäck, 2008). As politics becomes increasingly mediated – that is communicated through the media – it also becomes mediatised. Politics is shaped in order to adapt to a media logic. As a direct consequence, politics also becomes personalised (ibid., p. 238; Karvonen, 2010). For reasons of entertainment, storytelling and simplification, more focus is put on individual politicians and less on policy content. As politicians adapt to the media logic, they become more interested in managing their personal image.

Social network sites and other types of services generally lumped together under the fuzzy concept of social media are sometimes said to change the nature of political communication and political organisation (e.g. Bennett & Segerberg, 2012). The reporting of traditional mass media with important roles of a few influential editors morphs with new forms of media into a "hybrid media system" (Chadwick, 2013) where different actors can influence the way that information is produced, packaged, interpreted and disseminated. It can be argued that "social media fit into long-term on-going processes where political communication has become increasingly focused on personalities and personal traits of politicians" (Enli & Skogerbø, 2013, p. 758). Literature suggests that there is a homogenising effect of social media on political communication (cf. Enli & Skogerbø, 2013; Nilsson & Carlsson, 2014). Taken together with the cartel party thesis of state-party collusion (Katz & Mair, 1995), we would expect limited differences between individual parliamentarians when it comes to social media strategy. A competing perspective, underlining the need for contextualisation and opportunity structure, would lead us to expect major differences between parliamentarians. For instance, the concept of 'digital naturals' describes an approach to culture and society that is expressed through digital media in more individualist terms than that of other groups. These competing expectations will be explored in the present study.

Strategic dimensions of social media use

It was obvious that social network sites (SNS) were not seen as a favoured channel for internal communication in the parliamentary party, due to their semi-public nature. Instead, text messages were by far the preferred method, with SNS predominantly used as a means for reaching out to voters, journalists and fellow party members. E-mail is not seen as a viable means of communication as parliamentarians generally receive too much e-mail to be able to respond in a timely manner. SNS are a fast news source and often the way that parliamentarians first hear news. They are also a way of keeping track of fellow parliamentarians and other party members: what they are doing and what positions they take on political issues. In addition, parliamentarians can use SNS to get their message out to voters, fellow party members and journalists, as well as to inform the public and the media about what they are doing. This offers a way for parliamentarians to show the public what they spend their time on and that they are actively working for the electorate. As one respondent put it, parliamentarians who are less active on SNS risk being suspected of wasting their time at the taxpayers' expense. SNS also provide parliamentarians with a source of positive feedback on their performance. It is, however, also the case that management and strategy differ greatly on an individual basis: while Twitter is generally used as a tool to talk politics, Facebook can be a place to interact solely with political contacts (voters, party members) or with a mix of political and private contacts. Since Swedish parliamentarians usually write their updates themselves, strategies depend heavily on individual behaviour and path dependency: if you started your Facebook profile as a site of interacting with (real) friends and family, most likely you will keep doing this.

The different strategic themes that emerged in the interviews can be structured along four dimensions: *intensity, individualism, intuition* and *intimacy*. Although these dimensions are based on interviewees' own answers about their own behaviour and what they generally believe to be successful strategies, they can be anchored in literature and used to analyse actual behaviour in further studies of social media strategies. The following sections discusses the results of the interviews leading on from these dimensions.

Intensity

Under the theme of intensity, not only the frequency of updates and number of platforms are discussed, but also general attitudes to social media as a form of communication. In the general population, young people are heavily overrepresented in their use of social network sites (SNS) and in the intensity of that use. When it comes to using SNS for political purposes, young people are even more overrepresented (Gustafsson & Hoagland, 2011). This might lead one to believe that younger parliamentarians would be much more interested in using SNS. This is not the case; about 92% of all Swedish parliamentarians were Facebook and/or Twitter[2] users during the 2010–2014 term of office. The few non-users are found in all parties.

To accompany the interviews, a limited analysis of the social media profiles of the sample was conducted (all but one parliamentarian had a Facebook account). Their number of friends varied greatly, from a couple of hundred to several thousand. All Facebook users update regularly, usually a couple of times a day. Roughly half also had a Twitter account, with the number of followers again ranging from several hundred to several thousand. How often they tweeted ranged from one tweet now and again with a few days of inactivity in between to around 10–12 tweets a day, including retweets and discussions.

However, there were differing attitudes regarding the intensity of use, as well as general views on the format, which largely, but not exclusively, aligned along age patterns. There was a general sense that young parliamentarians were more intensive users of social media. One respondent, born in the late 1960s, said,

> I can sense the difference between those who are 20–25 years old and those who are older that everything is very fast and they are all very used to handle all these media that exhaust me. How do you keep up? How do you find the time?

This also addresses the cost-benefit analysis a lot of older parliamentarians seem to do when discussing their social media use. Whereas younger interviewees do not discuss a trade-off of social media versus other ways of using time, their seniors based decisions on how to use social media on alternative costs. One respondent born in the 1940s said he wondered at the amount of time some of his colleagues seemed to spend updating their profiles and how this affected their political competence and understanding of complex issues. He used his own Facebook account only for posting links to his electronic newsletter and maintained that he did not think that he would "learn anything from the chatter there".

It would perhaps be reasonable to believe that most differences in norms of communication and attitudes towards using SNS among the parliamentarians were attributable to age. If we look only to the interviewees' attitudes to social media as a career tool, there is no such connection. The tendency is instead that interviewees with high positions within the party or the group believed less in the merits of SNS use for internal success, whereas others tended to view SNS in a more favourable light, regardless of their age.

Individualism

The dimension of individualism relates to the tension between the personalisation of politics (Karvonen, 2010; Strömbäck, 2008) and the relatively strong collectivism of the parties in the Swedish Riksdag (Barrling Hermansson, 2004), as well more general arguments about individualism as a societal trend (Inglehart, 1977) and the idea that social media fits well into these trends (Bennett & Segerberg, 2012; Enli & Skogerbø, 2013). It also connects to discussions of transparency versus secrecy in internal affairs.

All interviewees acknowledged the tension between collectivism and individualism: it is built into the structure of a system that favours internal party cohesion *and* where internal competition is necessary for personal success. Some expressed the notion that this tension had grown stronger in later years, whereas others maintained it had remained stable over time. But it was clear that the way that individualism was expressed in social media was a source of irritation for many.

As one respondent, born in the 1980s, put it, "You can almost feel that some people are really screaming for affirmation!" The same respondent complained that Twitter had become "a platform for mutual admiration; it's a gang of people who are talking to each other all the time and try to outdo each other with who's got the funniest comment," and for some of her colleagues, "it's a strategy to keep in with journalists and like have this jargon that we're buddies."

It is clear that some in the PPGs are seen as being more outspoken than others. Some interviewees explain this by generational differences: people born in the 1980s are more outspoken. Others refer to differences in position: having a high formal position prevents you from being too frank.

One respondent claimed that instead of making internal debates more transparent, SNS have contributed to an even more secretive climate:

> If you post things like that in social media, then the group leadership knows that. 'What the hell, you're sitting here snitching about things you shouldn't talk about, you've signed the PPG rules!' So that you don't want to do, but a phone call is impossible to track. It's a difficult balance. On the one hand you want to be open. On the other hand private conversations must remain private, or else people won't dare to speak freely, and that becomes more and more difficult with Twitter and Facebook and text messages. It's almost the case that even when you're talking between four eyes, you're more careful.

There was no consensus over whether SNS have brought about an increased tension between individualism and collectivism. Generally the tension was felt more by Social Democrats and Moderates (which is in line with expectations, since these parties have more collectivist party cultures), but members of the Liberal and Green PPGs also claim this. Among those who said that individualism has become stronger in the parliamentary party, the role of SNS was disputed. One respondent referred to SNS as a cause of growing individualism. Others pointed to a general trend in society: building your personal brand becomes more important in all branches. Many interviewees claimed that young parliamentarians are more individualist.

One Social Democratic respondent went so far as to claim,

> (There are) parallel cultures right now. One where everything is open and transparent. And one where you still live in a world where we can fight secretly and then present something. But the citizens aren't buying it.

Intuition

The intuition dimension can be conceptualised as the extent to which social media use is integrated into the daily routines of the parliamentarian. A major difference between the party leadership and ordinary parliamentarians and indeed, as indicated earlier, more generally between the Swedish political system and those countries where they have more staff support, is that the parliamentarians manage their own social media accounts. This means that the actual posting has to be done by parliamentarians themselves during days filled by other tasks. As a result, the choice of social media strategy might not be so much an active choice as a result of whether social media feels intuitive – whether it can be fitted easily into the daily schedule. Those who feel that social media takes up time that would better used for other, more important tasks will refrain from using it, or use it in a limited way, whereas those who make it a natural part of life do it continuously, without feeling it is stealing time from other things.

> I can't use media that becomes an obstacle to me. Facebook for me is a natural way to communicate. And I do – not without having thought it through – but I do it without thinking 'Oh I have to do this now'. [. . .] [B]logging feels like shouting into the desert. The response is almost more important than what I post.

This quote, from a parliamentarian born in the 1960s, illustrates that 'intuitive' use of social media is not exclusively limited to younger generations, although there was a clear tendency towards the young finding it easier to integrate social media with other tasks. Digital naturals among the parliamentarians intuitively understand the social media logic (see Klinger & Svensson, 2014), whereas others have difficulties integrating social media into their public roles.

The importance of intuition in explaining differing social media use in the absence of professionalised, mainstreamed strategies seems banal when compared with research on 'ordinary' users, but that politicians behave like ordinary users is an important observation in the light of research trying to explain strategies with external factors. Individual traits are more important than any 'best practices'. The opposite is true for professionally managed accounts of leadership or party organisations, where strategies seem to be converging according to international inspiration.

Whether this makes digital natural parliamentarians more successful in internal competition is complicated by the fact that success in the intra-parliamentary arena means building support among a variety of actors. In any case, it is an empirical question that this study cannot answer.

Intimacy

The intimacy dimension relates to the norms and attitudes associated with what is seen as private and what is public. Social network site users must "write themselves into being" (boyd, 2008, p. 121) in that posted content forms the image of the user in the eyes of others. The semi-public character of sites like Facebook blurs private and public spheres. This may be especially true for many Swedish parliamentarians who have a profile with a mix of old classmates, family and friends as well as political contacts, journalists and citizens in general. Since content is decontextualised, it can be argued that "public and private become meaningless binaries" (ibid., p. 34).

The interviewees deem their own SNS conduct to be desirable and in accordance with norms of communication. They should be 'personal, but not private'. In order to be entertaining for followers and friends, SNS profiles should not be restricted to dry policy proposals and information about what meeting the parliamentarian is going to next. In SNS you are supposed to be human, and so interviewees occasionally post more personal things. What is personal and what is private is, however, a matter of definition. Elaborating on that boundary, one respondent viewed presence in SNS as being on a par with a profile interview in a tabloid. Others specified that posting pictures of their children would be off-limits. However, a simple check of the Facebook profiles of interviewees revealed that some of the very ones who had declared they would never post pictures of their children did just that.

It is clear that on one hand, there is a tension between different views of what is appropriate behaviour in social media for a parliamentarian, and on the other, between what the individual user/parliamentarian considers to be appropriate behaviour and what she or he actually does. If the first could be described as a cultural gap or a clash of norms, the second could perhaps best be described as a cognitive gap, or a clash between strategy and intuition.

A silent revolution?

SNS allow politicians to present a tailored personal image to voters, fellow party members and journalists. Since SNS almost inherently presuppose content of a personal nature, they lend themselves naturally to identity management (boyd, 2008, pp. 129f.; Gustafsson, 2010, p. 15). Users have to strike a balance between disclosure and privacy. However, earlier research has shown that there is "little to no relationship between online privacy concerns and information disclosure on online social network sites" (Tufekci, 2008, p. 20). The user interface in social network sites seems to make people more prone to voluntarily disclose information of a private or semi-private nature regardless of their stated attitudes. The interviewees in this study were aware that they had to 'lighten' their SNS presence with a personal note, but this did not seem to be felt as a burden. Norms of good identity management and being personal in SNS differ considerably between individuals. The lack of consensus on what the informal (or even formal) norm for parliamentarians' appearance in SNS really is creates insecurity and confusion for individual players in a collectivist and hierarchical institutional frame.

danah boyd (2008) uses the concept of invisible audiences and collapsed contexts to describe how SNS users deal with the changed communication infrastructure. Invisible audiences point to the fact that as a speaker, the individual user does not see the audience before her: it is invisible. Collapsed contexts refer to the fact that in social network sites, users usually bring in several distinct social networks (friends, family, colleagues, etc.). As a result, the different contexts that an individual is situated in collapse: she has to act like a unidimensional human being. Transferred to parliamentarians, their use of social network sites creates a collapse of the electoral and internal arenas: they can no longer separate different strategies for communication in the arenas, and this has repercussions on the parliamentary arena that they seek success in.

The party culture and the norms of communication in the parliamentary groups of the Social Democrats and the Left Party have been characterised as collectivist and focused on loyalty, whereas the parliamentary groups of especially the Liberal and Green Parties have been characterised as individualist. However, the interviews in this study show that norms might be under external pressure and that there might be a tension between competing norms of communication. Since it seems to be younger parliamentarians across all parties rather than parliamentarians in only some parties who embody this change in norms, and that the norms are more in the individualist-personal-active line, it would be likely to affect parties with collectivist norms more than parties with individualist norms. Tensions in relation to proper use of SNS seem to emanate from different opportunity structures depending on rank, the influence of different attitudes to SNS and transparency, and a general confusion and insecurity in the parliamentary parties over what exactly the norms of communication are in the wake of environmental changes and new technology.

It is not surprising that parliamentarians in high positions say that SNS are not an important factor for internal career building. Since they already have attained a secure position, they do not have to use an active SNS strategy to make their way within the party. For parliamentarians with a low position, SNS are seen as one useful strategy among many: they have more to win from using SNS, and since they are not official spokespersons, they are at liberty to use SNS in a more expressive way.

In this insecure environment, players with low positions and high ambitions are those who have the most to win to exploit potential changes in possible strategies. Players with high positions have more to lose: if they play their cards wrongly, they might lose the positions they have attained. But in reality the uncertainty is so high that there does not seem to be any connection between position and attitudes on one hand and behaviour on the other.

If there really are competing norms of communication in the parliamentary party, this could potentially become an even greater problem in the future, as insecurity and conflicts grow over the proper norms regarding the dimensions of intensity, individualism, intuition and intimacy. The lack of consensus on what really is the informal (or even formal) norm for parliamentarians' appearance in SNS creates insecurity and confusion for individual players in a collectivist and hierarchical institutional frame.

The differences between the strategies of individual parliamentarians offer a corrective to the cartel party thesis notion that party election strategies become more homogeneous (Katz & Mair, 2009). It could well be the case that *parties* are becoming more similar in this respect. However, *individual* strategies in a party-dominated system seem to be determined by personal traits to a higher extent.

Notes

1 The Social Democrats (11 interviews), the Moderates (10), the Green Party (5), the Liberal Party (4), the Left Party (3), the Centre Party (3) and the Sweden Democrats (1). Interviews were conducted June 2012–January 2014. The interviewed parliamentarians were chosen strategically to produce variation in age, gender and rank.
2 Based on my own estimate: I have not been able to find Facebook or Twitter profiles for the remaining 8%.

10 'Swarming' for democracy

Karl-Theodor Guttenberg's plagiarism case, the court of public opinion and the parliament of things

Hagen Schölzel and Howard Nothhaft

This chapter presents a case study of a prominent communicative conflict shaped mainly by Internet-based political activism. In a way, it is the story of a clash between conservative, established political power on one side and digital naturals on the other. We take a look at the two weeks that led to the resignation of former German defence minister Karl-Theodor zu Guttenberg on 1 March 2011. The first part gives an account of the case, paying attention to Guttenberg's attempts at handling the crisis. Next, we explain why Guttenberg's attempts failed. On the face of it, the reason was unprecedented 'swarm activism'. We want to clarify what the metaphor captures. We argue that (a) *the speed and thoroughness* with which the activists worked, (b) the *indisputability* of their results due to *impartiality* and *transparency* and (c) the *anonymity* and *loose collectivity* of the swarm members *undercut* 'traditional' strategies, such as 'accusing the accuser' or 'playing for time'. We conclude with a critical theorisation and suggest that the Guttenberg plagiarism affair can be construed not only as a clash of actors in the court of public opinion but also as a case of 'Dingpolitik' in the sense of actor-network thinkers like Bruno Latour.

We are well aware of the extensive body of literature systematising strategies of crisis communication as well as Internet-based activism. We chose not to discuss it for three reasons: (1) limitations of space, the focus being on the details of the case; (2) we assume that the repertoire is well known; and (3) there is no evidence the actors involved relied on any of the theories that would have been the subject of a literature review. This does not mean, of course, that a discussion of the case against the backdrop of crisis communication literature as read by an outside observer could not be rewarding. What is most important, however, is that the Guttenberg case illustrates how different elements of Internet activism come together. It demonstrates the use of web technology for organisational purposes and participation, the establishment of an alternative source of information, the coordination of online and offline activities, and the conduct of a symbolic political conflict going far beyond the idea of simply communicating a certain issue in public discussion.

The case of Karl-Theodor zu Guttenberg

Public discussion of Guttenberg's PhD dissertation began on Wednesday, 16 February 2011, when the newspaper *Süddeutsche Zeitung* reported that he had to defend himself against accusations that he had "deceived" ("getäuscht") in his dissertation.[1] Professor of law Andreas Fischer-Lescano (2011) had discovered "parallels with other texts". The journalists who reported the case after being contacted by Fischer-Lescano (Reimer & Ruppert, 2013, pp. 309–310) included some passages without pronouncing a clear judgement. They drew attention to the fact that "irregularities in citations do not necessarily mean that there is a fraudulent intent," but also cited Fischer-Lescano, who pronounced the work "an audacious plagiarism" and "a fraud" (Preuß & Schultz, 2011).

Guttenberg's first reaction, a written statement widely cited by the press, was to reject the accusation. He dismissed the plagiarism claim as "ludicrous" (e.g. "Uni Bayreuth prüft", 2011), and Guttenberg's former supervisor, professor emeritus Peter Häberle, called the accusations "absurd". In an interview with tabloid newspaper *Bild* Häberle praised Guttenberg as "one of my best seminarians and doctoral students" ("Guttenberg weist", 2011). The University of Bayreuth, which awarded Guttenberg his doctorate, announced that its commission of scientific self-control (Universität Bayreuth, 2011a) would look into the matter.

While most reactions were restrained or even expressed support, journalists and bloggers[2] searched for or reported further passages they claimed were plagiarised. One web activist, *PlagDoc* (a doctoral student from the south of Germany), opened a public document to collectively analyse the complete dissertation (PlagDoc, personal communication, 11 September 2013). Within hours, this collaboration attracted so many people that its website crashed. The community quickly moved to a new platform based on wiki technology, *GuttenPlag-Wiki*.[3] In an article published by *Frankfurter Allgemeine Zeitung Online*, only a few hours later, an anonymous activist explained the platform's success: "Tonight we observed that more and more users posted suspicious passages of Guttenberg's dissertation on weblogs and published them via Twitter. [. . .] We wanted to bundle these snippets on a common webpage to put things straight" (Georgi, 2011).

One initiator of *GuttenPlag-Wiki* described the swarm's motivation:

> We do not care about big politics but about facts. Not because we have something against Herr Guttenberg, but because we regard it as our function as serious scientists to clarify the case. [. . .] We want to defend serious science.
>
> (Georgi, 2011)

and

> If we indulge such plagiarism then it completely devalues a doctoral thesis.
>
> (Ruppert & Reimer, 2011)

Another activist, AnnaNym, explained,

> I hope very much that it will be recognized that we are working in favour of politicians' reputation, not against it. We convict cheaters. We want to improve

the reputation of science and politics, even if this probably won't work in the short run.

(Funk & Helbig, 2011)

Besides upholding scientific standards, other motives were dissatisfaction with politics or disappointment with Guttenberg (Reimer & Ruppert, 2011, p. 5), but the political motive was not necessarily connected to party preference – the activists included supporters of all relevant parties (ibid.). However, they did seem to share a general distrust in politics, from which Guttenberg, who had appeared as a new type of politician, was exempted in some cases. Activist KayH expressed this attitude: "I liked Guttenberg, thought that he was very talented. This was a great disappointment for me" (Bewarder, 2011). In a similar vein, activist Goalgetter said, "I thought he was cool, he appeared accurate to me. I was cheated as most others." He added, "This abuse of power has to be exterminated once and for all" ("Dieser Machtmissbrauch muss dauerhaft ausgerottet werden") (Haupt, 2011).

The collaboration and the public interest sustained the activists' motivation. On Wednesday, 17 February, more plagiarised passages were found. With 1,400,000 page views on its first day, about 10,000,000 page hits in two weeks, or up to 200,000 unique visitors per day (Reimer & Ruppert, 2013, p. 304), the *GuttenPlag* platform became a central actor. While the 'swarm' was carrying out its search, the minister travelled to Afghanistan, ostensibly to visit troops. The trip, which took place only hours after the first accusations, was regarded as a surprise by media observers. It had not been announced, and Guttenberg travelled without press representatives (e.g. "Überraschungsbesuch", 2011). There are reasons to believe, then, that the trip was an evasive manoeuvre. On his return, Guttenberg was observed sneaking into the *Kanzleramt* for a meeting with Chancellor Angela Merkel. The same day, columnist Franz Josef Wagner of *Bild* wrote a short commentary, probably expressing the majority opinion:

> *Dear Dr zu Guttenberg. What are the accusations of plagiarism in your doctoral thesis about? About purity of science? Or about disenchanting a superstar? Your popularity in the barometer of public opinion is titanic. [. . .] Germans expect you to assume higher responsibilities – prime Minister of Bavaria, chancellor of Germany. [. . .] I am clueless about doctoral theses. [. . .] After all, from outside, I can say: Don't fuck up a good man. Shit on the Doctor.*

(Wagner, 2011)

Bild is regarded as the single strongest influence on public opinion in Germany. Former chancellor Gerhard Schröder famously remarked that for governing he needed only "*Bild, Bild am Sonntag* and the gogglebox." *Bild* supported Guttenberg throughout the whole affair, initiating a campaign of articles, op-eds, telephone surveys and positive polls. Two days into the affair, Friday, 18 February 2011, Chancellor Merkel declared that she trusted Guttenberg fully ("volles Vertrauen"). Members of the government coalition deemed a "resignation improbable" (e.g. "Merkel", 2011). That same morning, news broke of an attack on the military camp Guttenberg had visited the day before. With three soldiers killed and six injured, the attack was the most momentous incident for about a year.

Unsurprisingly, the press corps expected a statement by the minister about the attack and the affair. And indeed, in the course of the morning Guttenberg did make a short statement to the journalists assembled in front of the ministry. Guttenberg apparently tried to put an end to discussions by apologising. He stated that his work was not plagiarism, and that he did not intend to mislead anyone. He would "gladly" refrain ("temporarily, I emphasize *temporarily*") from "bearing the academic title until investigations by the university lead to a result" (Friese & Linnenbrink, 2011). He clarified that he would communicate only with the university. Referring to the attack on soldiers in Afghanistan, he announced that he would, from now on, concentrate on his responsibilities as minister (ibid.).

The circumstances caused an éclat. The problem was that Guttenberg's statement took place at the same time the heavyweights of political journalism were attending *Bundespressekonferenz* – the official press conference instituted by the press corps. Here, only a stone's throw away, Guttenberg's spokesperson issued a terse statement that the minister was giving a declaration, right now, in front of "selected journalists" in the ministry of defence. On hearing that, many journalists left. The chairman protested – for the first time in history since 1945 (Friese & Linnenbrink, 2011). In the meanwhile, GuttenPlag activists identified more than 80 plagiarised passages. The *Berliner Zeitung* referred to the platform in reporting a passage plagiarised from an undergraduate term paper (Rest, 2011). Conservative newspaper *Die Welt* declared the day *Guttenberg's black Friday* (Alexander, 2011).

On Saturday, 19 February 2011, while conservative politicians supported and opposition members criticised the minister, an opinion poll by *TNS Emnid* showed the majority of German citizens (68%) wanted Guttenberg to stay; only 27% demanded resignation ("Guttenberg findet", 2011). In the same article, Emnid manager Klaus Peter Schöppner explained that Guttenberg did not need to resign, since "Germans willingly forgive the one who admits his mistakes." Political scientist Gerd Langguth was quoted as saying that Guttenberg could even gain in stature because a top-ranking politician "needs to pass storms of steel" (Stahlgewitter) since "that roots him in the ground, makes him more human" ("Guttenberg findet", 2011). The same afternoon, Guttenberg called suggestions of resignation "nonsense" ("Deutsche", 2011).

The following Monday, 21 February, leading members of the conservative party *CDU* once again expressed support ("Rücktritt", 2011). In a memorable turn of phrase, Chancellor Merkel declared that she had not hired Guttenberg as a scientific assistant: "I stand by him as a person and by the work he is doing" (Fras, Schmale & Von Bebenburg, 2011). Supporters also gathered on a Facebook page, which attracted "minute by minute . . . dozens of supporters" ("Guttenberg spaltet", 2011) and passed 130,000 likes that afternoon (Rücktritt, 2011). A news portal wrote that "Guttenberg divides the net," and *Bild* observed a veritable "battle for Guttenberg on the internet" between supporters and adversaries. The battle went on even after Guttenberg had resigned ("Guttenberg spaltet", 2011; Thewalt & Spieker, 2011). That evening, Guttenberg gave a speech at a conservative-party event in Kelkheim near Frankfurt, where he announced that he would permanently forgo his academic title (legally irrelevant). He again emphasised that although he had made mistakes, he did not "mislead consciously or in any way deliberately" (Von Bebenburg, 2011). An opinion poll by *Infratest dimap*, published in the TV magazine *Report München*, once again showed a majority of German citizens to be satisfied with Guttenberg's political performance. He remained Germany's most popular politician. Those polled also believed that the media did not report objectively and equitably about the case (Kuhn & Lingenfelser, 2011).

GuttenPlag activists, 60% of whom hold university degrees and 20% of whom have doctoral titles (Ruppert & Reimer, 2011), became even more motivated. One later said that "[m]y direct participation was due to the relatively easy-going handling of the accusations, up to that time, by the defence Minister" (ibid.). Another one, KayH, explained, "I was sure that the subject was meant to be played down. But I wanted nothing to be covered up" (Bewarder, 2011). Chancellor Merkel's personal support was a key factor: "[t]hat was a key moment for many" of the activists (Haupt, 2011). Marcusb suggested that "[t]his was a slap in the face for all those to whom science means something" (Bewarder, 2011). Another activist, AnnaNym, wrote, "The run on GuttenPlag came when many politicians slapped the face of science. That was a humiliation" (Funk & Helbig, 2011).

Two days later, on Wednesday, 23 February, the case was discussed during question time in the *Bundestag*. Opposition members severely attacked Guttenberg; conservatives supported; the governing coalition's smaller partner FDP avoided partisanship in Guttenberg's favour (Fischer, Gathmann & Wittrock, 2011). The plagiarism hunters had discovered that Guttenberg had plagiarised four expert reports requested from the parliament's very own research services. The opposition asked Guttenberg whether he had used others. The minister was not able to answer authoritatively (Fischer, Gathmann & Wittrock, 2011). The next day, evidence of plagiarism from other research services papers emerged ("Chronologie", n.d.). A "brown envelope" containing a detailed analysis of passages taken from the papers had been given anonymously to one publicly known activist (D. Weber-Wulff, personal communication, 6 September 2013). *GuttenPlag* activist KayH later revealed that the activists were tipped off by employees angered by the way Guttenberg handled science (Haupt, 2011).

At the end of the debate, the front lines were established: Guttenberg and his supporters conceded he had made mistakes, but he had apologised and relinquished his title. He did not deceive consciously, and the final judgement should properly rest with the university. Public discussions were an orchestrated campaign of slander. Opposition parties accused Guttenberg of fraud, plagiarism and downright lies. They demanded his resignation for reasons of personal ineptitude as a minister, in order to avoid damage to the academic system, to the armed forces he headed and to Germany's international reputation in the global scientific landscape.

In the evening, Bayreuth University revoked Guttenberg's title. It argued that his thesis "did objectively not adhere to scientific standards", so it was unnecessary to prove "deliberate intention at fraud" (Universität Bayreuth, 2011b). The decision sparked criticism by the opposition, because without addressing deliberate intentions the university "adopts Guttenberg's argument and facilitates his political survival". Chancellor Merkel, conversely, welcomed the decision as "correct and logical" ("Uni Bayreuth erleichtert", 2011). The decision "made sense", Merkel said, since it confirmed Guttenberg's own line of argumentation – that is that his dissertation was flawed but he did not deceive (ibid.).

But over the weekend, Guttenberg's support in the conservative party crumbled. Prominent critics included Bundestags president Norbert Lammert and Minister of Science and Education Annette Schavan (who would later herself be stripped of her PhD title). Despite that, an opinion poll by *Forschungsgruppe Wahlen* published by public broadcaster ZDF showed that Guttenberg, although he had lost sympathies, remained Germany's most popular politician, with 75% of citizens not seeing a need for his resignation ("Politbarometer", 2011). But Merkel's statement that she did not hire a 'scientific assistant' provoked German doctoral students to initiate an open letter to the chancellor, which gained nearly 64,000 signatures (Bunde *et al.*, 2011). At least one *GuttenPlag* activist, professor Debora Weber-Wulff, was involved (ibid.). The organisers held that the government's handling of the affair was a "mockery".

On Monday, 28 February, the open letter was sent to the chancellery. The next morning, 1 March, Guttenberg resigned. In a short, terse statement he declared that he did not do so because of the academic community's pressure, although he did understand their outrage. His explanation was that he could not bear a situation where the debate about his person and PhD thesis overshadowed the tragic incident in Afghanistan and the important Army reform. He concluded by saying he was always willing to fight but that he had reached the limits of his strength ("habe die Grenzen meiner Kräfte erreicht") ("'Ich'", 2011).

Analysing the 'swarm'

When Guttenberg resigned, he demonstrably was Germany's best-liked politician. He enjoyed the support of the tabloid *Bild*, with an estimated 12 million readers. Arguably, he had the full support of his party, which placed high hopes on him as a crown prince, although the fact that he began to be a rival to Angela Merkel cannot be discounted entirely. In the course of his stellar career, Guttenberg had demonstrated mastery of public relations, moreover, expertly stage-managing visits to the troops in Afghanistan at Christmas, not forgetting to bring along his young wife, Stefanie, born Countess Bismarck-Schönhausen, a TV celebrity in her own right. The question, then, is why did an immensely popular, well-connected politician, a PR genius, fail to ride out the storm?

A metaphorical answer would be that Guttenberg was attacked by a 'killer swarm' against which traditional defence strategies proved futile. That the *Gutten-Plag-Wiki* was a swarm phenomenon quickly became a common narrative in the media. Nowadays, even activists, when reflecting about their activities, reconstruct themselves as "a swarm" (PlagDoc & Kotynek, 2012). Yet, although metaphors can be helpful, sometimes they obscure more than they enlighten. What exactly is the swarm, how did it work and what does it mean for strategic communication?

Aware that Guttenberg's position, given the blatancy of his plagiarisms, might have been untenable from the beginning, our analysis emphasises three factors which were novel at the time: (1) the immense *speed* and *thoroughness*; (2) the *indisputability* and *impartiality* of the activists' work; and (3) the *anonymity* and *open collectivity* of the group.

Speed and thoroughness

The wiki became a central source of information for two reasons, its very speed and its professionalism. Two statements may serve as indicators. Hauke Jansen, chief fact checker of news magazine *Der Spiegel*, compared *GuttenPlag* to his own department: "[i]t develops a strong power, a 'bang', that we can't keep up with. I can't say: *Everyone on Guttenberg, no matter what.* We had to work on the issue's other stories as well" (Ruppert & Reimer, 2011). Hans Leyendecker, journalist at *Süddeutsche Zeitung*, analysed crowdsourced research as follows: "Even those [media] with the most resources at their disposal cannot compare to what an internet community can achieve together with regard to an issue" (ibid.).

When federal minister for education and research Annette Schavan (CDU) was accused of plagiarism, the formal procedure which led to the revocation of the title took nine months: from 29 April 2012, the day when activist "Robert Schmidt" informed the university, to 5 February 2013, the day the title was revoked. It took almost 11 months until Schavan's contestation of that decision was finally rejected in court on 20 March 2013. In Guttenberg's case, Bayreuth University revoked the title *seven days* after the first public accusations. The difference lay in three aspects: (1) there was no swarm in Schavan's case – her case was initially driven by only one activist, "Robert Schmidt"; (2) the Schavan case was taken on by Düsseldorf University and conducted as a proper academic investigation with a strong emphasis on legality and equal treatment for the incumbent minister; and (3) scholarly opinion was genuinely divided as to whether the 24-year-old Schavan committed plagiarism *at all*.

Although Schavan lost her title and resigned, the issue at hand was very different from that of Guttenberg. Schavan, a "grey woman" respected for her solidity, was probably aware that her position as minister would become untenable should her title be revoked. Not only was Guttenberg's title withdrawn, but also he relinquished it *himself*, temporarily, and then permanently. Guttenberg's actions suggest that he changed his strategy early on, from defending his title to defending his job and future political career.

But the strategy did not work. Despite attempts to construe the situation otherwise, Guttenberg was hounded out of office. Although he prepared the grounds for a return with a book in which he is interviewed about the affair by journalist Giovanni di Lorenzo (the book is called *Vorerst gescheitert*, "Failed for now"), two comeback attempts so far have foundered for the same reason – whatever Guttenberg says, he is no longer believed. Again, the speed and thoroughness with which the *GuttenPlag* community worked were probably the deciding factors: On 3 April 2011, one month after his resignation, the *GuttenPlag* community concluded their investigation. They had found plagiarised passages on 371 of 393 pages (94.8%), and 10,371 (63.8%) lines copied without proper reference from 135 different sources (GuttenPlag, 2011a). This is very different from the University of Bayreuth's bland verdict that the thesis objectively does not fulfil the criteria of a PhD dissertation. Anyone who looked at the various diagrams illustrating the blatant copy and paste, in one case stretching over five consecutive pages, could not but conclude that for Guttenberg to deny *intentional* fraud he must be a shameless liar, the victim of a very bad ghostwriter (which would have been even worse) or a madman.

That Guttenberg is no longer believed is not only due to the investigation's final results, but also arguably even more due to the dynamics of the communicative conflict. Guttenberg's attempts to downplay the plagiarism, to slow down the process of investigation, to claim ignorance of details, to shift the matter away from public scrutiny and to avoid admitting intentional fraud were answered quickly by more detailed research, by providing factual answers to contested questions within hours, by concentrating attention again on the case and by producing more evidence of fraud. Thus, although it is still not known what Guttenberg actually did when writing his thesis, the affair ruined his personal credibility.

Indisputability and impartiality

GuttenPlag was recognised as an indisputable source of information because the activists did professional work which was respected by professional journalists as the process and results were transparently documented. Kai Gniffke, chief of the national broadcaster ARD's editorial department, stated that "[t]he GuttenPlag-Wiki's practice seemed so professional and solid to me that I had no problem with using this by citing the reference" (Ruppert & Reimer, 2011).

The degree of professionalism achieved by *GuttenPlag* was not a coincidence, however. *GuttenPlag-Wiki*, PlagDoc and Kotynek (2012) clearly state, was "no unmanaged, magically self-organizing crowd of equals". On the contrary,

> *the collaborative process was guided by a common objective. There were clear arrangements on purpose, principles and modes of operation within the swarm: We only document, don't set political demands, we verify everything twice, we don't judge anything, which is not covered by data; in doing so we arrange things among each other.*
>
> (PlagDoc & Kotynek, 2012)

About 20 moderators and 100 supporters served as a "task force" which managed the platform, organised workflows, arranged content, cleaned the platform from vandalism and moderated conflicts – some of them having long experience of collaboration on other wiki platforms – for example *Wikipedia* (PlagDoc, 2013; PlagDoc & Kotynek, 2012). When conflicts arose – for example when *GuttenPlag* won the prestigious *Grimme Online Award* and the question occurred of whether the group's anonymity should be lifted for the ceremony – decisions were taken by vote in a core group in a private chat room. Activists also had personal phone calls in the case of some severe and personal controversies. Important for running the system day and night was the fact that the platform's two founders and main administrators, friends acting together under the same nickname *PlagDoc*, lived in different time zones – one in Germany, the other in the United States (PlagDoc, personal communication, 11 September 2013); PlagDoc, 2013). There were communication and coordination behind the scene, then, but the research work was public and transparent: every single step was documented and remained traceable on the platform. Full transparency was deemed a precaution to defend against public demands to disclose activists' identities:

> *[W]ho allows anonymity on a research-platform has to take specific care for all steps being reproducible afterwards, and all co-helpers acting on ethical and practical principles of investigative journalism and science: collecting evidence without forestalling results, no prejudgements, searching in all directions, handling both incriminating and exculpating material, using several sources.*
>
> (PlagDoc & Kotynek, 2012)

Apart from the careful processes in getting results, the way the results were published constituted a second indicator for the seriousness of *GuttenPlag*. The policy was to publish only double-checked facts. The vocabulary showed prudence and restraint. Activists spoke of "analogy of texts", "peculiarities" or "strong indications"; the term "plagiarism" was used only later. Speculation was avoided on the platform because, according to PlagDoc and Kotynek (2012), this "can become legally dangerous".

Activists cooperated with mass media, but their selective cooperation was based on personal decisions to answer journalists' requests and did not follow a certain communication strategy (PlagDoc, 2013). The group published only two preliminary reports: one filed on Monday, 21 February 2011, was a reaction on public discussions of the case, and the second on Wednesday, 1 March 2011, the day after Guttenberg resigned (GuttenPlag, 2011b, 2011c).

The "barcode" (GuttenPlag, 2011a), an animated visualisation which showed the transformation of a "clean" white surface representing the textual corpus of Guttenberg's dissertation into a collection of black and red (representing pages with plagiarised passages), was widely adopted by the media. But, contrary to its later use in public communication, that visualisation was intended for internal communication – that is to better coordinate work process on the *GuttenPlag-Wiki* (PlagDoc, personal communication, 11 September 2013).

On the other side, mass media and journalists also supported and shaped activists' work. One element documenting a close relationship between the two, and journalists' trust in the group, was the delivery of a digitalised copy of Guttenberg's thesis to *PlagDoc* by a reporter of the *Süddeutsche Zeitung* (PlagDoc, 2013). Furthermore, a survey showed that nearly 60% of *GuttenPlag* users became aware of the platform via traditional mass media or their respective websites (Reimer &

Ruppert, 2013, p. 308). Within activist circles, PlagDoc explains, the media attention made "everyone in the Wiki aware that one can't afford mistakes and never be suggestive of partiality" (ibid.).

Anonymity and open collectivity

Public criticism returned again and again to activist anonymity, which was seen as facilitating "swarm intelligence" but also "swarm gutlessness" (Spreng, 2011). However, anonymity was no obstacle to being recognised by journalists as a serious source. Activists themselves expressed different reasons for their anonymity, especially strategic and personal. Anonymity was also relevant for establishing the swarm's open collectivity.

First, anonymity and nicknames helped to focus attention on the matter of concern, not on individuals. One activist, AnnaNym, explained,

> *It is understandable that politicians and journalists want to know who works on the projects. But what would be better when we were publicly known? The facts wouldn't differ, however. We are doing nothing different than a book review. We just investigate on a published work. Anyone can do that. Our namelessness is an advantage, because it helps to focus discussion on the message not on its bearer.*
>
> (Funk & Helbig, 2011)

Another activist added that "[t]he idea that scientific credibility is related to single persons and single carriers needs to be overcome" (Haupt, 2011). KayH, pointed at the strategic dimension:

> *This demand for real names has only one objective. . . . That's the wish to personalize a discussion, which cannot be maintained by focusing on persons: Our objective is first and foremost a description of facts as objectively grounded as possible.*
>
> (Bewarder, 2011)

A second reason was that working with *GuttenPlag* did not go together with other personal or business interests. Activist Goalgetter pointed out for example that as a self-employed person he feared for business relations with politically conservative clients (Haupt, 2011). In at least one case, when anonymity was lifted, the person indeed did have to deal with unpleasant consequences in his professional life (D. Weber-Wulff, personal communication, 6 September 2013). PlagDoc worried about disadvantages in the scientific field, but also feared personal hostility:

> *We carefully adhered to anonymity at Guttenplag from the beginning. We didn't know what consequences this would have. Uncovering grievances in science is not necessarily rewarded. Sometimes you count as a traitor then. I*

have many other interests in life, and I don't want to suffer drawbacks in my life because of Guttenplag. If I only think of the e-mails we received . . . at the platform. One of our members once wrote a letter to the editors of a local newspaper under his real name, and the next day he found a threat in his letterbox. The message was: "We will catch all of you." I don't want to experience that myself.

(Funk & Helbig, 2011)

Anonymity not only protected individuals but also helped to keep the swarm together. PlagDoc explained that anonymity corresponded to its non-hierarchical organisation: "[W]e would not at all know who should represent us". As the platform's founder he also referred to the problematic example of another activist group:

I learned from the *Wikileaks* affair. When a person like Julian Assange stands so much out of a group project, then it is disadvantageous for the whole community. That's why I don't want to stand with my name in the foreground.

(Funk & Helbig, 2011)

The open collectivity of the 'swarm' organisation was also relevant for the process of knowledge production. Here it was not only a matter of culture but also closely related to the wiki platform and other technology (scanners, mailings, chat rooms, etc.). These technologies were crucial for facilitating, first, the partition of the research process into many single steps accomplished by many different persons, and second, the recombination of the snippets gathered into one coherent document. Partition not only facilitated collaborative work but also allowed different concrete research practices by different activists. There was manual literature research, automated comparison of digitalised texts (Bewarder, 2011) and the anonymous delivery of a brown envelope containing detailed analyses of certain parts of the thesis (D. Weber-Wulff, personal communication, 6 September 2013).

Strategic communication, democracy and the parliament of things

We have seen how activism confronted Germany's best-liked politician with a problem that even a PR genius could not solve. We have argued that the novel factors were as follows: (1a) The *speed* with which the activists established (some would say 'created') facts rendered ineffective well-known defence strategies, such as playing for time and changing the agenda. (1b) The *thoroughness* with which the activists demonstrated, visually, the blatant scale of Guttenberg's plagiarism negated the strategy of downplaying the incident or muddying the water. No one who has seen the barcode can believe that plagiarism on 94.8% of pages just 'happens'. (2) The time-honoured strategy of undermining the credibility of the attack was negated, moreover, by strict *impartiality* and *transparency* that, in turn, made the activists' results virtually *indisputable*. (3) The *anonymity* and *open collectivity* of the activists, finally, refocused the debate again and again on the facts, and made it impossible to undermine the accusations by accusing the accuser.

The conventional reconstruction by strategic communication scholars of a case like Guttenberg would be that two 'actors' clashed *in the court of public opinion*. What the swarm metaphor captures in such a reconstruction is the peculiarity of the swarm actor. The activists *organised*, constituted an *open collectivity*, but they did not form an *organisation* in the full sense of the word. The metaphorical swarm afforded protection by making the individual not only *anonymous* but also *unimportant* – that is irrelevant as a target of a defence strategy. Swarm activity, just as swarming in nature, undercuts predatory attacks by making the singling out of prey difficult.

This, however, is where the usefulness of the swarm metaphor ends. Faced with a professionally coordinated activist collective, it is difficult to uphold the myth of a mysteriously self-organised entity. The metaphor also suggests that the swarm strategically 'attacked' Guttenberg. This is not the best description: the activists made little effort to communicate with mass media, press agencies and online media. They carried out no specific PR activities. In a way, they did not communicate strategically at all. Their work, the documentation, *attracted public attention without the authors communicating publicly in a traditional sense*. GuttenPlag's public impact developed as an effect of the work process itself, which distributed in time *and* space the amount of work *and* the different steps necessary to conclude it. Both work process and knowledge attracted the attention of individual visitors and mass media journalists (arguably, a self-amplifying dynamic). With perhaps one exception, one could say that *they* did not campaign, but rather that *it campaigned*. The one exception was the phase of punch-for-punch campaigning at the height of the crisis, when individuals associated with the swarm searched for and published evidence as a *direct reaction* to Guttenberg's public statements, to prove him a liar on the spot or to put pressure on supporters – for example his doctoral supervisor (Bewarder, 2011).

But there is another, theoretically interesting aspect: the workings of contemporary political publics as "hybrid forums" (Callon, Lascoumes & Barthe, 2011). Established concepts of political publics capture phenomena by placing emphasis on persons, organisations (collective actors) or social subsystems (collectives of collective actors). It is 'actors', theory consequently assumes, who act and communicate. Acts and communications of actors are then amplified via media actors, 'communicators'. In contrast, theorists in the actor-network tradition show how an *issue* (or 'thing') serves as the constitutive reference for the non-strategic development of a specific public forum. That forum cannot be reduced to personal or organisational power or a key technology, although it included what can be called "material participation" (Marres, 2012). It is not just another element of a "hybrid media system" in the sense of Chadwick (2013). It is an ephemeral entity in itself. So the fascinating aspect of the Guttenberg affair is that 'the thing' claimed its right as a member of what Bruno Latour conceptualised as the 'Parliament of Things'. Guttenberg's case may be construed, thus, as a case of 'Dingpolitik' – with allusion to the old Germanic notion for a political assembly still present in today's names of Scandinavian parliaments, such as the Swedish *Landsting*, the Danish *Folketing*, the *Storting* in Norway or the *Althing* in Iceland (Latour, 1993, 2005). We do not want to go deep into Latour's and other actor-network theorists' ideas here (although our account followed their methodological suggestions), but if the core idea is taken seriously, modern democracy is not necessarily only about including more and more humans in more and more discourses. It is also about giving non-humans, 'things', their due: first and foremost, of course, the planet, nature. In *Politics of nature*, Latour extends the idea even further: *"By defending the rights of the human subject to speak and to be the sole speaker, one does not establish democracy; one makes it increasingly more impracticable every day"* (Latour, 2004, p. 69, italics in original).

Maybe the most far-reaching insight of the Guttenberg case is that the hybrid combination of a factual issue attracting many actors can be a very powerful *actant* (a term used by Latour), even if the individual intentions of the many human actors overlap only partly. It then takes only a small step to slip into Latour's mode of thinking and say that the human activists were spokespersons giving voice to 'inscriptions' on the object, Guttenberg's PhD thesis.

The irony of the Guttenberg case is that this strange nonentity, this hybrid-actor, prevailed against its exact opposite. The hybrid-actor prevailed, if the term is appropriate, not only because it established and demonstrated, by astonishing collaborative work, *the fact* that Guttenberg *objectively* had plagiarised on a grand scale but also because the swarming process transformed that fact into relevant knowledge nobody could ignore. And in this context the most important strategic message the swarm sent to the people was entirely unstrategic: *go to Guttenplag-Wiki, see for yourself.* Our hope for the future is that something similar happens with regard to climate change or the destruction of biodiversity.

11 Deliberation and adjudication as democratic practice in post-fact society

Marja Åkerström

In September 2012 a 15-year-old Afghan boy called Ali arrived in Sweden to claim asylum. He had come from Italy, the first country on his journey from Afghanistan, but was forced to move on after being violently assaulted in a refugee camp and severely mistreated by the police.

Although Sweden is the country in Europe that accepts the largest number of unaccompanied minors seeking asylum (Migration board, 2013-04-13) the decision was taken to return him to Italy. The Swedish response was in line with European Union rules (Dublin Regulation) which state that his asylum application should be decided in the first country to which he arrived. The decision caused a storm of protest in the media. Desperate, Ali believed had no choice but to mount a graphic protest – he sewed up his mouth.

The most intense period of media debate concerning the legal side of the case lasted for approximately three months (September–December 2012), but the media coverage continued into 2014 (see overall results ahead). This case can be seen as a process of communication and a story in which discussion of law, legal decisions and various aspects of democracy is central and connected to various media channels in specific ways. Communication around the Ali case took place on digital forums as well as in print press, radio and TV. Various arguments were put forward by traditional media organisations as well as across more or less organised networks.

Only days after the story first broke on Swedish radio (Sveriges Radio, 2012)) calls to change the wording of the law to loosen restrictions became intense. In June 2014 the Swedish parliament enacted a new law, which applied from 1 July (Amendment 2013/14: SfU21). Crucially, critical momentum was building even before the case appeared in print, and the more extreme opinions on either side of the case appeared online rather than through traditional media outlets. As this chapter makes clear, the dynamic of the discourse raises many interesting questions surrounding the democratic potential of digital media, not least in the ways in which norms negotiated in the new media landscape can become assimilated by the judicial process. This chapter uses the Ali case to question some of the assumptions underlying claims that democracy is facilitated by digital media technology, and applies the "spiral of silence" theory (Noelle-Neumann, 1973, 1974). It concludes by raising questions around the broader implications for the future of democracy. Throughout, the core argument is that the new media landscape tends to nurture alternative realities rather than deliberate communication and stimulate collective intelligence. The empirical findings suggest that deliberation is more remote than ever in a media landscape where antagonism has taken precedence over sound criticism and agonistic pluralism (Manjoo, 2008; Mouffe, 2007, 2009).

The chapter begins with an overview of the research field on democracy and digital media, and then describes the aims of the study, the material and methodology, and the results. It concludes with an analysis of the broader picture of how communication and democracy can be understood in the contemporary media landscape.

Background

To give an overview of the problem and questions of the study, this section starts by describing the earlier and contemporary debate on the optimistic versus pessimistic consequences of digital media. Furthermore it gives a brief background of the Swedish discourse of democracy and finally on how communicated norms interact as a part of democracy.

Dialectic functions of digital media, utopians and dystopians of today

Every character and function that interactive digital media facilitates can be seen as double-sided, where the dark side inevitably connects to the light. Some scientific as well as public debate suggests online technologies may bring about a good and enlightened society, but simultaneously there is an ongoing debate portraying its societal risks and democratic threats. This goes for example with the aspect of anonymity, absence of physical presence, hyper-textual ability to surf on the Web and the interactivity itself, which is claimed to facilitate deliberative communication and vivify democracy. Every trait of the Internet holds both utopian and dystopian visions of future.

Critics claim it is important that the issue of how to develop the Internet is taken seriously as the current situation is in many aspects depoliticised and anarchical, driven by a minority of large conglomerates which conduct online affairs on behalf of unknowing 'digital illiterates' who are not equipped to understand their power or their procedures. Moreover, this situation is handled arbitrarily at a judicial level, due to insecurity in the processes of adjudication (Snickars & Strömbäck, 2012).

Algorithms selecting and determining information output, partisan groups mobilising hostile opinions and national surveillance of civic behaviour are just few examples of undesirable outcomes which hinder realisation of profound values commonly associated with democracy. Critics of the development of the new media landscape (Lessig, 1999; Morozov, 2011; Rydell, 2012) argue that freedom of expression and freedom of information are severely restricted in a technological environment where the architecture of the Internet is concealed backstage and invisible to most of us. The World Wide Web involves technological, strategically communicative and judicial considerations and actions taken on an individual, organisational, institutional and transnational level. It also demands cross-boundary cooperation and agreements in order to shape the future of the Internet in desirable directions (Levine, 2012; Rydell, 2012; Snickars & Strömbäck, 2012).

Yet for all the debate, the dream of enlightenment and deliberation discussed in Chapter 2 still lingers, visible both in theory and in practice. The optimistic discourse of digitalised interactive media and democracy is thriving and still awakens optimism. Almost ten years ago O'Reilly (2005) published an influential article, stating that Web 2.0 can be seen as a democratising force, a worldwide radical experiment in trust that can reinforce possibilities for collective intelligence and give wisdom to the crowds, encourage collective activity and through the collective power online equalise power inequalities in the so-called offline world. Many political and market-driven decisions have their ontological basis in this optimistic vision as the underlying assumption states that this deliberates democracy and brings power (back) to the people.

The deliberative discourse of Sweden

Even before the 'digital revolution' official reports on democracy and civic engagement contained visions and ambitions for citizens' empowerment. The Swedish Power Investigation emphasised the need to equalise power in society and cautioned against the dominance of representational democracy and the consonant influence of mass media (Petersson, 1991). Even where critique of the deliberation model has been expressed and scholars oppose the optimistic techno-deterministic view of the Internet's democratic potential, the reference point is the same, analogous to Habermas's deliberation ideal and his theory of consensus and reasoned action (Habermas, 1996). For two decades now many Swedish municipalities have been implementing digital information and communication channels aimed at facilitating dialogue and civic empowerment, and there are no signs the trend is slowing.

Legislative proposals put forward by the Swedish government point to the strengthened possibilities for deliberative dialogue between the main actors of societal communication (citizens, politicians, employees and journalists) to vitalise Swedish democracy – for example Prop. 2001/02:80 and Prop. 2009/10:55. The latter proposition extends the participatory part to embrace "civic society", defined as a counterpart to the state, commercial interests and individual households. Communicative networking between more or less organised extra-parliamentary groups is emphasised, with the aim to strengthen collaboration and thus democracy (Prop. 2009/10:55).

The three pillars of democracy

Democracy in Sweden is realised through the power of the people "through a representative and parliamentary form of Government and through local self-government. Public power is exercised under the law" (*The Instrument of*

Government, chap. 1, article 1). The first sentence in article 1 states that "All public power in Sweden proceeds from the people" (ibid.). A common interpretation is that the parliamentarian representative system needs a complimentary system of alternative channels and more opportunities to deliberate and to exercise direct democracy so that people can participate and influence politics on a daily basis and in between elections. Sweden has a strong and long tradition of participatory elements at both local and national levels.

The relations between norms and deliberative communication

Furthermore, besides representative democracy (which guarantees efficiency in decision-making processes) and civic democracy (which favours civic deliberation and empowerment) there is a third fundamental pillar, the constitutional state – that is law –under which public power is executed. This third pillar interacts with the other two in such a way that norms of society are negotiated and developed through dialogue and public debate. This process may gradually change law and eventually the discourse on democracy per se (Petersson *et al.*, 1998, 2005; Rothstein *et al.*, 1995). This interplay between the debate conducted in the digital media landscape and consequent transformation of norms is brought into focus by the Ali case.

Aim of the study, the empirical case and methodology

Many other cases involving children and migration have told similar stories and activate democratic media debate. Although they centre on different individuals, and might be packaged in slightly different ways, they can be seen as following the same process and pattern. That is they activate the same kind of arguments, and as they are repeated over and over again, they form the discourse of an issue (Foucault, 1993, 2002, 2008). The Ali case is thereby thematically framed in the same way as many other articles portraying the experience of child refugees, and follows the same format and media logic (Weibull & Wadbring, 2014). Together they might be analysed and understood as constituting a normative discourse formation.

The overall question that guided the empirical study was if and how digital media has deliberating qualities and if they are used in such a way that new discourses about normative issues can emerge.

The first research question asks how norms emerge and are negotiated in the new media landscape. Can we see an adjudication process and does digital media deliberate communication on legal matters? And if so, how can the processes of adjudication and deliberation be understood? Secondly, if digital media holds such qualities, how can the interplay between digital and traditional media be described and understood, and what are the implications for future democracy?

Adjudication as democratic practice describes the process of how norms are negotiated through deliberation and public debate and gradually may change law and/or the law enforcement. Using the case study method, the empirical material was collected and analysed in four steps (Merriam, 2006). The study began with a quantitative media analysis of the single case of migration and migration politics. The case was chosen because it was controversial and rendered intense debate and varied argument. The ambition was firstly to map out an overall view of the migration issue. The search string 15-år* Ali* + migrationsverk* (migration board) and "stitch* up lip* yielded approximately 380,000 hits from Google, Twitter and Facebook, including articles that held pro-migration opinions as well as a lot of adverse contra-migration opinions mostly visible in hostile and xenophobic blogs and sites. The second step was to use the same search strings on the Lund University database, Retriever, to make a qualitative analysis to identify central arguments and stakeholders, and to follow the process of the 'story'. This rendered 86 relevant articles from traditional media (newspapers and public service broadcast TV and radio), of which approximately 40% were published online and 60% in print. Thus 'contra-' and 'pro-Ali' organisations and websites were identified, giving more detailed information on actors and arguments, and how these were legitimised in the debate.

Results and analysis

The analysis sheds light on how norms emerge and transform in the new media landscape and how public opinion is distributed. It also reveals the adjudication process of the case by answering the question of whether digital media can deliberate communication on legal matters. Finally it reveals the nature of deliberation and gives insights about how public opinions are formed and distributed in the new media landscape.

The process of emerging norms and the distribution of public opinion

The decision by Swedish authorities to expel Ali sparked intense social media debate. Besides gaining public attention, the case activated many different opinions and parties, and showed how different values of democracy tend to collide with each other and with different regulations and laws.

Online established media set the agenda

The case of Ali was first reported by Swedish Public Service broadcast radio (Sveriges Radio, 2012), and there was significant online coverage within 24 hours, even before it appeared in print. The agenda was set by established news organisations, but through their online platforms. Following the case chronologically, the agenda process worked in ways where online established media have been one step ahead, followed by print press and various actors that comment and discuss the news and decisions made on the way. Even though the contrary has been found in other studies, the agenda-setting process in the Ali case was set by established media online channels. They thereby set the "common ground" for the "public opinion" (Johnson, 2014). This means that mass media also determined the direction of opinion on migration issues per se, favouring perspectives of Ali and human rights. Hostile articles questioning Ali's individual credibility or migration politics were not visible in established media; such opinions were submitted to the online communities.

Interpretation and quick fluctuation of opinions and decisions initially

The first articles examined the way different institutions *interpreted* Swedish law on migration in relation to other laws and regulations, like the United Nation's Universal Declaration of Human Rights and especially the UN Convention of the Rights of the Child (Unicef, 2014). The argument is that as Sweden is one of the 193 countries to have ratified the convention, it is obliged to comply. But in contrast some actors argued for invoking the Dublin Regulation, an EU law that aims to determine which member state is responsible for an asylum claim (Council of the European Union, Regulation No. 604/2013). Here, two crucial laws and regulations differ and collide. News sites reported that the police would expel Ali – even though the Migration Board had decided to reconsider the case. Over the next 24 hours criticism of the Swedish police intensified, expressed on many websites as well as by prominent actors, like the EU parliamentarian Cecilia Wikström. The pressure and temperature of the debate in different web forums heightened, and the next day, after the issue had been published in the print media, the head of border police decided to halt Ali's deportation – at least temporarily (Lindberg, 2012). This means that the issue didn't reach print and offline media channels until the day after it had been heavily debated online. That said, the decision to suspend deportation came only after print press had covered it. Opinions changed very quickly, and established media both online and offline almost immediately positioned themselves as defending Ali by referring to morality and human considerations, framing Ali as an issue of principle. The situation was (and still is) represented differently in digital channels; various anti-migration websites were flooded with antagonistic and racist opinions on Ali specifically and Swedish migration politics and law in general. Some actors were pro-Ali, and they more frequently commented on pro-Ali websites, blogs and established media organisations, whereas contra-Ali opinions were more often (but temporarily) seen in comments to established media and, most often, on their own partisan websites. Unlike the online communication, which displayed a variety of opinions on anti-migration as well as pro-migration websites, the established media channels were overall pro-migration.

Quick and strong polarisation of opinions

The time period of interpretation and fluctuation of opinions in the media debate was intense but short-lived and followed up by a strong polarisation between opinions displayed in established media compared to channels and forums on the Web. The vast majority of established media were critical of the Swedish government, arguing that a democratic state must guard and defend humanitarian values instead of legitimising decisions to deport children by referring to bureaucratic rules (like the Dublin Regulation). On the other hand many Internet actors organised in hostile groups, such as "Avpixlat" (http://avpixlat.info/), "Petterssons blogg" (http://petterssonsblogg.se/) and "Exponerat" (www.Exponerat.net), which were (and are) extremely hostile to foreigners, claiming Ali was a liar, as are many others trying to cross the Swedish border.

These actors are also critical of *all* politicians in the Swedish parliament, labelling them as the "seven-leaf-clover", lumping left-wing and right-wing parties all together and claiming that they are "destroying the nation and Swedish culture" (Avpixlat, 2014). Their arguments are based on mistrust and xenophobia, stating that Ali and others "like him" lie about their age in order to be defined as children and thereby benefit from more generous asylum regulations. On some sites even more racist arguments thrived and thrive. For example "Nordfront", which is a website for the "Swedish Resistance Movement" (www.nordfront.se/) and quite active in Sweden, encourages its followers to hand out flyers reminiscent of 1930s propaganda in Germany. The group claims that only persons who are "genuinely Swedish" should be allowed to stay in Sweden. The website has specific categories, like "Race History", "Science" and "Third Reich". Articles like "Der ewige Jude" (Nordfront, 2014-11-28) are typical, as are online surveys with statements like, "Of course it should be legal to label Hitler as a hero of the people" (Nordfront, 2014-12-01).

It might seem easy to dismiss these websites as expressing extreme opinions, but they attract a lot of visitors who interact and communicate with each other. Furthermore, as there are numerous similar websites which in turn interact with each other and with like-minded networks and organisations in other EU countries and beyond, there are good reasons to take them seriously. This has severe implications for society, democracy and virtual politics.

Adjudication process – From specific case to normative discussion of legal justice principles

Some days after the case had become clear and the polarisation was settled (see earlier), the perspective shifted from an ethical/moral topic to a legal/juridical description of the case. A few weeks later, Ali had become just one example among many and the critique against the police, the migration board and the government deepened. Humanitarian non-profit organisations like the Red Cross, the influential Save the Children (Rädda barnen), Amnesty International and UNICEF gave voice to their arguments and also started to criticise related regulations, like the REVA, which permitted police to demand that people on the street show their identity card if the police suspected them to be foreigners.

From normative intense online discussion to adjustments in Swedish migration law

The volume of critical voices raised against Swedish migration politics became increasingly pressing as more influential actors in the front line joined the debate. The polarisation became even more intense. In mid-September 2012, the Swedish migration minister defended the Dublin enactment and thereby the legislation for the deportation of children like Ali. The Swedish ombudsman for children ("barnombudsmannen") criticised the decision, and many other front actors joined in opposition. Established media actors, like the newspaper *Aftonbladet* and especially the Swedish Green Party (Miljöpartiet), scrutinised how the Ali case had been handled and showed mistakes had been made.

Clicktivism put pressure on the adjudication process

There was considerable online activity among citizens, and many readers shared, commented and acted upon this case. The case itself is special as it activates questions of humanity, morals, law and order, and democracy. Many of the online actors held negative attitudes towards foreigners, and the demand to 'choose sides' was intense.

Even though one can argue that people who click 'like' and share comments do not 'truly' engage in legal cases and in democratic practice, the amount of comments and debate matters. Politicians have to interpret, negotiate and reconsider such cases. Those in the front line consider the amount of debate, and if they *perceive* the situation as intense and requiring action, they may try to change decisions quite quickly. One might even suggest that the speed of transformation of normative processes of adjudication is greater today. Certainly, this was salient in the case of Ali.

Demands for further changes in law due to the intense debate

After intense media coverage both online and offline, the Swedish government decided to change the rules, softening the legal wording to make it easier for unaccompanied children to gain asylum in Sweden. As mentioned before, the law applied from July 2014. The specific case of Ali now became of minor importance and was used as one of many examples, but the legal changes and principles continued to be widely debated; many actors demanded and still want the UN Convention on the Rights of the Child to be incorporated into Swedish law. Politicians and others who hold pro-migration opinions claim that the law is going to be further improved at the EU level as well. By the end of 2014 the debate was still ongoing.

The adjudication process in the fragmented media landscape

It is clear that the Ali case made a difference in Swedish virtual politics. This research has shown how a single case developed into an *issue of principle*, which became used as a combat weapon between polarised contending parties that do not correspond to conventional 'offline' party dividing lines. On the one hand, Ali was used by the organisations defending human rights by referring to Swedish and international regulations and UN declarations, and on the other by combatant organisations that want to limit migration, which referred to the Dublin Regulation and questioned the truthfulness of information given by refugees. On both sides of the online battlefield the Ali case has become embedded in a wider context of migration politics and in Swedish national politics (see ahead).

Spiral of silence and the distribution of opinions today

This study shows that norms on migration and unaccompanied minors are heavily debated in media today, but the results also display an important difference when it comes to the *distribution of opinions*. This will be clarified by returning to the spiral of silence, a theory which Elisabeth Noelle-Neumann formulated at a time when most scholars considered the effects of mass media to be limited. She disagreed, arguing that the "cumulation, ubiquity and consonance of mass communication combine and produce powerful effects on public opinion" (Severin & Tankard, 1997, p. 305).

The spiral of silence was formulated when mass media was the major source of reference information. To give a short description, my understanding of Noelle-Neumann is as follows: (1) Individuals are social beings and need a sense of fellowship with their fellow human beings. (2) Especially on *controversial* issues, people form impressions about the distribution of opinion. (3) Individuals fear isolation and try to determine if they are in majority or in minority, and then they try to sense whether public opinion is changing. (4) If they *perceive* themselves as being in the majority, they will give voice to their opinions. If they, on the other hand, perceive themselves as unsupported by others, they will not express their opinion. (5) The more they remain silent, the more the other people feel that the specific point is not represented, and the more they remain silent (Noelle-Neumann, 1973, 1974).

If one applies Noelle-Neumann's theory to the Ali case, my main argument is that it was harder to break the spiral of silence before digital media made its entrance. For better and worse, the contemporary (divided) media landscape has given opportunities for diversified distribution of opinions and made it harder on a societal level to maintain and preserve spirals of silence. Furthermore, the opportunities to *break* different spirals of silence have multiplied due to heteronormative activity on digital media. Hostile opinions that don't correspond to the opinions put forward in mass media may be expressed and grow intense as individuals *perceive* a sense of fellowship with peers on their own partisan websites. They can give voice to their anti-migration opinions without fearing isolation. They might even sense that the public opinion is changing, and act upon this perception. This is also what happened in the Swedish election in September 2014 when Sweden Democrats gained about 13% of the votes, giving them a pivotal position in Parliament.

Spiral of silence and the adjudication process

As shown, the overall picture is of public opinion being divided between established media and digital channels, together holding both contra-migration and pro-migration perspectives. Crucially, the results do not display a *singular* media landscape where fluent societal communication takes place between different channels and smoothly opens up possibilities for deliberation. Rather, the distribution of opinions is divided between two spheres, where mass media sets the agenda and becomes the reference point of opinions still defined as 'common ground'. Different actors can in turn react to this and indeed have done so, as mentioned earlier.

In the case of Ali and the issue of migration overall, mass media took the position of defending human rights. They had the power to define the common ground and the process of adjudication, and the outcome of a new law was strongly dependent on communication that took place in the sphere of established media. The magnitude of the debate on established media *online*, though, played a significant part by putting pressure on politicians to act. To be more specific, and from the point of view of Noelle-Neumann, it was the *perceived visibility on digital media* as well as the coverage in established media that together formed the impression of pressure that caused politicians to react and led to the adjudication. For better or worse, the interplay between the two spheres seems to have made the adjudication process more dynamic than before.

Spiral of silence and 'deliberation' in a fragmented media landscape

According to the spiral of silence people fear isolation and don't express opinions if they perceive themselves as being in minority, but do tend to reveal their opinions when they feel safe. This study shows that opinions that are not 'allowed' in established media can flourish on websites. So the communities online and the traditional channels function differently. The established media in Sweden can still be considered as creating a common ground in the sense that they display a *variety* of news and perspectives. Especially in Sweden, where public service broadcast channels retain significant audiences, there are lot of issues and agendas to which people have to respond. The breadth of issues, agendas and perspectives forces us to think critically, to relate and prioritise, and eventually to compromise.

The situation is different with website communities. Online media analysis suggests that most website communities are limited to considering a couple of aspects that combine to create an alternative reality. This is most salient on anti-migration and pro-migration websites where: (1) there is one single agenda; (2) people on the website stick to that single agenda and don't bring in other agendas or contradictory arguments; and (3) they legitimise these arguments by using their own sources and facts and/or their own interpretations of public statistics.

Several of the anti-migration websites have tables and diagrams which at first sight *look* and *feel* to be factual. In some cases references are given but in other cases not even that. Some references are official and clickable, but the interpretations are adjusted to the anti- *or* pro-migration agenda that defines the web community. Other strategies for creating a homogenous 'truth' are also adopted. For instance, the Nordfront website has its own book store (www.nordfront.se/), offering books that are unavailable elsewhere. It describes 'facts' that were outdated long ago and 'truths' that are simply false.

This means that the spiral of silence *is working not only between established mass media versus digital online communities* but also *within each community* since only one agenda is discussed, counterarguments are not 'welcome' and 'facts' are chosen to correspond with permitted opinion. As people don't want to experience isolation or cognitive dissonance (Festinger, 1957), they choose communities that correspond to their perception of reality.

Conclusion: alternative realities in post-fact society

Different websites create their own versions of reality. The new media landscape might now be described as a world of *alternative realities*, where 'truth' is differently cultivated depending on your preferred online community. All together this makes it hard to build *collectivity* in many senses. It makes it hard to build a society that can take collective action. It makes it harder to build parliamentarian majorities, and it makes it harder to come to decisions, both on specific cases like Ali and on migration issues per se. So while these digital communities make connections easier between people, they facilitate a closeted view of reality (Manjoo, 2008). Additionally, these niches make the adjudication process more difficult as 'truth' becomes more negotiable and relativistic. It has become not just an issue over Ali or migration and what to do about it, but rather an issue over what is true and false, the fundamental state of the world. One must acknowledge that some things *are* true and some things are not. But it rather seems we live in a post-fact society.

Although digital communities are much-feted for their capacity to return power to people, to increase deliberation and to build collective intelligence, in reality these effects appears illusory. Although the Ali case worked to soften what can be seen as unfair rules, the wider picture is that such discourse doesn't build collective intelligence but rather promotes pluralistic ignorance.

12 The gamification of democracy

Computer games as strategic communication tools and cultivating forces

Howard Nothhaft and Jens Seiffert

Media scholar Peter Dahlgren (2009, p. i) begins his inquiry in *Media and Political Engagement* by remarking that declining political engagement by citizens is one of the most difficult problems facing Western democracy today. Dahlgren then treats his topic, the nexus of 'citizens, communication and democracy', in eight chapters of impressive sweep. He considers different aspects of democracy, civil engagement and agency, analyses television and popular public spheres and considers the Internet's civic potential and its practices and cultures. The book concludes with a section of media generations which is, in a way, a discussion of digital naturals:

> Today, the factor of generation takes on special importance, because many of the trends we see in regard to media use, political horizons and democratic participation are shaped by changes that have to do with specific patterns among younger age cohorts.
>
> (Dahlgren, 2009, p. 200)

Dahlgren is an author with a broad conception of politics and a firm grasp on the role of *popular culture*. Yet one of the most popular entertainment media of our time is conspicuously absent in his analysis: neither the term 'computer game' nor 'video game' appears in the index. Television, cinema, yes. Computer games, no.

We believe that computer games do have a sociopolitical bearing. We will explain in what way and why it matters for researchers and scholars in strategic communication. We note, of course, that 'gamification' has been a buzzword for several years now. During the last five years, the concepts of 'gamification' and 'serious games' have burgeoned not only in the business, management and marketing literature (Chatfield, 2011; Zichermann & Cunningham, 2011; Zichermann & Linder, 2013) but also in human resources (Bishop, 2013), education (Kapp, 2012; Niman, 2014) and environment and health (Shea, 2014). Not surprisingly, the concept has also gained a foothold in politics (see e.g. Electoral Reform Services, 2014). We contend, however, that the civic dimension of computer games goes beyond attempts to 'gamify' politics with apps and voting advice (Fossen & Andersson, 2014). Our thesis is that the *lives* of digital naturals are gamified to varying degrees.

We are not at a point where we can *prove* our hypotheses, and this point may never be reached conclusively. However, the other research strands devoted to the influence of digital media on political participation rarely investigate the nexus from a strictly causal angle either. What we see is a mosaic of studies held together by a few key concepts, such as deliberative democracy or 'empowerment' or 'network society', and a plausible line of argumentation (see e.g. Loader & Mercea, 2011, for an overview). We hope to advance a similarly plausible argumentation and to stimulate research.

In brief, we theorise that computer games have a bearing on modern democracy in three ways:

1. Computer games are media in the ordinary sense of the word – that is they mediate *text* or *content* to players and, by doing so, lay a claim to *representation of reality*. In many cases, the representation they offer is of a special quality: representation by *simulation*, not by *narration*. This makes computer games powerful tools of strategic communication, the true heirs of the propaganda newsreel.
2. Computer games are media in a profoundly special, *procedural* sense of the word – that is they deploy what game researcher Ian Bogost terms 'procedural rhetoric'. This makes computer games subtle tools of strategic communication in a sense not yet fully understood by scholars.
3. Finally, given (1) and (2), we believe computer games as a genre lead to procedural cultivation effects. These effects may explain some of the 'specific patterns among younger age cohorts' Dahlgren draws attention to – namely disenchantment with traditional politics.

Computer games and political culture: the missing and dismissed media

In the 1940s social scientists began to inquire why democracy remained stable in some countries while it collapsed or never developed in others (see Almond & Verba, 1963; Berelson, Lazarsfeld & McPhee, 1954; Dahl, 1956;Shils, 1960). For 70 years or so, political scientists and communication scholars have tracked the evolution of media systems; a concern for democracy has always been a driver energising the scrutiny of media technology, media structures, trends in content and consumption patterns. The twenty-first century did not change that. "There are many factors that shape the character of democracy and of political engagement within it," Dahlgren (2009, p. 34) summarises, "but one of the key elements is of course the nature and role of the media." Some theorists go further and hold that the evolution of the media landscape is the *one* factor that explains most of the shifts and changes in the contemporary political landscape (for an overview of the debate, see e.g. Meyen, 2009). *Mediatisation*, one of the watchwords at the intersection of communication studies and political science, captures the idea that our societies are media societies in the sense that the *legitimacy* of other societal subsystems, such as the political, economic, legal, scientific or cultural system, is ultimately negotiated in the mediasphere. This creates a pressure on functionally differentiated subsystems to adapt to the media logic – with mass media having and creating their own reality (Luhmann, 2009). In other words, what Aronoff describes as 'political culture', "the socially constructed and tenuously shared meanings which endow or challenge legitimacy in the political institutions, offices, and procedures of a polity" (2001, p. 11640), becomes an extension of *media logic*, subjected to *media logic*. Conversely, if Dahlgren is right and declining political engagement among the young is the greatest problem facing Western democracy, decoding the media logic of digital naturals becomes the key to the future.

The missing media

In general, researchers and scholars in the late twentieth and early twenty-first centuries have been reasonably quick in decoding the *logic* of the ever-evolving 'new' media. Computer games remain the one exception. Computer games are older than the Internet. If *Pong* is considered the first commercially successful game, they have been around, first as arcade games, then as home entertainment, since the mid-1970s. Their rise as a mass medium began with the second generation of consoles (e.g. Atari 2600) and the home computer (for a brief history, see e.g. Beck & Wade, 2006, p. 30–32). The bestselling home computer, the Commodore 64, sold up to 30 million units between 1982 and 1994. By the early 1980s, IBM PCs and Macs became available for home use and gaming. But the true legacy of the arcade machines lies in the game consoles. It is with the fifth generation, from 1993 to about 1999, that the sales figures explode. Sony's *Playstation*, released in September 1994, sold around 100 million units. Its sixth-generation successor, *Playstation 2*, was the most successful console so far, selling in excess of 150 million units, with main contenders Nintendo, Sega and Microsoft achieving sales in the double-digit millions.

Given these numbers – several hundred million units, without counting handhelds – it is legitimate to say that several generations of Westerners (and Easterners) from the 1980s onwards grew up with computer games. They are 'digital naturals' in that respect, and that respect is not to be neglected. As we have shown elsewhere (Seiffert & Nothhaft, 2014), today's computer games are a major industry and play a major role in daily life. In 2014 gaming boasted greater economic importance than the music industry, and has surpassed Hollywood in revenue. Often, computer games take the lead in the entertainment value chain – whereas once a game accompanied the film, now the film often accompanies the game (*Tomb Raider*, *Doom*, *Resident Evil*). Moreover, the virtual worlds created by computer games are increasingly discovered as advertising spaces, with in-game advertising becoming ever more sophisticated and substantial: the Entertainment Software Association (ESA) predicted that the global in-game advertising market will grow to 7.2 billion USD by 2016 (see ESA, 2014). What is ultimately important, however, is that computer games take a larger and larger share of the average citizens' media consumption budget. An independent study in Germany reported for example that about one quarter of the population play 'frequently', spending approximately 50 minutes per day (Quandt *et al.*, 2013, p. 485). Simply speaking, people spend a lot of time playing computer games, alone or together with others.

The dismissed media

Despite whole generations growing up with games produced by a multibillion-dollar industry, there has been very little interest in their *sociopolitical impact*. The one impact they are routinely associated with in public debate is *violence*. Whenever a youth runs amok, media coverage will emphasise that the perpetrator was playing 'killer games'. As a consequence, there is considerable research into the connection of violent computer games and aggressive behaviour, although the ultimate question – whether violent games *cause* violent behaviour – has not been answered authoritatively yet.[1] However, another variation on the 'killer games' theme made headlines in February 2012, when Chen Rong-yu, a young Taiwanese, was found dead in an Internet café. According to reconstructions (Breeze, 2013), Chen started playing around 10:00 p.m. on Tuesday, was seen talking on his phone while still playing *League of Legends* around noon the next day, and was found dead nine hours later, arms outstretched at the console. Unsurprisingly, this event and similar ones as early as 2003 triggered research into *game addiction* (Wood *et al.*, 2007). Interestingly, some researchers see the highest potential for addiction in the MMORPGs (massively multiplayer online role-playing games), which heavily feature interpersonal relationships with other players, albeit mediated through character avatars (see Jennett, 2010, p. 22; see also Caplan, Williams & Yee, 2009; Freeman, 2008; Hsu *et al.*, 2009). Viewed from that angle, with the emphasis on *mediated sociality* as the key factor, addiction to MMORPGs seems closely related to Facebook addiction.[2]

Ludology: computer games in their own right

Computer game scholars, unsurprisingly, tend to complain that their subject is trivialised and vilified. Bogost (2007, p. viii) writes that games "are considered inconsequential because they are perceived to serve no cultural or social function save distraction at best, moral baseness at worst." Chesher and Costello condense the attitude underlying intellectual (non-) engagement with games into a telling paragraph. Computer games, they hold, are considered "simplistic, patriarchal and militaristic, promoting obesity, violence and anti-social behaviour. Their narratives are paper-thin and puerile. They are not legitimate objects of study, lacking the richness of higher art forms" (Chesher & Costello, 2004, p. 5).

Although united in resisting trivialisation and vilification, the community of *ludologists* (Frasca, 2003) is not homogenous. Roughly speaking, there are two approaches: as a *designed product* on one side and as *artefacts* on the other. The questions asked by game design scholars are, what makes computer games successful, and what keeps players playing? A simple yet powerful idea here is the *compulsion loop*. It is from this research that the burgeoning literature on gamification takes its cues. The second strand approaches computer games as cultural and aesthetic artefacts and explores for example the experiences of players and the representation of phenomena in games, often against the backdrop of sophisticated sociological theory or in a phenomenological vein. The first peer-reviewed journal in the field (inaugurated 2001), *Game Studies*, emphasises that its "primary focus" lies on "aesthetic, cultural and communicative aspects of computer games", although "any previously unpublished article focused on games and gaming is welcome" as long as "it attempt[s] to shed new light on games, rather than simply use games as metaphor or illustration of some other theory or phenomenon" (Game Studies, 2014).

Representation and simulation

After substantiating our contention that computer games are significant, we turn to the ways in which computer games become relevant for political culture, civic engagement and, by extension, strategic communication. Here, we suggest that the computer game is the true heir of the propaganda newsreel. Computer games can become politically relevant, we argue, when the virtual environment (VE) involves players in politically contested issues by *simulation. Experiencing* something in a simulation, we theorise, leads to *familiarity*; familiarity, in turn, leads to *acceptance*.

Computer games are media in the ordinary sense that they expose players to coherent stimuli, content. By doing so, computer games lay a claim to *representation of a reality (or 'the' reality)*, as every media product does. It is not surprising, therefore, that early computer game researchers approached their subject with a stance rooted in the *humanities*. As Frasca puts it, "So far, the traditional – and most popular – research approach from both the industry and the academy has been to consider video games as extensions of drama and narrative" (2003, p. 221).

Computer games differ from movies or books by being *interactive*. Using the documentary game *Fort McMoney* (see Seiffert & Nothhaft, 2014) we have shown that interactivity can be employed to break up seriality and make players 'explore' a complex issue (in this case tar sand mining in Canada), in a playful way, at their own pace. De-linearisation of representation does not capture the difference between playing *Fort McMoney* and reading a book about Fort McMurray, however. The true potential of computer games, Frasca (2003) points out, lies in representation *by simulation*. Computer games do not tell *one* unique story. They are cybernetic systems that 'generate' chains of events *in interaction with the player.* This shift, Frasca theorises, is what makes computer games so hard to understand for scholars with a 'literary mind': "Video games imply an enormous paradigm shift for our culture because they represent the first complex simulational media for the masses" (Frasca, 2003, p. 224).

In the next section, we will explore further the idea that computer games, being simulations, generate not unique 'stories' but instances or 'versions' of stories. Our argument in this section is that interactivity, the involvement of the player, favours *immersion* in the virtual environment or VE: the player gets 'sucked into' the simulated world, an effect researched as 'real-world dissociation' or RWD (Jennett, 2010; see also Jennett *et al.*, 2008). One may experience something similar with a book or film, or even a crossword puzzle, but the difference lies in *quality* and *degree*. The so-called SCI model differentiates three levels – namely sensory, challenge-based and imaginative immersion (Ermi & Mayra, 2005). Solving a crossword puzzle leads to challenge-based immersion. Reading *The Lord of the Rings* leads to imaginative immersion; watching the movie most likely leads to sensory immersion. Only the computer game is capable of immersing a player simultaneously on challenge-based, sensory and imaginative levels. The VE in computer games is not narrated or 'retold' by a narrator, however unobtrusive. More so than in television or movies, the player does not perceive an *angle of representation*, but experiences events with a great degree of immediacy. As Jennett (2010, p. 30) puts it, "the player is not empathising with their character's frustration at losing a race; they are frustrated at themselves for losing the race." Games very rarely comment critically, not only because they are predominantly entertainment products but also because they don't need a narrator. This uncritical immediacy is what makes games powerful as a propaganda tool.

Not every piece of entertainment must be compulsively subjected to social justice scrutiny, of course. Sometimes, there are no victims and no reason to believe that actions depicted in the game cause emulation in the real world. But if one accepts that games are highly *immersive* – so immersive that compulsive players ignore signs of impending physiological collapse – then strategic communication researchers are well advised to develop some sensitivity for games as 'persuasive devices' (Bogost, 2007). The employment of private military companies (PMCs) in armed conflicts is a case in point. The *Arma* series is a first-person military simulation or 'tactical shooter'. The series is considered a highly realistic representation of small unit combat action; the developer, Bohemia Interactive (BI), was even contracted to develop training software (VBS 1, VBS 2) for the US Marine Corps. In its original version, *Arma II* featured forces from the United States, Russia and the fictitious Takistan. However, BI soon boosted the game with expansion packs. As the first featured *British Armed Forces* (BAF), players naturally expected that the second pack would add national forces from other national armies – for example Germany. In the event, the second expansion, 'PMC', featured the operators, vehicles and weapons of a fictitious *private military company*.

The representation of mercenaries or PMCs in a 'soldier sim' marketed as highly realistic can be construed as simply reflecting the reality of twenty-first-century warfare. Paramilitary and military work in Iraq and other hotspots is often carried out by security firms, like Blackwater (now Academi) or Aegis Defence Services. But it must be remembered that games like *Arma* make players *step into the shoes* of a PMC operator. This, we argue, creates *familiarity* and by that, arguably, *acceptance*. That the effect might not be intended by the developer is largely irrelevant. Private military contractors can be viewed as the smart solution to the realities of modern conflicts – and they can also be viewed as a key constituent of a dangerous industry with a vested interest in ongoing armed conflict, a business that undermines the democratic control of armed force – a nexus Naomi Klein identified as the "disaster capitalism complex" (Klein, 2007). All we say is that scholars who are puzzled by an apparent lack of engagement in similar issues (armed drones, cluster bombs, landmines, war crimes, etc.) should be aware that milsimmers get their information virtually 'first-hand'. Depicting PMCs as 'normal' in a tactical shooter can be construed as legitimising their mandate. Scholars who wish to reconstruct the 'discourses' that led to seemingly uncritical acceptance should take a look at computer games played by hundreds of thousands of people for millions of hours.

Computer games as *procedural media*

Next we argue that computer games are sociopolitically relevant because players will transfer what they learn about the *rules* governing abstract systems by playing games to the real world – maybe not fully, but partly. This is what makes computer games powerful strategic communication media in a subtle and yet scarcely researched way.

That even scholars sensitive to popular culture tend to dismiss computer games is, to a degree, a theoretical shortcoming. A lot of games, when viewed through the lens of orthodox media theory, admittedly appear devoid of meaning, "lacking the richness of higher art forms" (Chesher & Costello, 2004, p. 5). Computer games researchers, like Frasca or Bogost, point out, however, that this is because orthodox scholars are looking for the wrong thing. Bogost's (2007) theory of procedural rhetoric highlights that the true 'meaning' of computer games is to be found on the *procedural level* – that is in the rules or algorithms that govern the game (for an exposition of procedural rhetoric, see Bogost, 2007; see also Seiffert & Nothhaft, 2014) and are learned by the players.

To inquire into the political relevance of 'procedural rhetorics', we take a look at two video games that simulate politics: the 'serious game' *Democracy 3* and the mass-market bestseller *Civilization*.

In *Democracy 3*, the player takes the role of a head of government. The core activity is passing legislation on tax, welfare, military spending, environmental regulation and so on, in order to gain or secure the support of voters whose attitudes are continually monitored by virtual opinion polls. The key to playing successfully is to legislate smartly – that is in a way as to stay in power, while taking into account that there is a limit to the legislative powers of the head of government, as every piece of legislation 'costs'; it affects the national budget – that is drains money from the budget – and influences voter opinion.

There are three problems with *Democracy 3*. The first problem is that the underlying game dynamics and algorithms are clearly based on the United States and the UK, do not reflect national cultures and reproduce neo-liberal doctrine about how an economy works. During tests, the co-author chose to play Germany even though 'gun control' emerged as a continuously hot issue. As one player comments, "You can choose which country you want to govern, but it feels like it doesn't make any difference" (King of Tritation, 2014). The second problem is that

Democracy 3 appears as a highly complex, multifaceted democracy simulation, but neglects various aspects of real politics (e.g. the bi- or multi-partisan cooperation that is so important to balance contrary political positions) in favour of an emphasis on budget and reputation. For all its dazzling complexity and arrays of interconnected issues, *Democracy 3* is a simple simulation at its core. *Democracy 3* reduces policymaking to a financial and reputational calculus, where right or wrong, justice or fairness or other values or beliefs are subjected to staying in power. Objective problems which have puzzled the cleverest politicians are easily solved by smart decisions. As one player put it, "Fixed America's economy and repayed [sic] all its debt within 3 quarters. Come on Obama" (Almighty Sosa, 2014). Another player added, "You reach a point were [sic] there are no problems, you make money and have a large reserve and win elections with upwards of 95% of the vote going your way" (King of Tritation, 2014). The third problem is maybe the most fundamental and procedural: *Democracy 3* presents democracy as a game where re-election, not sticking to your values, is the one and only measure of success.

The procedural effect of a game like *Democracy 3*, we theorise, is the repeated virtual experience that successful politics ultimately boils down to a game of smart resource allocation in which the goal is to win re-election. At the same time, researchers in political science point out the increasingly common portrayal of politics as a game (e.g. the 'horse race frame') in political journalism (see Aalberg, Strömbäck & de Vreese, 2011). While inquiring into possible negative implications for informed citizenry, including cynicism towards politics, the question as to where the paradigm might come from is rarely raised.

We do not suggest, of course, that games played by few people, like *Democracy 3*, are the source of the paradigm. But if serious games like *Democracy 3* rarely attract large numbers of players, *Civilization* attracts millions (the first instalment of the game was published in 1991). The time spent playing is illustrated by one review of *Civilization V* on the game platform *Steam*: "I only played a little but it was fun," writes BenjiOfTheZulu (2014). 'Little', in this case, amounted to 2,154 hours, around 90 days. While *Civilization* is less sophisticated than *Democracy 3* in emulating the intricacies and details of politics[3] – the goal is to build a civilisation over the course of human history and to prevail against other civilisations – the core mechanisms are similar. Progress and success equal smartly amassing and distributing resources. Since the game offers different paths to victory – for example culture, science, diplomacy or power – the measures of success may change: for a science victory the player has to launch the first spaceship; a diplomatic victory is achieved by a vote in the United Nations assembly; a military victory by total domination of the planet. No matter what the success parameter is, however, the smart allocation of *quantified* in-game resources (points) is always the key to success. Cause and effect are always *known* to the player and clearly stated, and decisions by the players are always promptly and accurately implemented. Once again, it is suggested to the players, *procedurally*, without saying so, that politics comprises discrete loops of rather deterministic decision making: if you do this, it will bring this advantage and this disadvantage; if you have this problem, technology will solve it; if your reputation goes down, invest more in PR.

Cultivation and the compulsion loop

Finally, we theorise that the most powerful effect on the generation who grew up with computer games, since the early 1990s at the latest, might be a long-term, cumulative *cultivation effect*. The origin of cultivation theory lies with George Gerbner and colleagues (1986), who posited that the more time people spend watching TV, the more they believe TV represents reality. What drove Gerbner's research is that the world portrayed in TV is *systematically different* from reality. TV portrays considerably more violence and crime for example than average citizens are statistically exposed to (in one of Gerbner's studies, heavy TV viewers estimate their weekly chances to become victim of a violent crime to be 1:10, moderate viewers as 1:100, while the actual chance at the time was 1:10,000).

Expanding on Gerbner *et al.* (1986), Dmitri Williams (2006) tested the hypothesis of *virtual cultivation*. Using candidates who played the MMORPG *Asheron's Call 2*, which involves frequent attacks by armed monsters, Williams showed that increasing exposure to the game went hand in hand with an increased perception of likelihood to become a victim of *armed robbery*, specifically, *in the real world*:

> After playing the game, the participants in the treatment condition were more likely than those in the control group to say that people would experience robbery with weapons in the real world. This finding was substantively very large (more than 10 points on a 100-point scale) and significantly powerful and was strongest among the male participants.
>
> (p. 79)

The interesting twist in Williams's research is that perception of the likelihood of *other* violent crimes – rape, murder and physical assault – *which did not have parallels in the game*, did *not* change significantly.

Williams's research indicates that heavy game exposure has directed and specific cultivation effects after a couple of months. Williams points out, however, that "[c]ultivation requires there to be a consistent metamessage" (2006, p. 74), a condition he judged as realised because the candidates played at the cost of almost any other media use. Given the requirement of a consistent metamessage, the cultivation effect we would expect from lifelong computer gaming in young adults is not content-related, therefore. The contents of games differ too much. We expect the metamessage to be *procedural* – that is about the rules of the world, how things work or should work. We theorise that gamers will have slightly heightened expectations in three dimensions:

1. Problems and tasks should be clear-cut and well defined and that the tools and resources to master a challenge should be at hand.

2. Efforts, even minor ones, should be rewarded immediately or at least in direct connection with the accomplished task.
3. Life should show a progression, a constant expansion of opportunities.

The theoretical framework that led us to expect these cultivations is a pattern almost universal in mass-market games: the so-called *compulsion loop*. The concept, which is difficult to ascribe to a single author, captures the fact that most games are driven by repetition of the same core events. In the most addictive genre, fantasy MMORPGs, the loop might be kill monster, earn reward, buy stuff, kill bigger monster and so forth. The *Civilization* games, famous for their one-more-turn syndrome (Magnuson, 2010), exhibit the very same pattern, but, interestingly, a lot of educative or serious games do not implement it fully (that is why *Democracy 3* gameplay is awkward). What turns this *core loop* – that is the cycle of what is going on – into *a compulsive loop* is the fine-tuning of the underlying anticipation-action-reward structure. To avoid a frustration spiral, the player must be presented with a progression of challenging but ultimately manageable tasks (in social games, and MMORPGs are immensely social, anticipation and reward might be located at least partly outside the game). A successful game constantly activates the agency of the player and immerses her in a positive loop or 'flow', to return to the SCI model, of mastering challenges, experiencing satisfying sensory input, being engrossed in new exciting imaginary worlds and expecting the next step in the progression. As one of the legends of game design, Chris Crawford, points out, this is not a peripheral aspect. 'Escapism' is the central feature of the most immersive genre of entertainment:

> Videogamers slip out of a world of overbearing parents, demanding teachers, and dismal failure, to enter a world of simple challenges and frequent glorious successes. Their loss of awareness of the world around them is no happenstance; it's an important part of the appeal of the experience.
> (Crawford, 2003, p. 47)

Given the near ubiquity of the compulsion loop in successful games, we suggest a cultivation of players in the sense that the computer game generation expects *organised life experiences* – like going to university or a career in a corporation or 'politics' – to be as *rewarding* and *immersive* as games. In other words, should game-cultivated individuals experience something other than clear-cut problems, meaningful, engaging tasks, immediate rewards and constant progression, they tend to suspect that inept teachers or incapable managers are *actively* frustrating them (which might or might not be true).

There is some hindsight in our suggestions; we grew up with computer games. Moreover, the idea of a 'gamer generation' that differs from non-gaming generations is not new. Beck and Wade point out for example how "[g]ames have become this generation's ultimate weapon against all the dead time that life throws their way. As they see it, there is never a good reason to be bored" (Beck & Wade, 2006, p. 73). Beck and Wade even try to ascribe the recklessness of young entrepreneurs in the dotcom-crisis of 2000/2001 to a cultivation in the sense that the world is a game, and 'game over' simply means 'restart'. They claim that the older investor generation did not understand the game mentality of the young, although it is, in retrospective, clearly captured in attitude tests: "Consistently, on item after item, the respondents who had grown up playing games reported sharply different attitudes about the very foundations of business: risk, achievement, the value of experience, their own capabilities" (ibid., p. 44).

We would not wish to go that far, but psychologists researching generational differences point to similar trends. Jean Twenge has researched generational differences by meta-analysing survey data and standardised psychological tests, mostly drawn from US college students, going back to the 1930s. By doing so, she was able to track how key psychological traits of college students changed from generation to generation (see Twenge & Campbell, 2008). Twenge's best-known assertions, that of a steadily growing narcissism and sense of entitlement among young adults, is encapsulated in her label "Generation Me". Another aspect Twenge traces among the young is high self-esteem curiously coupled with a low self-reliance and an external locus of control. This makes it necessary for teachers to give clear guidance; otherwise students will blame the teachers for their own unsatisfactory performance: "They like to know exactly what they need to do to earn good grades and they become stressed when given ambiguous instructions" (Twenge, 2009, p. 403). Twenge advises teachers at medical schools to remember that

> Today's students frequently need the purpose and meaning of activities spelled out for them. Previous generations had a sense of duty and would often do what they were told without asking why. Most young people no longer respond to appeals to duty; instead, they want to know exactly why they are doing something and want to feel they are having a personal impact.
>
> (Twenge, 2009, p. 404)

One could almost say that the young people have the expectation, not entirely unreasonable, that the game should make sense.

Conclusion

In *Media and Political Engagement*, Peter Dahlgren (2009) identified declining political engagement as one of the most difficult problems facing Western democracy. Dahlgren's broad analytic approach, which displays great sensitivity to popular culture, certainly identifies some of the key explanations of declining engagement in traditional, institutionalised politics. But the analysis must be extended to include computer games. After substantiating that computer games are not negligible, we proposed that computer games have a sociopolitical bearing in three ways. First, they represent otherwise inaccessible reality by simulating it. Since familiarity leads to acceptance, experience by simulation provides a powerful strategic communication tool – one that has hitherto been under the radar of critical coverage. Second, computer games represent reality *procedurally*, which makes them a *subtle* strategic communication tool – not only under the radar but also de facto in stealth mode. Third, computer games as a genre *cultivate* expectations about organised life experiences in players.

While we do believe that critical scholars interested in discourses should no longer ignore how computer games are employed as strategic communication tools on the *simulative level* (*America's Army* is the paradigm example) and in a more subtle and covert way on the *procedural level*, the long-term, cumulative cultivation effects are maybe the most important. An expectation of clear-cut problems, meaningful tasks, immediate rewards and constant progression is obviously at odds with traditional civic engagement. Participation in institutionalised politics, especially at local and regional levels, is often concerned with mundane, ill-defined issues. Council and committee work is slow and cumbersome, with few 'frequent glorious successes' and much frustration. Real politics, not the politics in *House of Cards* or *Civilization V*, contains very little in terms of a compulsion loop, and much in duty. No wonder, then, that Åkerström & Young (Chapter 8) found in focus groups with students that the young do not 'do politics' in the traditional sense, but rather influence their friends – with instant rewards in the form of 'likes'. Others choose single-issue activism as a field for self-actualisation, which is, of course, far sexier.

It must be remembered, however, that there is nothing wrong with a young generation which is, after all, facing a far more uncomfortable and uncertain future than their parents. As Twenge (2009, p. 404) puts it, "'Generation Me' is doing exactly what it has been taught to by parents, teachers and media." Cultivation of expectations works only if there is a 'consistent metamessage' (Williams, 2006). And the consistent metamessage of the twenty-first-century capitalist consumer society, it seems, is that life *should turn out* as a progressive series of action-reward-anticipation loops: get a promotion, buy a new handbag or golf clubs, be empowered for the next great step in your career. In reality, it does not play like that, of course – but then there must be some frustrating force at work.

The carving up of life into *environments* by service providers that then organise a positive experience and leave frustration outside the door works well as a business practice. Unfortunately that is the opposite of what the roots of the word *politics* denote: the totality of everything that concerns the *polis*, the community. It is here, it seems to us, that the true gamification of democracy lies: in the fact that politics is considered another game or 'loop' among many others, and that it turns out to be a bad, unsatisfying loop. No wonder, then, that democracy is the game of what is left.

Notes

1 Playing violent games has been found to raise levels of aggressive behavior, aggressive cognition, aggressive affect and physiological arousal in the short term (Anderson *et al.*, 2010; Anderson, Gentile & Buckley, 2007) in men and women across cultures. There are also studies that found no effects (cf. Adachi & Willoughby, 2011, p. 259). Anderson

et al. (2010, p. 152) come to the conclusion that "violent video game research mirrors findings from the violent TV and film research, with some evidence that the violent video game effects may be somewhat larger." Adachi and Willoughby (2011) found indications, however, that aggression after playing computer games might derive from in-game competition (i.e. losing), not the experience of violence in itself.

2 Game addiction and the effects of killer games, in the double sense of word, have not been the only focus of research. Researchers have inquired into the effects of computer games on the development of children and young adults and into ways of learning via computer games. Brain development and plasticity, motor skills, spatial representation, empathy and a host of other parameters have been researched in connection with computer games. Another angle that has attracted attention recently, especially after the events referred to as 'gamersgate', is the feminist critique of misogynic stereotypes, tropes and clichés in computer games.

3 Politics are present in the game, especially in the later stages of gameplay, when the player is allowed to adopt an ideology: autocracy, freedom or order.

13 Digital media and new terrorism

Jesper Falkheimer

The relationship between the news media and terrorism is crucial, for, as former UK prime minister Margaret Thatcher said, media exposure is the "oxygen of terrorism" (Wilkinson, 1997, p. 53). One of the core goals of terror is to win attention for political and religious ideas, and there is an intrinsic connection between propaganda, strategic communication and terrorism. In 2014, a social media propaganda war raged between the terrorist group IS (Islamic State) and counterterrorism communication units in different nations. Videos on YouTube, tweets, messages on Facebook and so forth were posted from different sources, and people all over the world saw horrible images of beheadings of journalists and volunteers. This shows even terrorists can be digital naturals.

Terrorism expert Neuman (2009) describes how the structure, aim and methods of terrorism have changed in late modernity and makes a division between old and new terrorism. New terrorism is said to be more brutal, transnational and media-oriented than it has ever been before. Against this background and drawing on earlier research into propaganda, terrorism and media, this chapter examines how digital media changes the premises and circumstances for terrorists as well as governments. The field of propaganda, terrorism and media has received increased interest from researchers, but is still an under-researched area in terrorism studies (Schmid, 2011).

In this chapter I challenge the normative idea that digital media and its utilisation by digital naturals lead us to a new brave world. The core argument is that digital media technology may be used in good ways and bad, and that old forms of propaganda are not gone but have taken new forms. In fact, I propose that propaganda strategies and tactics have enjoyed a renaissance in the age of digital media, and I will illustrate my argument with examples from earlier research and cases collected from IS terrorists' use of social media.

I begin by introducing concepts such as propaganda and terrorism. I then link to the role of the media, especially digital and social media. In the final part I give examples of how terrorists use social media strategies and tactics, and discuss counterterrorism social media strategies.

As discussed throughout this book, digital media technologies have changed the media structure and turned old communication models upside down. Many of the changes carry high expectations, not least from a democratic perspective, and are often predicated on a belief that the new systems favour two-way symmetric communication. Together, widespread individual access to publishing (Web 2.0) and the privileging of transparency and authenticity in online channels would seem to have consigned mass communication and propaganda to the past. Certainly, the old governmental and corporate monopoly of production and distribution of media content is challenged by media technologies that make it possible for citizens, groups and other social entities to communicate and reach large groups of people all over the world. Technological optimists such as Shirky (2009, p. 71) conclude that "anyone in the developed world can publish anything anytime, and the instant it is published, it is globally available and readily findable." Propaganda grew with radio, TV, cinema newsreels and mass circulation newspapers, channels with reach and, it appeared, persuasive impact. In democracies professional journalists were gatekeepers in this mass communication. At the same time as mass communication models have disintegrated, social media provides a way of jumping the traditional gatekeepers. Terror used to be good for grabbing news attention, but it was harder for terrorists to get messages out and frame narratives since mainstream media didn't offer a platform. Now a terror group, in the same way as an individual blogger or a corporation, can launch its own media channel and direct this towards certain target groups and a wider public. Social media is indeed a double-edged sword, since research also indicates that social media has a positive impact on political participation (Loader & Mercea, 2012), even if socio-economic factors still are very important (Gustafsson, 2013). But, as mentioned earlier, social media has a dark side and opens the way for new and direct forms of propaganda.

Propaganda and terrorism

The term 'propaganda' is contested and hard to define. For most people propaganda is associated with political and religious deception and distortions of truth through the use of different communicative strategies and tactics. O'Shaughnessy (1996) characterises propaganda as one-directional, biased, ideological, simplified, exaggerated and totally avoiding argumentative exchange or interaction. Jowett and O'Donnell (2015, p. 7) have defined propaganda as "the deliberate, systematic attempt to shape perceptions, manipulate cognitions, and direct behaviour to achieve a response that furthers the desired intent of the propagandist".

The history of propaganda is beyond the scope of this chapter, but it should be mentioned that when the term 'propaganda' was first used it was viewed as something good; the Roman Catholic Church created the *Congregation de Propaganda Fide* in 1622 as a platform for spreading the religion to non-Catholic parts of society, and the Communist leader Vladimir Lenin defined propaganda as political enlightenment and education. The impact of propaganda is parallel and integrated with the rise of mass communications, but O'Shaughnessy (2012, p. 34) concludes that the traditional premises for propaganda have changed due to the development of digital media: "Classical propaganda was something produced by powerful factions and forces or governments or parties. The rise of the internet has changed that balance, with YouTube and social networking allowing private citizens to sponsor their own propaganda campaigns."

Terrorism is defined as asymmetrical warfare, meaning that weaker parties (usually non-state actors) apply methods that are not accepted in symmetrical warfare against a stronger or institutionalised opponent, such as a state. Terrorism propaganda is a category of asymmetrical warfare and difficult to counteract or attack for democratic states, since "true asymmetry involves those actions that an adversary can exercise that you either cannot or will not" (Barnett, 2003, p. 12).

Moloney (2000) makes a division between manipulative public relations (weak propaganda) and ethically sound public relations. From a historical standpoint the line between propaganda and public relations is unclear, and propaganda was not viewed as negative in itself during the first decades of the last century. Manipulative communication is still practised, but public relations does not have to be propagandistic in itself. If propaganda is about shaping perceptions, it has a strong connection to public relations.

Holbrook (2014, p. 145) writes about terrorist propaganda and public relations initiatives and concludes that "some conceptual approaches to PR allow for the incorporation of propaganda as an element or descriptive aspect of some of the overall qualities of PR activities." In the same article Holbrook mentions an attempt by al-Qaeda to interact with the public. In 2008 al-Qaeda invited the public to ask questions online at an Islamist fundamentalist web forum. Some weeks later the questions, several of them very critical, and answers were published. According to Holbrook (ibid., p. 145) this "particular initiative was never repeated. It seems probable, however, that terrorist efforts will encounter more direct feedback of this kind in the future, particularly as usage of social media networks such as Twitter increases."

If propaganda is a contested concept, so too is terrorism. Acts of terrorism with political, religious or ideological motives have a longer history than the term terrorism. Archaeologists have found artefacts outside Mosul in present Iraq showing how Assurnasirpal II, king of Assyria during 883–859 BC, practiced terror against civilians during conquests (Matusitz, 2013). During the first century AD Jewish fundamentalists, called Zealots, practiced terror in their struggle against the Roman Empire and its allies. The Zealots were religious and puritanical men who became notorious for stabbing people to death in public places to get attention. Eventually they inspired a major revolt against the Roman Empire, which ended when the Zealots fled to the desert fortress of Masada, where they held out against the Romans for three years. Instead of giving up, the remaining Zealots committed collective suicide; only two women and five children escaped (Tuman, 2010). The Shia group Ismailites exerted terror in the twelfth century in a similar manner as the Zealots. The Ismailites, who were later known as Assassins, also killed people with knives in public places, often during religious holidays to get maximum attention. Sometimes the assassin had a hidden identity and had created a relationship with the person he killed. The terrorist tactic of killing people randomly in public spaces to create attention and horror is still around. A recent example is the Sunni jihadist extremist group IS (Islamic State) that has urged its followers, also via social media, to randomly behead ordinary people in public spaces in Europe, Australia and other parts of the Western world.[1]

Despite the historical examples, the term 'terrorism' did not emerge until the French Revolution in the late 1700s. The Jacobins and their leader, Maximillian Robespierre, introduced *le régime de la terreur* and the guillotine in order to impose revolutionary ideals.

Defining terrorism is not easy. Terrorism is a value-loaded term and is used rhetorically-politically. Etymologically, terrorism is derived from the Latin word *terrere* (fear), and the French verb suffix *isme* (to act). Most definitions consider terrorism asymmetric warfare, which uses the threat or use of violence against civilians to achieve political or religious goals. Some of those whom many today call terrorists use different terms to describe themselves – for example jihadists, nationalists (often right-wing extremists) and freedom fighters. Beliefs about terrorism reflect both the actions of contemporary terrorists and its portrayal in the media. In the 1970s, most people in Europe probably associated the term with terrorist organisations such as the Irish Republican Army (IRA) and German RAF (Red Army Faction) and the taking of hostages or hijacking. Today, most people's perceptions are probably dominated by images of Islamic fundamentalists and suicide bombers. Popular culture, such as the TV series *Homeland*, also has a crucial role in the creation of images of terrorists and terrorism.

In a simplified view, there are three forms of terrorism: state terrorism (when authoritarian states use political violence), national or domestic terrorism (directed against their own government) and transnational terrorism (rooted in a global network, directed against states, international institutions or movements). It has been accepted for many years that the importance of exposure in the media cannot be underestimated; the attention that the terrorist act creates is perhaps its fundamental driving force (Laqueur, 1987).

> Terrorist attacks are often carefully choreographed to attract the attention of the electronic media and the international press. Holding hostages increases the drama. If certain demands are not satisfied, the hostages may be killed. The hostages themselves often mean nothing to the terrorists. Terrorism is aimed at the people watching, not at the actual victims. Terrorism is theatre.
>
> (Jenkins, 1974, p. 7)

Terrorism researchers, such as Neuman (2009), argue that we must make a division between old and new terrorism. This division is easily linked to the social theoretical analysis of the transformation from modernity to late modernity (e.g. Bauman, 2000; Giddens, 1990). Neuman (2009) points out several characteristics of new terrorism that reveal changes in structure, aim and method. While old terrorism was hierarchical, organised in cells and with a physical centre, new terrorism is typically transnational and organised in diffuse networks formed around personalised relationships, sometimes without any operational connections at all. While old terrorism movements were mainly grounded in Marxist and nationalist ideologies, new terrorism mainly emanates from radical and fundamentalist religious ideologies. Finally, the methods have changed, even if the result remains the same – namely the death of civilians. But terrorist attacks have become more brutal (Neuman, 2009) and mass casualties are routine: "Faced with media saturation and desensitization, terrorists need to engage in ever more vicious forms of violence in order to 'get through' and achieve the psychological effect on which the strategy of terrorism relies" (Neuman, 2009, p. 5).

Terrorism, media and strategic communication

As stated before, publicity is an important goal for terrorists. Terrorist attacks in themselves are newsworthy, planned and designed according to the media logic and dramaturgy (Papacharissi & Oliveira, 2008, p. 53). But publicity is not the only communicative goal. Media researcher Picard (1989) emphasised several decades ago that a terrorist's target is not only publicity *per se* but also part of a much more sophisticated communication strategy:

> Labelling perpetrators of terrorism as seekers of publicity for its own sake is simplistic and ignores their very significant efforts to direct news coverage to present their cause in favourable ways and to disassociate groups from acts that will bring significant negative responses to the cause.
>
> (Picard, 1989, p. 14)

In their analysis of the terrorist attacks in Madrid (2004) and London (2005), Canel and Sanders (2010, p. 450) describe terrorism as strategic communication designed to attack the legitimacy of democracy by undermining public confidence, influencing and polarising politics and damaging the reputation of other organisations. Terrorists consider the logics of news both when planning their attacks and for amplifying the impact of their consequences. In a study of the 9/11 attacks of 2001 which focused on the US government and the media, Norris, Kern and Just (2003, p. 3) conclude that the media should be viewed as a double-edged sword. On the one hand, media coverage may favour the terrorists by giving exposure, spreading their political messages and unintentionally encouraging further attacks and creating new networks. On the other hand, media coverage may lead to the incumbent government or regime reinforcing its position and its ability to implement sanctions – for example lessening public resistance to new legislation that may be questionable in the long term from a democratic perspective.

After the 9/11 attacks, the discussion of terrorism as a strategic communication intensified (Falkheimer, 2014; Norris, Kern & Just, 2003; Richards, 2004; Somerville & Purcell, 2011). But so too is counterterrorism legitimised through effective strategic communication. Former US president George W. Bush coined the term 'war on terror' in the aftermath of 9/11 and created maximum polarisation as a basis for military intervention in Iraq and Afghanistan. As for terrorists, Loew (2003, p. 212) concluded that the al-Qaeda attacks in 2001 had communication goals that went beyond publicity for example to create fear, provoke reactions, communicate political messages and demonstrate US vulnerability. They also served to help the recruitment of like-minded people, create political radicalisation and reinforce a common identity among terrorist groups in relation to what is defined as US hegemony.

The first steps towards the professionalisation of terrorism as strategic communication took place back in the 1970s when German Red Army Faction began to systematically evaluate media coverage of its attacks (Rothenberger, 2015). The planning and execution of the 9/11 attacks may nonetheless be considered a turning point in terms of terrorism adaptation to media logic. The attacks on three fundamental institutions of power – political, economic and military – were also a strategic communicative attack on three symbols of Western society. Richards (2004, p. 171) believes that the attack on the World Trade Centre in New York was adapted to the conditions of the media in that film crews would be in place to bring live coverage as the second aircraft struck the Twin Towers.

Tuman (2010) argues that terrorism should be seen as rhetorical communication with multiple audiences. Rothenberger (2014) argues in accordance with Picard (1989) that the terrorists' strategic communication is complex and has communication goals that go beyond inducing fear – namely to:

- polarise public opinion
- attract new members
- publish a manifesto
- mislead enemies
- announce further measures
- create a media image
- facilitate internal communication between networks of terrorists
- get information about the hostages and counterterrorism.

This list will sound familiar to those versed in strategic communication.

One may add that terrorists use digital media for behavioural instruction. Jowett and O'Donnell (2015, p. 14) mention the Boston Marathon attack in 2013 as an example. One month before the attack in Boston, an al-Qaeda faction posted a compilation of "do-it-yourself articles with jaunty English text, high-quality graphics and teen-friendly shorthand [. . .] [stating] 'There's no need to travel abroad, because the frontline has come to you.'" The two Boston terrorists used this website and other instructions published by al-Qaeda to plan the attack and make the bombs which killed three people.

Contemporary terrorists use digital and social media proactively and reach individuals and publics without communicating through journalists. Weimann (2008) analysed 6,714 international terrorist incidents between late 1960 and early 1990 and showed that terrorist acts are increasingly adapted to the media logic. Before the Internet, groups such as the RAF and IRA depended on traditional mass media, but by the mid-1990s more and more were proactively using online channels. Weimann notes that in 1998 less than half of the international terrorist organisations identified by the US authorities had websites of their own. In 1999, almost all of these organisations were active on the Internet, and this trend has escalated through social media. Weimann concludes that terror sites have many characteristics in common: they present violence as the only way to deal with the opponent, they blame the violence on the past actions of the opponent, they dehumanise the adversary and they define themselves as freedom fighters and as representatives of marginalised minorities or groups.

Democratic states have become increasingly concerned about the social media strategies employed by terrorists in recent years. In 2010 the US State Department launched its Center for Strategic Counterterrorism Communication (CSCC) "to coordinate, orient, and inform government-wide foreign communications activities targeted against terrorism and violent extremism, particularly al-Qaida and its affiliates and adherents".[2] A digital outreach team, employing around 50 social media experts, counters terrorist propaganda and works actively in different languages. In 2014 IS propaganda has been a main target. By posting anti-IS films, messages and so forth on Facebook, YouTube and Twitter (*#Think Again Turn Away*), the Center tries to impact the recruitment of jihadists. In the *New York Times* undersecretary of state for public diplomacy Richard A. Stengel said that the old strategies of public diplomacy and persuasion no longer work.

"Sending a jazz trio to Budapest is not really what we want to do in 2014," said Mr. Stengel, referring to the soft-edged cultural diplomacy that sent musicians like Dave Brubeck on tours of Eastern-bloc capitals to counter communism during the Cold War. "We have to be tougher, we have to be harder, particularly in the information space, and we have to hit back."[3]

In a literature review on terrorism, risk and crisis communication, Ruggiero and Vos (2013) found several characteristics of terrorism crises that are relevant from a communication perspective. While all crises can evoke strong emotions, terrorist attacks which are low-probability but high-risk incidents "create more fear and anxiety than a naturally occurring crisis with similar consequences" (Ruggiero & Vos, 2013, p. 156). Although earlier research showed that the notion of public panic is overblown (Sheppard *et al.*, 2006), terror threats may lead to strong emotional and behavioural effects, not least on a societal level due to politisation and polarisation between groups.

Examples of terrorism social media strategies and tactics: the Islamic State

The following section shows *how* terrorists use social media to meet their aims. I use examples collected from earlier research, military reports and news media to focus on a terrorism movement that is currently receiving a lot of attention for its digital and social media strategies. The Islamic State (IS), formerly known as Islamic State in Iraq and the Levant (ISIL), is a transnational Sunni and Jihadist terrorist movement based in Iraq and Syria, which aims to create a worldwide Islamic caliphate. With its origin in al-Qaeda in Iraq, IS was defined as a terror group by the UN and EU in 2004, and has deployed a minor army in a war in Iraq and Syria since the beginning of 2014. Led by Abu Bakr al-Baghdadi, it has changed name several times and gained significant attention by its macabre use of violence, torture, executions, ethnic cleansing – and media strategies.

IS is not only a terrorist organisation but also an international brand. The black flag of IS is a central brand carrier. In an article in *Time* magazine, reporter Prusher (2014) finds that the black flag with white texts and a seal (the words translated: "There is no God but God" and "God Messenger Muhammed") is a strategic symbol. Mentioning Muhammed means that the flag becomes sacred, and the Prophet Muhammed's war banner was black. Quoting the terrorism researcher Magnus Ranstorp, the reporter concludes that "there's a kind of Islamic end-of-the-days element in the flag, pitting the forces of Islam against the Christian West."

IS established media and propaganda production centres several years ago. The al-Hayat Media Center was launched in 2014 to focus on Western publics and produce propaganda in several languages. Twitter shut down several IS accounts in August 2014, and when IS tried to create new accounts they too were shut down. IS has also tried to communicate through other social media, but have been shut down in most cases. Still, IS propaganda is relatively easy to find as the group launches new accounts and uses third parties. One example is the recruitment movie *Flames of War* (IS, 2014). The movie, designed in the style of a typical Hollywood action trailer, with explosions in slow motion and a short sequence with Barack Obama as the enemy, romanticises violence. It lasts 52 seconds and ends with the text "Coming soon".

Another example is the Android app The Dawn of Glad Tidings (described in the *Sydney Morning Herald*, Powell, June 2014). The app, launched in April 2014 and available on Google Play for several months, delivered an IS Twitter stream of updates and images. Quoting international relations researcher Andrew Philips, a *Sydney Morning Herald* article concludes that "Beyond intimidating their opponents, the two key target markets for groups like ISIL are donors and recruits, particularly disenfranchised second- and third-generation Muslim immigrants in Western countries." The IS social media strategy is well coordinated and professional. Different accounts are directed towards different targets with differing modes of communication, following the same logics and trends as large corporations do. One such trend is *co-production*, the integration of users and participants in media production. Here mujaheddin fighters communicate about everyday life from the war front, mixing private and public issues. Another trend is streaming live images and films and creating attention through massive campaigns with simple messages adapted to the social media platforms. Military analyst Elkjer Nissen (2014) argues that IS is combining a central top-down strategy with elements of bottom-up tactics. The top-level strategy is to produce and disseminate professional content, especially videos. At a second level IS regional and provincial accounts post live reports from the field. At a third level fighters post updates from everyday life, often with a personal approach. Finally, at the fourth level actors (disseminators, fans and the like) repost content and participate in the process, in different languages.

Kaya (2014) found four central themes when analysing the IS Turkish news website takvahaber.net. First, IS is eager to communicate that the organisation has power and resources and is successful. Second, IS communicates examples of how they provide services to the public – for example building water canals or providing food to children. Third, IS is creating integration and disintegration (Ellul, 1973), and a clear division between us and them. The United States and its allies are named "invaders" and "the evil coalition". Fourth, and linked to the third theme, IS develops narratives and gives examples of how the "evil coalition" has massacred civilians in Iraq.

The communication strategy, as understood from the outside, is very clear and employs tactics that reflect the latest strategic communication practice. Through the use of several channels (a multichannel strategy), a strong narrative with a clear goal (to create a caliphate), visual appearance with intertexts relating to well-known action genres, and inviting fans and co-members to take part in the productions, IS has created a transnational brand (Elkjer Nissen, 2014, p. 2). The stories, movies and images that are communicated have a strong emotional appeal: ranging from beheadings to mujaheddins posting cute images of cats. By posting a massive amount of messages and content in different channels, IS spreads these messages to both potential followers and others.

> Another dimension of this strategy is to rely on these 'disseminators' using hashtags crafted to look like grassroot initiatives exploiting 'astro-turfing' techniques, in some cases also hijacking existing hashtags, and thereby lending third party credibility to their narrative.
>
> (Elkjer Nissen, 2014, p. 3)

Counterterrorism social media strategies

It is clear that digital media technologies have created new possibilities for propaganda and terrorists have indeed capitalised on them. The boundaries between media strategies used by corporations, governments, activist movements and terrorism groups have become blurred. The examples given from the IS social media strategy are one example of this hybridisation. A follow-up question is, of course, how can democratic states counteract social media campaigns from terror groups? Earlier, the Center for Strategic Counterterrorism Communication (CSCC) in the United States was mentioned as an organised counterterrorism attempt focusing on social media, and there are similar examples in several countries. The attitudes of digital naturals are relevant to counterterrorism. The premises for such operations are complicated. IS, as an example, follows no regulations and seems to have no limitations, while democratic states cannot or should not use disinformation and deception. Counterterrorism social media strategies have to be developed further, but giving concrete advice goes beyond the aim of this chapter. That said, some general remarks may be made. A counterterrorism strategy may focus on four operational aspects. First, there is a need for monitoring and surveilling terrorism social media propaganda. Second, when possible there is a need to move fast to close down terrorists accounts and platforms. But banning websites and social media accounts is not enough:

> Not only does the decentralized, global structure of the Internet make it virtually impossible to remove particular types of content for long, the volume of 'radical' and 'extremist' material that is currently available would necessitate a truly Orwellian structure to ensure complete control over what can be accessed.
>
> (Neuman, 2009, p. 156)

Third, there is a need to develop efficient antiterrorism content (messages, visuals, etc.) posted in all possible channels, arguing against and questioning terrorism narratives and stories by using both facts and emotions. Developing coordinated strategic communication functions at different levels in government and communicating according to the logic of digital naturals and new networks are necessary. Fourth, the top-down strategy must be combined with efforts to engage victims and citizens as disseminators of antiterrorism content. Still, counterterrorism social media strategies are complicated and may have paradoxical effects, as mentioned by Ruggiero and Vos (2013, p. 157) when they refer to research about communication campaigns as a tool for raising awareness about potential school shootings and terrorism and conclude that "communication campaigns about terrorism have to be framed with caution in order to avoid negative reactions towards minorities." There is also another possible unintended consequence of communication campaigns focusing on terrorism. As mentioned earlier, despite the fact that the probability of a terror attack is low compared to most other risks, it is perceived by the public as a major problem. There may be several reasons behind this risk perception. On the one hand, this indicates that terror methods do fulfil the strategic aim of creating horror, but on the other hand the media publicity and framing of attacks have strong effects. This leads to a paradox for counterterrorism communication strategists. Creating major campaigns trying to persuade potential recruits not to join terrorist movements may cause some individuals to turn against terror, but they may also lead to increased stigmatisation and persuade potential terrorists to join. The exposure in itself may lead to increased safety measures and public resistance, but may also help terrorists reach their main target: to set the agenda and influence debate and discussion.

Notes

1 www.theguardian.com/world/2014/sep/18/terrorism-raids-police-arrests-raids-sydney-brisbane.
2 www.state.gov/r/cscc/.
3 www.nytimes.com/2014/09/27/world/middleeast/us-vividly-rebuts-isis-propaganda-on-arab-social-media.html.

Conclusion

Although opinion will continue to be divided as to how fundamental the changes to strategic communication brought by the advance of digital technologies really are, it is beyond doubt that every chapter in this book has analysed phenomena, circumstances and behaviours that differ significantly from those experienced even a decade or so ago. All illustrate the incontestable reality that strategic communication has to evolve, both as theory and as practice.

Not surprisingly, there is little here to fully vindicate the aspirations of digital optimists, and many writers are urging policymakers to face up to some very real challenges. The picture that emerges is of rapid evolution rather than revolution, with change happening at different speeds across differing demographic, social and economic arenas. Being aware of trends and anticipating and reacting to new circumstances, attitudes and social norms are part and parcel of being a communicator, but there are worrying signs in many chapters that practitioners, and those who strive to shape civic life, are struggling to stay abreast of the challenges.

NEMO authors have found it useful to apply the digital naturals framing to develop their understanding of shifting patterns. We believe the digital naturals framing helps to capture the texture of change, and provides a flexible and fruitful platform for gaining deeper insights. One of the advantages of the digital naturals approach is that it seeks to be inclusive rather than exclusive, and acknowledges that the lives of almost everyone in the developed world are being influenced – for good or ill – by the move online. Crucially, it doesn't characterise the online world as being somewhere distinct and different, the arena of particular interests or self-selecting elites. In countries such as Sweden, going online is not a leap into cyber-space, requiring great technical skill and the mental agility of a young mind; rather it is just another part of daily life. Not everyone is addicted to Instagram, or feels compelled to check Facebook before getting out of bed (as many do!), but they do shop, check bus timetables, buy rail tickets, read news and run bank accounts. Almost everyone experiences purposeful (and probably persuasive) strategic communication activity by organisations in forms that are enabled by digital channels.

Even as prices fall, it is undeniable that access to digital platforms *does* cost money, but the number of people excluded for economic reasons is dwindling, in part because online access is becoming an essential buy rather than a luxury, displacing other items in many a core budget. Digital exclusion has a monetary dimension, and it also has a skills requirement; linguistic fluency is a useful social asset, whether it is measured against an ability to comprehend information, or to express oneself fluently and in a way that commands respect from peers. Online communication leaves a trail of social clues that can be permanent, and can inhibit expression and participation in debate.

Notice that the vast majority of actors discussed in this book have reasonably sophisticated communication skills, be they professional politicians, Instagrammers recording life in Landskrona or activists checking the work of a German minister. Notice, too, that our definition of the digital natural describes someone who is comfortable in the online environment. The notion of comfort is necessarily complex: being comfortable in your ability to check the opening hours of a shop online or buy a bus pass is not the same thing as being comfortable surrendering a significant amount of personal information in exchange for being allowed to join a social networking site.

Very broadly, the findings of Åkerström and Young's focus groups, that digital naturals have (or at least feel they have) wider access to a greater amount of information than those who came before, are reflected in other chapters. At the same time, there is a recognition that having access to information and actually using it as an instrument for change are far from inevitable. Yes, some agents, not least the terrorists discussed by Falkheimer, can make extraordinary use of the expanded platform for expression that emerges with the demise of traditional gatekeeping, but it is hard to find studies that suggest great democratic benefit is accruing from new technologies. Some would argue that the digital natural environment is as reactionary in its preservation of elites as anything that has gone before.

Gustafsson's investigations shed an interesting light on the digital natural thesis, in that age does appear to be significant factor in determining use of social media, but closer examination shows that this has more to do with career stage than aptitude. The older politicians have different priorities and different time pressures, and it is not surprising that this is more significant than some intrinsic quality of youth. Gustafsson's opening sketch, where the Swedish politician is more relaxed in her delineation of borders between political and private life than her American counterpart, may reflect age, but surely has more to do with culture. The same process underpins claimed variations in notions of privacy between younger and older people; teenagers may share some information that their elders would guard as personal, but they also fight hard for private space, whether through 'secret' slang and idiom or the firmly shut bedroom door.

Many of the shifts discussed flow from the way in which Web 2.0 technologies have opened up access to the spreading and sharing of content and messaging. The role of formal journalism is increasingly contested, and the influence of actors ranging from swarm activists to the co-creators of city image is bringing social as well as economic transformation. The chapters on terrorism (Chapter 13) and adjudication (Chapter 11) show implications of widening access in ways that empower racists and violent, even murderous, militancy.

Transparency and the groundswell of righteous indignation are of ever more importance. Elites can be rocked by collective action, as vividly illustrated by the demise of Defence Minister Guttenberg, the PR wizard who didn't understand the importance of matching words and deeds (Chapter 10).

Social media may have improved institutional capacity for engagement and conversation (much contested terms, as we saw in Chapter 3), but it has also served to let competing disciplines gatecrash territory claimed by strategic communication.

Considering the realities of modern PR practice, the emergence of digital has laid bare fault lines in some fundamental conceptions. Using paradox as a lens, Chapter 2 made a strong case for believing that the discipline will need to rethink the way in which it seeks to define and distinguish the practice. Certainly, its ongoing identity crisis shows no sign of easing. If we accept that the digital naturals have raised expectations for dialogue, transparency and mutual understanding, it does increase tensions juxtaposed against arguments that PR is also about "one-way communication, sugar-coating and one-sided persuasion" (p. 17).

As Merkelsen, Möllerström and von Platen argue,

In terms of future theoretical developments new distinctions will be needed, too. And perhaps, if the paradoxical nature of public relations is accepted as a starting point, these distinctions will be productive. If the problematic relationship between theory and practice is to improve, a good starting point would be to make a distinction at a higher order: a distinction between the distinctions that define practice and the distinctions that define theory.

(p. 24)

As ever, the conclusion must be that the impact of digital naturals on strategic communication and democratic processes demands continued, rigorous and ever deeper investigation. There is no indication that the pace of change is slowing – far from it!

Bibliography

Aalberg, T., Strömbäck, J. & de Vreese, C. H. (2011). The framing of politics as strategy and game: A review of concepts, operationalizations and key findings. *Journalism 13*(2), 1–17.

Adachi, P. & Willoughby, T. (2011). The effect of video game competition and violence on aggressive behavior: Which characteristic has the greatest influence? *Psychology of Violence, 1*(4), 259–274.

Åkerström, M. (2010). *Den kosmetiska demokratin: En studie av den diskursiva praktiken i Sjöbo och Ystad.* Lund: Lund University.

Albert, S. & Whetten, D.A. (1985). Organizational identity. *Research in Organizational Behavior, 7,* 263–295.

Alexander, R. (2011, 19 February). Guttenbergs schwarzer Freitag. *Die Welt Online.* Retrieved 5 May 2015 from www.welt.de/print/die_welt/politik/article12590727/Guttenbergs-schwarzer-Freitag.html

Almighty Sosa. (2014). In steam community [Reviews on democracy 3]. Retrieved 14 December from http://steamcommunity.com/app/245470/reviews

Almond, G. A., & Verba S. (1963). The civic culture: Political attitudes and democracy in five nations. Princeton, NJ: Princeton University Press.

Alvesson, M. & Empson, L. (2008). The construction of organizational identity: Comparative case studies of consulting firms. *Scandinavian Journal of Management, 24,* 1–16.

Anderson, C. A., Gentile, D. A., & Buckley, K. E. (2007). *Violent video game effects.* Oxford, UK: Oxford University Press.

Anderson, C. A., Gentile, D. A. & Buckley, K. E. (2007). *Violent video game effects.* New York, NY: Oxford University Press.

Anderson, C. A., Ihori, N., Bushman, B. J., Rothstein, H. R., Shibuya, A., Swing, E. L. & Saleem, M. (2010). Video game effects on aggression, empathy, and prosocial behavior and eastern and western countries: A meta-analytic review. *Psychological Bulletin, 136,* 151–173.

Aronoff, M. J. (2001). Political culture. In N. Smelser (ed.), *International encyclopedia of the social and behavioral sciences* (pp. 11640–11644). Amsterdam: Elsevier.

Aronovitch, H. (2012). Interpreting Weber's ideal types. *Philosophy of the Social Sciences, 42*(3), 356–369.

Arpan, L. M. & Pompper, D. (2003). Stormy weather: Testing "stealing thunder" as a crisis communication strategy to improve communication flow between organizations and journalists. *Public Relations Review, 29,* 291–308.

Åsblom, J. (2012, 17 February). Facebook modell när företagen blir sociala: Webbaserade molntjänster håller de anställda uppdaterade. *Computer Sweden,* p. 14.

Ashby, W. R. (1956). *Introduction to cybernetics*. London, UK: Chapman & Hall.

Avery, E. J., Lariscy, R. W., Kim, S. & Hocke, T. (2010). A quantitative review of crisis communication research in public relations from 1991 to 2009. *Public Relations Review*, *36*(2), 190–192.

Avpixlat. (2014). http://avpixlat.info/

Bal, M. (2003). Visual essentialism and the object of visual culture. *Journal of Visual Culture*, *2*(1), 5–32.

Ballantine, P. W. & Martin, B. A. (2005). Forming parasocial relationships in online communities. *Advances in Consumer Research*, *32*, 197–201.

Bark, M. (1997). *Intranät i organisationens kommunikation*. Uppsala: Konsultförlaget.

Bark, M. & Heide, M. (2002). Introduktion. In M. Bark & M. Heide (eds.), *Intranätboken: Från elektronisk anslagstavla till dagligt arbetsverktyg* [The intranet book: From electronic dashboard to daily work tool] (pp. 8–13). Malmö: Liber.

Barnard, C. I. (1968). *The functions of the executive*. Cambridge, MA: Harvard University Press (Original work published 1938).

Barnett, R. W. (2003). *Asymmetric warfare: Today's challenges to US military power*. Washington, DC: Brasseys.

Barrling Hermansson, K. (2004). *Partikulturer: Kollektiva självbilder och normer i Sveriges riksdag*. Acta Universitatis Upsaliensis 159. Uppsala: Uppsala University.

Barton, L. (2001). *Crisis in organizations II* (2nd ed.). Cincinnati, OH: College Divisions South-Western.

Bateson, G., Jackson, D. D., Haley, J. & Weakland, J. (1956). Toward a theory of schizophrenia. *Behavorial Science*, *1*(4), 251–254.

Bauman, Z. (2000). *Liquid modernity*. Cambridge, UK: Polity.

Bebbington, J., Larrinaga, C. & Moneva, J. M. (2008). Corporate social reporting and reputation risk management. *Accounting, Auditing & Accountability Journal*, *21*(3), 337–361.

Beck, J. C. & Wade, M. (2006). *The kids are alright: How the gamer generation is changing the workplace*. Boston, MA: Harvard Business School Press.

BenjiOfTheZulu. (2014). In steam community [Reviews on *Civilization V*]. Retrieved 14 December 2014 from http://store.steampowered.com/app/8930

Bennet, S., Maton, K. & Kervin, L. (2008). The "digital natives" debate: A critical review of the evidence. *British Journal of Educational Technology*, *39*(5), 321–331.

Bennett, W. L. & Segerberg, A. (2012). The logic of connective action: Digital media and the personalization of contentious politics. *Information, Communication & Society*, *15*(5), 739–768.

Benoit, W. L. (1995). *Accounts, excuses, and apologies: A theory of image restoration*. Albany: State University of New York Press.

Berelson B., Lazarsfeld P. & McPhee, W. (1954). *Voting: A study of opinion formation in a political campaign*. Chicago, IL: University of Chicago Press.

Bernays, E. (1923). *Crystallizing public opinion*. New York, NY: Liveright.

Bessette, Joseph. (1994). *The mild voice of reason: Deliberative democracy and American national government*. Chicago, IL: University of Chicago Press.

Bewarder, M. (2011, 19 June). So arbeiten die Plagiatsjäger von GuttenPlag. *Berliner Morgenpost Online*. Retrieved 5 May 2015 from www.morgenpost.de/politik/article1676145/So-arbeiten-die-Plagiatsjaeger-von-GuttenPlag.html

Biddle, B. (1979). *Role theory: Expectations, identities, and behaviors*. New York, NY: Academic Press.

Bishop, J. (2013). *Gamification for human factors integration: Social, education, and psychological issues*. Hershey, PA: IGI Global.

Black, G. S. (1972). A theory of political ambition: Career choices and the role of structural incentives. *American Political Science Review, 66*(1), 144–159.

Bogost, I. (2007). *Persuasive games: The expressive power of videogames.* Cambridge, MA: MIT Press.

Booth, S. A. (2000). How can organisations prepare for reputational crises? *Journal of Contingencies and Crisis Management, 8*(4), 197–207.

Bouwmeester, O. & van Werven, R. (2011). Consultants as legitimizers: Exploring their rhetoric. *Journal of Organizational Change Management, 24*(4), 427–441.

boyd, d. (2008). *Taken out of context: American teen sociality in networked publics* (Unpublished doctoral dissertation). University of California, Berkeley.

boyd, d. (2014). *It's complicated: The social lives of networked teens.* New Haven, CT: Yale University Press.

Bradley, A. J. & McDonald, M. P. (2011). *The social organization: How to use social media to tap the collective genius of your customers and employees.* Boston, MA: Harvard Business Review Press.

Breeze, M. (2013, 12 February). A quiet killer: Why games are so addictive. Retrieved 5 May 2015 from http://thenextweb.com/insider/2013/01/12/what-makes-games-so-addictive

Bruce, C.T. (1998) The Disappearance of Technology: Toward an Ecological Model of Literacy, in David Reinking, Michael C. McKenna, Linda D. Labbo, & Ronald D. Kieffer (Eds.), *Handbook of literacy and technology: Transformations in a post-typographic world* (pp. 269–281). London, UK: Routledge.

Bruns, A. & Highfield, T. (2013). Political networks on Twitter. *Information, Communication & Society, 16*(5), 667–691.

Bunde, T., Fliegauf, M. T., Klöppler, H., Mirow, W., Staemmler, J., Trettin, F. & Wihl, T. (2011). *Causa Guttenberg: Offener Brief von Doktoranden an die Bundeskanzlerin.* Retrieved 5 May 2015 from http://offenerbrief.posterous.com

Burt, S., Johansson, U. & Thelander, Å. (2007). Retail image as seen through consumers' eye: Studying international retail image through consumer photographs of stores. *International Review of Retail, Distribution and Consumer Research, 17*(5), 447–467.

Callon, M., Lascoumes, P. & Barthe, Y. (2011). *Acting in an uncertain world: An essay on technical democracy.* Cambridge, MA: MIT Press.

Canel, M. J. & Sanders, K. (2010). Crisis communication and terrorist attacks: Framing a response to the 2004 Madrid bombing and 2005 London bombing. In T. Coombs & S. Holladay (eds.), *The handbook of crisis communication* (pp. 449–466). West Sussex, UK: Blackwell.

Caplan, S., Williams, D. & Yee, N. (2009). Problematic internet use and psychosocial well-being among MMO players. *Computers in Human Behavior, 25*, 1312–1319.

Castells, M. (1996). *The rise of the network society: The information age: Economy, society and culture* (Vol. 1). Oxford, UK: Blackwell.

———. (1997). *The power of identity: The information age: Economy, society and culture* (Vol. 2). Oxford, UK: Blackwell.

———. (1998). *End of millennium: The information age: Economy, society and culture* (Vol. 3). Oxford: Blackwell.

———. (2013). *Communication power.* Oxford, UK: Oxford University Press.

Chadwick, A. (2013). *The hybrid media system: Politics and power.* Oxford, UK: Oxford University Press.

Chalfen, R. (1987). *Snapshot versions of Life.* Bowling Green, OH: Bowling Green Popular Press.

Chalfen, R. (1998). Interpreting family photographs as pictorial communication. In J. Prosser (Ed.), *Image based research* (pp. 190–208). London, UK: Routledge.

Chambers, S. (2003). Deliberative democratic theory. *Annual Review of Political Science*, *6*, 307–326.

Chatfield, T. (2011). *Fun Inc.: Why games are the twenty-first century's most serious business*. London, UK: Virgin.

Cheney, G. & Christensen, L. T. (2001). Public relations as contested terrain: A critical response. In R. L. Heath (ed.), *Handbook of public relations* (pp. 167–187). Thousand Oaks, CA: Sage.

Chesher, C. & Costello, B. (2004). Why media scholars should not study computer games. *Media International Australia Incorporating Culture & Policy*, *110*, 5–9.

Child, J. T. & Shumate, M. (2007). The impact of communal knowledge repositories and people-based knowledge management on perceptions of team effectiveness. *Management Communication Quarterly*, *21*, 29–54.

Christensen, L. T. & Langer, R. (2009). Consistency, hypocrisy, and corporate change. In R. L. Heath, E. L. Toth & D. Waymer (eds.), *Rhetorical and critical approaches to public relations II* (pp. 129–153). New York, NY: Routledge.

Christensen, L. T., Morsing, M. & Cheney, G. (2008). *Corporate communications: Convention, complexity and critique*. Thousand Oaks, CA: Sage.

Chronologie der Plagiatsaffaire: Guttenbergs Weg in den Rücktritt. (n.d.). *Spiegel Online*. Retrieved 5 February 2015 from www.spiegel.de/flash/flash-25408.html

Claeys, A. S. & Cauberghe, V. (2010). Crisis response and crisis timing strategies: Two sides of the same coin. *Public Relations Review*, *38*(1), 83–88.

Clark-Ibanez, M. (2004). Framing the social world with photo-elicitation interviews. *American Behavioural Scientists*, *47*(12), 1507–1527.

Collier, J. & Collier, M. (1999). *Visual anthropology: Photography as a research method*. Albuquerque: University of New Mexico Press (Original work published 1967).

Coombs, W. T. (1995). Choosing the right words: The development of guidelines for the selection of the "appropriate" crisis-response strategies. *Management Communication Quarterly*, *8*(4), 447–476.

———. (2010a). Crisis communication: A developing field. In R. L. Heath (ed.), *Handbook of public relations* (2nd ed., pp. 477–488). Thousand Oaks, CA: Sage.

———. (2010b). Sustainability: A new and complex "challenge" for crisis managers. *International Journal of Sustainable Strategic Management*, *2*, 4–16.

———. (2014). *Applied crisis communication and crisis management*. Thousand Oaks, CA: Sage.

———. (2015). *Ongoing crisis communication: Planning, managing, and responding* (4th ed.). Los Angeles, CA: Sage.

———. (in press). Revising situational crisis communication theory: The influences of social media on crisis communication on theory and practice. In L. L. Austin & Y. Jin (eds.), *Social media and crisis communication*. New York, NY: Routledge.

Coombs, W. T., Claeys, A. S. & Holladay S. J. (in press). Social media's value in a crisis: Channel effect of stealing thunder? In L. L. Austin & Y. Jin (eds.), *Social media and crisis communication*. New York, NY: Routledge.

Coombs, W. T. & Holladay, S. J. (2002). Helping crisis managers protect reputational assets: Initial tests of the situational crisis communication theory. *Management Communication Quarterly*, *16*, 165–186.

———. (2012a). Amazon.com's Orwellian nightmare: Exploring apology in an online environment. *Journal of Communication Management*, *16*(3), 280–295.

———. (2012b). Internet contagion theory 2.0: How internet communication channels empower stakeholders. In S. Duhé (ed.), *New media and public relations* (2nd ed., pp. 21–30). New York, NY: Peter Lang.

———. (2012c). The paracrisis: The challenges created by publicly managing crisis prevention. *Public Relations Review, 38*(3), 408–415.

———. (2014). How publics react to crisis communication efforts: Comparing crisis response reactions across sub-arenas. *Journal of Communication Management, 18*(1), 40–57.

———. (in press). Public relations' "relationship identity" in research: Enlightenment or illusion. *Public Relations Review*.

Cornelissen, J. (2014). *Corporate communication: A guide to theory and practice*. Thousand Oaks, CA: Sage.

Crang, M. (1997). Picturing practices: Research through the tourist gaze. *Progress in Human Geography, 21*(3), 359–373.

Crawford, C. (2003). *Chris Crawford on game design.* Indianapolis, IN: New Riders.

Crouch, Colin. (2004). *Post-democracy*. Cambridge, UK: Polity Press.

Crozier, M., Huntington, S. & Watanuki, J. (1975). *The crisis of democracy: Report on the governability of democracies to the trilateral commission.* New York, NY: New York University Press.

Curators of Sweden. (n.d.). Retrieved 8 November 2014 from www.curatorsofsweden.com

Dahl, R. A. (1956). *A preface to democratic theory.* Chicago, IL: University of Chicago Press.

———. (1999). *Demokratin och dess antagonister.* Stockholm: Ordfront Förlag.

Dahlberg, L. (2010). Cyberlibertarianism 2.0: A discourse theory/critical political economy-examination. *Cultural Politics, 6*(3), 331–356.

Dahlgren, P. (2006). Doing citizenship: The cultural origins of civic agency in the public sphere. *European Journal of Cultural Studies, 9*(3), 267–286.

———. (2009). *Media and political engagement: Citizens, communication, and democracy.* Cambridge, UK: Cambridge University Press.

Davies, N. (2008). *Flat earth news.* London, UK: Chatto & Windus.

Deephouse, D. L. (2000). Media reputation as a strategic resource: An integration of mass communication and resource-based theories. *Journal of Management, 26*(6), 1091–1112.

Deetz, S. (1992). *Democracy in an age of corporate colonization: Developments in communication and the politics of everyday life.* Albany: State University of New York Press.

Delli Carpini, M., Cook, F. & Jacobs, L. (2004). Public deliberations, discursive participation and citizen engagement: A review of the empirical literature. *Annual Review of Political Science, 7*(1), 315–344.

Depauw, S. & Martin, S. (2008). Legislative party discipline and cohesion in comparative perspective. In D. Gianetti & K. Benoit (eds.), *Intra-party politics and coalition governments* (pp. 103–120). London, UK: Routledge.

Derrick, J. L., Gabriel, S. & Tippin, B. (2008). Parasocial relationships and self-discrepancies: Faux relationships have benefits for low self-esteem individuals. *Personal Relationships, 15*(2), 261–280.

DeSanctis, G. & Fulk, J. (1999). *Shaping organizational form: Communication, connection, and community.* Thousand Oaks, CA: Sage.

Deutsche wollen Guttenberg behalten. (2011, 19 February). *Focus Online.* Retrieved 5 May 2015 from www.focus.de/politik/deutschland/plagiataffaere-deutsche-wollen-guttenberg-behalten_aid_601406.html

DiNucci, D. (1999). Fragmented future. *Print.* Retrieved 5 May 2015 from www.darcyd. com/fragmented_future.pdf

DiStaso, M. W. (2012). Measuring public relations Wikipedia engagement: How bright is the rule? *Public Relations Journal, 6*(2), 1–22.

DiStaso, M. W. & Messner, M. (2010). Forced transparency: Corporate image on Wikipedia and what it means for public relations. *Public Relations Journal, 4*(2), 1–23.

Earl, S. & Waddington, S. (2012). *Brand anarchy.* London, UK: Bloomsbury.

———. (2013). *Brand vandals.* London, UK: Bloomsbury.

Edensor, T. (2001). Performing tourism, staging tourism: (Re)producing tourist space and practice. *Tourist Studies, 1*, 59–81.

Edwards, L. (2012). Defining the "object" of public relations research: A new starting point. *Public Relations Inquiry, 1*(1), 7–30.

Ehling, W. P., White, J. & Grunig, J. E. (1992). Public relations and marketing practices. In J. E. Grunig (ed.), *Excellence in public relations and communication management* (pp. 357–393). Hillsdale, NJ: Erlbaum.

Eisenegger, M. & Schranz, M. (2011). Reputation management and corporate social responsibility. In O. Ihlen, J. L. Bartlett & S. May (eds.), *The handbook of corporate social responsibility* (pp. 128–146). Malden, MA: Blackwell.

Electoral Reform Services. (2014). Gamification and its role in democratic engagement. Retrieved 27 November 2014 from www.electoralreform.co.uk/news-blogs/blogs/ gamification-and-its-role-democratic-engagement

Elkjer Nissen, T. (2014). Terror.com: IS social media warfare in Syria and Iraq. *Military Studies Magazine: Contemporary Conflicts.* Retrieved 4 February 2015 from http:// forsvaret.dk/FAK/eng/news/magazine/articles/Pages/Issue-2-Volume-2-2014/Terror-com-IS-Social-Media-Warfare-in-Syria-and-Iraq.aspx.

Ellul, J. (1973). *Propaganda: The formation of men's attitudes.* New York, NY: Vintage.

Emirbayer, M. (1997). Manifesto for a relational sociology 1. *American Journal of Sociology, 103*(2), 281–317.

Enli, G. S. & Skogerbø, E. (2013). Personalized campaigns in party-centred politics. *Information, Communication & Society, 16*(5), 757–774.

Eriksson-Zetterquist, U., Lindberg, K. & Styhre, A. (2009). When the good times are over: Professionals encountering new technology. *Human Relations, 62*, 1145–1170.

Ermi, L. & Mayra, F. (2005). Fundamental components of the game play experience: Analysing immersion. Proceedings of DiGRA 2005 Conference: Changing Views – Worlds in Play. Retrieved 4 May 2015 from www.digra.org/wp-content/uploads/digital-library/06276.41516.pdf.

ESA Entertainment Software Association. (2014). *In-game advertising.* Retrieved 19 December 2014 from www.theesa.com/wp-content/uploads/2014/11/Games_Advertising-11.4.pdf

Falkheimer, J. (2014). Crisis communication and terrorism: The Norway attacks on 22 July 2011. *Corporate Communications: An International Journal, 19*(1), 52–63.

Falkheimer, J. & Heide, M. (in press). A reflexive perspective on public relations: On leaving traditional thinking and uncover the taken-for-granted. In J. L'Etang, D. McKie, N. Snow & J. Xifra (eds.), *The Routledge handbook of critical public relations.* New York, NY: Routledge.

Fawkes, J. & Gregory, A. (2000). Applying communication theories to the Internet. *Journal of Communication Management, 5*(2), 109–124.

Festinger, L. A. (1957). *A theory of cognitive dissonance.* Stanford, CA: Stanford University Press.

Fincham, R. (1999). The consultant–client relationship: Critical perspectives on the management of organizational change. *Journal of Management Studies*, *36*(3), 335–351.

Fischer, E. & Reuber, R. (2007). The good, the bad, and the unfamiliar: The challenges of reputation formation facing new firms. *Entrepreneurship Theory and Practice*, *31*(1), 53–75.

Fischer, S., Gathmann, F. & Wittrock, P. (2011, 23 February). Opposition spricht von Lüge, Regierungsseite verteidigt Guttenberg. *Spiegel Online*. Retrieved 4 February 2015 from www.spiegel.de/politik/deutschland/liveticker-aus-dem-bundestag-opposition-spricht-von-luege-regierungsseite-verteidigt-guttenberg-a-747232.html

Fischer-Lescano, A. (2011). Karl-Theodor Frhr. zu Guttenberg, Verfassung und Verfassungsvertrag: Konstitutionelle Entwicklungsstufen in den USA und der EU. *Kritische Justiz*, *44*(1), 112–119.

Fishkin, James. (1991). *Democracy and deliberation*. New Haven, CT: Yale University Press.

Fombrun, C. J. (2005). A world of reputation research, analysis and thinking: Building corporate reputation through CSR initiatives: Evolving standards. *Corporate Reputation Review*, *8*(1), 7–12.

Foremski, T. (2006). Die press release! Die! Die! Die! Retrieved 4 February 2015 from www.siliconvalleywatcher.com/mt/archives/2006/02/die_press_relea.php

Fossen, T. & Anderson, J. (2014). What's the point of voting advice applications? Competing perspectives on democracy and citizenship. *Electoral Studies, 36*, 263–271.

Foucault, M. (1980). *Power/knowledge*. New York, NY: Pantheon.

———. (1993). *Diskursens ordning*. Stockholm: Brutus Östlings Bokförlag Symposion.

———. (2002). *Vetandets arkeologi*. Lund: Arkiv Förlag.

———. (2008). *The political technology of individuals*. In *Diskursernas kamp – Texter i urval av Thomas Götzelius och Ulf Olsson*. Stockholm: Brutus Östlings Förlag.

Frandsen, F. & Johansen, W. (2010a). Apologizing in a globalizing world: Crisis communication and apologetic ethics. *Corporate Communications: An International Journal*, *15*(4), 350–364.

———. (2010b). Crisis communication, complexity, and the cartoon affair: A case study. In W. T. Coombs & S. J. Holladay (eds.), *The handbook of crisis communication* (pp. 425–448). Boston, MA: Wiley-Blackwell.

———. (2011). The study of internal crisis communication: Towards an integrative framework. *Corporate Communications: An International Journal*, *16*(4), 347–361.

Fras, D., Schmale, H. & von Bebenburg, P. (2011, 21 February). Guttenberg will auf Doktortitel verzichten. *Frankfurter Rundschau Online*. Retrieved 5 February 2015 from www.fr-online.de/politik/guttenberg-verzichtet-auf-seinen-titel,1472596,7241324.html

Frasca, G. (2003). Simulation vs narrative: Introduction to ludology. In M.J.P. Wolf (ed.), *The video game theory reader* (pp. 221–235). New York, NY: Routledge.

Freeman, C. (2008). Internet gaming addiction. *The Journal for Nurse Practitioners*, *4*, 42–47.

Friberg, K. (2011, 29 March). Ledningen skräms av sociala intranät. *Computer Sweden*, p. 17.

Friedl, J. & Verčič, A. T. (2011). Media preferences of digital natives' internal communication: A pilot study. *Public Relations Review*, *37*, 84–86.

Friese, G. M. & Linnenbrink, M. (2011, 18 February). Guttenberg verzichtet vorerst auf Doktortitel. *DW.de*. Retrieved 16 December 2014 from www.dw.de/guttenberg-verzichtet-vorerst-auf-doktortitel/a-14851179–1

Fuchs, C. (2014). *Social media: A critical introduction*. London, UK: Sage.

Fulk, J., Schmitz, J. & Steinfield, C. W. (1990). A social influence model of technology use. In J. Fulk & C. W. Steinfield (eds.), *Organizations and communication technology* (pp. 117–140). Newbury Park, CA: Sage.

Funk, V. & Helbig, F. (2011, 20 May). Den Ruf der Politik verbessern. *Frankfurter Rundschau Online*. Retrieved 5 May 2015 from www.fr-online.de/politik/fr-gespraech-mit-plagiatsjaegern—den-ruf-der-politik-verbessern-,1472596,8473032.html

Game Studies. (2014). About game studies. Retrieved 19 December 2014 from http://gamestudies.org/1401/about

Georgi, O. (2011, 17 February). Die Stunde der Plagiatssucher. *Frankfurter Allgemeine Zeitung Online*. Retrieved 5 February 2015 from www.faz.net/aktuell/politik/inland/vorwuerfe-gegen-guttenberg-die-stunde-der-plagiatssucher-1595524.html

Gerbner, G., Gross, L., Morgan, M., & Signorielli, N. (1986). Living with television: The dynamics of the cultivation process. In J. Bryant & D. Zillman (Eds.), *Perspectives on media effects* (pp. 17–40). Hilldale, NJ: Lawrence Erlbaum Associates.

Giddens, A. (1984). *The constitution of society*. Cambridge, UK: Polity.

———. (1990). *The consequences of modernity*. Cambridge, UK: Polity/Blackwell.

———. (1991). *Modernity and self-identity*. Cambridge, UK: Polity.

———. (1994). *Beyond left and right: The future of radical politics*. Cambridge, UK: Polity Press.

Goffman, E. (1959). *The presentation of self in everyday life*. Garden City, NY: Doubleday.

———. (1974). *Frame analysis*. Lebanon, NH: Northeastern University Press.

Graeber, D. (2011). *Debt: The first 5,000 years*. New York, NY: Melville House.

———. (2012). *Kampf dem Kamikaze-Kapitalismus: Es gibt Alternativen zum herrschenden System*. London, UK: Random House.

———. (2013). *The democracy project: A history, a crisis, a movement*. London, UK: Penguin.

Gregory, A. (2012). Reviewing public relations research and scholarship in the 21st century. *Public Relations Review*, 38(1), 1–4.

Gulati, G. J. & Williams, C. B. (2013). Social media and campaign 2012: Developments and trends for Facebook adoption. *Social Science Computer Review*, 31(5), 577–588.

Gustafsson N. & Höglund, L. (2011). Sociala medier och politiskt engagemang [Social media and political engagement]. In H. Oscarsson, S. Holmberg, & L. Weibull (Eds.), *Lycksalighetens ö* (pp. 511–524). Gothenburg, Sweden: University of Gothenburg.

Gustafsson, A., Kristensson, P. & Witell, L. (2012). Customer co-creation in service innovation: A matter of communication? *Journal of Service Management*, 23, 311–327.

Gustafsson, N. (2010). This time it's personal: Social networks, viral politics and identity management. In D. Riha & A. Maj (eds.), *Emerging practices in social networking and cybercultures*. Amsterdam: Rodopi, 1–22.

Gustafsson, N. (2013). *Leetocracy: Political participation, social network sites and inequality* (Doctoral Thesis). Lund, Sweden: Department of Political Science, Lund University.

Guttenberg findet tausende Unterstützer bei Facebook. (2011, 21 February). *Focus Online*. Retrieved 5 May 2015 from www.focus.de/politik/weitere-meldungen/plagiatsaffaere-guttenberg-findet-tausende-unterstuetzer-bei-facebook_aid_602106.html

Guttenberg spaltet das Netz. (2011, 21 February). *RP Online*. Retrieved 4 February 2015 from www.rp-online.de/digitales/internet/guttenberg-spaltet-das-netz-aid-1.2182799

Guttenberg weist Plagiatsvorwurf zurück. (2011, 16 February). *Bild.de*. Retrieved 5 May 2015 from www.bild.de/politik/2011/karl-theodor-zu-guttenberg/professor-erhebt-plagiats-vorwurf-16005102.bild.html

GuttenPlag. (2011a). GuttenPlag – kollaborative Plagiatsdokumentation. Retrieved 5 February 2015 from http://de.guttenplag.wikia.com/wiki/GuttenPlag_Wiki

———. (2011b). 1. Zwischenbericht. Retrieved 5 February 2015 from http://de.guttenplag.wikia.com/wiki/1._Zwischenbericht

———. (2011c). 2. Zwischenbericht. Retrieved 5 February 2015 from http://de.guttenplag.wikia.com/wiki/2._Zwischenbericht

Habermas, J. (1981/1984). *A theory of communicative action*. London, UK: Heinemann.

———. (1996). *Between facts and norms: Contributions to a discourse theory of law and democracy* (William Rehg, Trans.). Cambridge, UK: Polity.

Hadenius, S.,Weibull, L. & Wadbring, I. (2008). *Massmedier – Press, radio och tv i den digitala tidsåldern*. Falun: Bonniers Förlag.

Halliday, J (2013) Facebook: four out of five daily users log on via smartphone or tablet. *The Guardian*. www.theguardian.com/technology/2013/aug/14/facebook-users-smartphone-tablet

Hampton, K. N., Rainie, L., Lu, W., Dwyer, M., Shin, I. & Purcell, K. (2014). *Social media and the "spiral of silence"*. Washington, DC: Pew Research Center.

Hansen, M. T., Nohria, N. & Tierney, T. (1999, March–April). What's your strategy for managing knowledge? *Harvard Business Review*, pp. 106–116.

Haraway, D. (1991). A cyborg manifesto: Science, technology, and socialist feminism in the late twentieth century. In D. J. Haraway (ed.), *Simians, cyborgs and women: The reinvention of nature* (pp. 149–181). New York, NY: Routledge.

Hardt, M., & Negri, A. (2000). *Empire*. Cambridge, MA: Harvard University Press.

———. (2005). *Multitude: War and democracy in the age of empire*. London, UK: Hamish Hamilton.

———. (2009). *Commonwealth*. Cambridge, MA: Belknap.

Harige, O. & Tourish, D. (2004). How are we doing? Measuring and monitoring organizational communication. In D. Tourish & O. Harige (eds.), *Key issues in organizational communication* (pp. 234–251). London, UK: Routledge.

Harkaway, N. (2013). *The blind giant: How to survive in the digital age*. London, UK: John Murray.

Harper, D. (1998). On the authority of the image: Visual methods at the crossroads. In N. K. Denzin & Y. S. Lincoln (eds.), *Collecting and interpreting qualitative materials* (pp. 130–149). London, UK: Sage.

———. (2002). Talking about pictures: A case for photo elicitation. *Visual Studies, 17*(1), 13–26.

Hartmann, T., Stuke, D. & Daschmann, G. (2008). Positive parasocial relationships with drivers affect suspense in racing sport spectators. *Journal of Media Psychology: Theories, Methods, and Applications, 20*(1), 24–34.

Haupt, F. (2011, 16 May). "Die Scanner." *Frankfurter Allgemeine Zeitung Online*. Retrieved 5 February 2015 from www.faz.net/aktuell/feuilleton/2.1781/jagd-auf-plagiatoren-die-scanner-1635922.html

Hazleton, V. (2006). Toward a theory of public relations competence. In C. H. Botan & V. Hazleton (eds.), *Public relations theory II* (pp. 341–357). Mahwah, NJ: Erlbaum.

Hearit, K. M. (1995). "Mistakes were made": Organizations, apologia, and crises of social legitimacy. *Communication Studies, 46*(1–2), 1–17.

————. (2006). *Crisis management by apology: Corporate response to allegations of wrongdoing*. Mahwah, NJ: Erlbaum.

Heath, R. L. (2006). Onward into more fog: Thoughts on public relations' research directions. *Journal of Public Relations Research, 18*(2), 93–114.

Heide, M. (1997). Intranät – produkt eller processkapare [Intranet – product or process creator]. In M. Bark (ed.), *Intranät i organisationens kommunikation* (pp. 109–122). Uppsala: Konsultförlaget.

————. (2002a). *Intranät: En ny arena för kommunikation och lärande* [Intranet: A new arena for communication and learning]. Lund: Sociologiska institutionen, Lunds universitet.

————. (2002b). Intranät och knowledge management [Intranet and knowledge management]. In M. Bark & M. Heide (eds.), *Intranätboken* (pp. 43–59). Malmö: Liber.

Heide, M. & Simonsson, C. (2011). Putting co-workers in the limelight: New challenges for communication professionals. *International Journal of Strategic Communication, 5*, 201–220.

————. (in press). Struggling with internal crisis communication: A balancing act between paradoxical tensions. *Public Relations Inquiry*.

Held, D. (1987). *Models of democracy*. Cambridge, UK: Polity.

————. (2006). *Models of democracy* (3rd ed.). Cambridge, UK: Polity.

Hermes, J. (2000). Cultural citizenship and crime fiction: Politics and the interpretive community. *European Journal of Cultural Studies, 3*(2), 215–232.

Hoerner, J. (1999). Scaling the web: A parasocial interaction scale for world wide web sites. *Advertising and the World Wide Web, 99*, 135–147.

Holbrook, D. (2014). Approaching terrorist public relations initiatives. *Public Relations Inquiry, 3*(2), 141–162.

Holladay, S. J. (2009). Crisis communication strategies in the media coverage of chemical accidents. *Journal of Public Relations Research, 21*, 208–215.

Horton, D. & Wohl, R. R. (1956). Mass communication and parasocial interaction: Observations on intimacy at a distance. *Psychiatry, 19*(3), 215–229.

Hsu, S. H., Wen, M. H., & Wu, M. C. (2009). Exploring user experiences as predictors of MMORPG addiction. *Computers and Education, 53*, 990–999.

Huntington, S. (1968). *Political order in changing societies*. New Haven, CT: Yale University Press.

Hutton, J. G. (1999). The definition, dimensions, and domain of public relations. *Public Relations Review, 25*(2), 199–214.

Iacono, S. & Kling, R. (2001). Computerization movements: The rise of the internet and distant forms of work. In J. Yates & J. Van Maanen (eds.), *Information technology and organizational transformation: History, rhetoric, and practice* (pp. 93–135). Thousand Oaks, CA: Sage.

"Ich habe die Grenzen meiner Kräfte erreicht". (2011, 1 March). *Süddeutsche Zeitung Online*. Retrieved 5 May 2015 from www.sueddeutsche.de/politik/guettenbergs-erklaerung-im-wortlaut-ich-habe-die-grenzen-meiner-kraefte-erreicht-1.1066386

Ihlen, Ø., Van Ruler, B. & Fredriksson, M. (Eds.). (2009). *Public relations and social theory: Key figures and concepts*. New York, NY: Routledge.

Ihlen, Ø. & Verhoeven, P. (2012). A public relations identity for the 2010s. *Public Relations Inquiry, 1*(2), 159–176.

Inglehart, R. (1977). *The silent revolution: Changing values and political styles among western publics*. Princeton, NJ: Princeton University Press.

Iosifidis, P. (2011). The public sphere, social networks and public service media. *Information, Communication & Society, 14*(5), 619–637.

IS. (2014). *Flames of war* (film). Retrieved 7 November 2014 from http://vimeo.com/106389534.

Jablin, F. M. & Putnam, L. L. (2001). *The new handbook of organizational communication: Advances in theory, research, and methods.* Thousand Oaks, CA: Sage.

Jablin, F. M., Putnam, L. L., Roberts, K. H. & Porter, L. (1987). *Handbook of organizational communication: An interdisciplinary perspective.* Newbury Park, CA: Sage.

Jackson, N. A. & Lilleker, D. G. (2009). Building an architecture of participation? Political parties and web 2.0 in Britain. *Journal of Information Technology & Politics, 6,* 232–250.

Jansen, B. J., Zhang, M., Sobel, K. & Chowdury, A. (2009). Twitter power: Tweets as electronic word of mouth. *Journal of the American Society for Information Science and Technology, 60*(11), 2169–2188.

Jenkins, B. M. (1974). *International terrorism: A new kind of warfare.* Rand Paper Series (Vol. P-5261). Santa Monica, CA: Rand.

Jenkins, H. (2007). Reconsidering digital immigrants. Retrieved 5 May 2015 from http://henryjenkins.org/2007/12/reconsidering_digital_immigran.html

Jennett, C. I. (2010). *Is game immersion just another form of selective attention? An empirical investigation of real world-dissociation in computer game immersion.* London, UK: University College London. Retrieved 5 May 2015 from http://discovery.ucl.ac.uk/20225

Jennett, C. I., Cox, A. L., Cairns, P., Dhoparee, S., Epps, A., Tijs, T. & Walton, A. (2008). Measuring and defining the experience of immersion in games. *International Journal of Human-Computer-Studies, 66*(9), 641–661.

Johnson, T. J. (ed.). (2014). *Agenda setting in a 2.0 world. New agendas in communication.* New York, NY: Routledge.

Jowett, G. & O'Donnell, V. (2015). *Propaganda and persuasion* (6th ed.). Thousand Oaks, CA: Sage.

Jurgenson, N. (2011). Digital dualism vs augmented reality. Retrieved 22 June 2014 from http://thesocietypages.org/cyborgology/2011/02/24/digital-dualism-versus-augmented-reality

Kaplan, A. M. & Haenlein, M. (2010). Users of the world, unite! The challenges and opportunities of social media. *Business Horizons, 53,* 59–68.

Kapp, K. M. (2012). *The gamification of learning and instruction. Game-based methods and strategies for training and education.* San Francisco, CA: Pfeiffer.

Karvonen, L. (2010). *The personalization of politics: A study of parliamentary democracies.* Wivenhoe Park, UK: ECPR Press.

Katz, R. S. & Mair, P. (1995). Changing models of party organization and party democracy: The emergence of the cartel party. *Party Politics, 1*(1), 5–28.

———. (2009). The cartel party thesis: A restatement. *Perspectives on Politics, 7*(4), 753–766.

Kaya, K. (2014). ISIS's information operations: Analyzing their themes and messages. In *OE Watch, Foreign News & Perspectives of the Operational Environment.* US: Foreign Military Office. Retrieved 4 May 2015 from http://fmso.leavenworth.army.mil/OEWatch/201410/Special_Essay_01.html.

Kelleher, T. (2006). *Public relations online: Lasting concepts for changing media.* Thousand Oaks, CA: Sage.

Kent, M. L. (2010). What is a public relations "crisis"? Refocusing crisis research. In W. T. Coombs & S. J. Holladay (eds.), *Handbook of crisis communication* (pp. 705–712). Malden, MA: Blackwell.

Khang, H., Ki, E. J. & Ye, L. (2012). Social media research in advertising, communication, marketing, and public relations, 1997–2010. *Journalism and Mass Communication Quarterly, 89,* 279–298.

Kietzmann, J. H., Hermkens, K., McCarthy, I. P. & Silvestre, B. (2011). Social media? Get serious! Understanding the functional building blocks of social media. *Business Horizons, 54,* 241–251.

King, B. G. (2011). The tactical disruptiveness of social movements: Sources of market and mediated disruption in corporate boycotts. *Social Problems, 58*(4), 491–517.

King of Tritation. (2014). In steam community [Reviews of *Democracy 3*]. Retrieved 2 December 2014 from http://steamcommunity.com/app/245470/reviews

Klein, N. (2007). *The shock doctrine.* New York, NY: Picador.

Klinger, U. & Svensson, J (2014). The emergence of network media logic in political communication:A theoretical approach. *New Media & Society,* doi: 10.1177/1461444814522952.

Kuhn, J. & Lingenfelser, M. (2011, 21 February). Zu Guttenberg unter Druck: Von den Massen geliebt – von Medien angegriffen. *Report München.* Retrieved 5 May 2015 from http://mediathek.daserste.de/sendungen_a-z/431936_report-muenchen/6537978_zu-guttenberg-unter-druck-von-den-massen-geliebt-

Laqueur, W. (1987). *The age of terrorism.* Boston, MA: Little, Brown.

Larsen, J. (2005). Families seen sightseeing: Performativity of tourist photography. *Space and Culture, 8,* 416–434.

Latour, B. (1993). *We have never been modern* (C. Porter, Trans.). Cambridge, MA: Harvester Wheatsheaf/Harvard University Press.

———. (2004). *Politics of nature: How to bring the sciences into democracy.* Cambridge, MA: Harvard University Press.

———. (2005). From Realpolitik to Dingpolitik or how to make things public. In B. Latour & P. Weibel (eds.), *Making things public: Atmospheres of democracy* (pp. 4–31). Cambridge, MA: MIT Press,

Lave, J. & Wenger, E. (1991). *Situated learning: Legitimate peripheral participation.* Cambridge, MA: Cambridge University Press.

Legge, K. (2002). On knowledge, business consultants and the selling of total quality management. In T. Clark & R. Fincham (eds.), *Critical consulting: New perspectives on the management advice industry* (pp. 74–90). Chichester, UK: Wiley Blackwell.

Leistner, F. (2012). *Connecting organizational silos: Taking knowledge flow management to the next level with social media.* Hoboken, NJ: Wiley.

Lerbinger, O. (1997). *The crisis manager: Facing risk and responsibility.* Mahwah, NJ: Erlbaum.

Lessig, L. (1999). *Code and other laws of cyberspace.* New York, NY: Basic Books.

L'Etang, J. (2006). Public relations and propaganda: Conceptual issues, methodological problems, and public relations discourse. In J. L'Etang & M. Pieczka (eds.), *Public relations: Critical debates and contemporary practices* (pp. 23–40). Mahwah, NJ: Erlbaum.

Levine, R. (2012). Snålskjuts – *Myten om affärsmodellen.* In P. Snickars & P. Strömbäck (eds.), *Myten om Internet* (pp. 15–38). Stockholm: Volante Förlag.

Levine, R., Locke, R., Searle, D. & Wenberger, D. (1999). *The cluetrain manifesto.* Retrieved 5 May 2015 from http://cluetrain.com/book

Li, C. & Bernoff, J. (2008). *Groundswell: Winning in a world transformed by social technologies.* Boston, MA: Harvard Business Press.

Lindberg, A: (2012, September 6). *Det är ju det här du vill Billström.* Retrieved 4 May 2015 from www.aftonbladet.se/ledare/ledarkronika/anderslindberg/article15395145.ab

Loader, B. D. & Mercea, D. (2011). Networking democracy? Social media innovations and participatory politics. *Information, Communication & Society, 14*(6), 757–769.

————. (Eds.). (2012). *Social media and democracy: Innovations in participatory politics.* London, UK: Routledge.

Loew, E. P. (2003). The war against terrorism: A public relations challenge for the Pentagon. *International Journal for Communication Studies, 65*(3), 211–230.

Lüders, M. (2013). Networking and notworking in social intranets: User archetypes and participatory divides. *First Monday, 18*, 4–10.

Luhmann, N. (1988). Tautology and paradox in the self-descriptions of modern society. *Sociological Theory, 6*(1), 21–37.

————. (1994). "What is the case?" and "what lies behind it?" The two sociologies and the theory of society. *Sociological Theory, 12*(2), 126–139.

————. (1995a). The paradoxy of observing systems. *Cultural Critique, 31*, 37–55.

————. (1995b). *Social systems.* Stanford, CA: Stanford University Press.

————. (2009). *Die Realität der Massenmedien.* Wiesbaden: VS Verlag.

Lundgren, L., Strandh, K. & Johansson, C. (2012). *De sociala intranätens praxis: Användning, nytta och framgångsfaktorer.* Rapportserie 5. Sundsvall: Mid-Sweden University, Demicom.

Magnuson, J. (2010). Civilization: The good kind of addicted: Necessary games. Retrieved 10 March 2014 from www.necessarygames.com/reviews/sid-meiers-civilization-iv-game-commercial-mac-os-x-windows-turn-based-strategy-historical

Malthouse, E. C., Haenlein, M., Skiera, B., Wege, E. & Zhang, M. (2013). Managing customer relationships in the social media era: Introducing the social CRM house. *Journal of Interactive Marketing, 27*, 270–280.

Mangold, W. G. & Faulds, D. J. (2009). Social media: The new hybrid element of the promotion mix. *Business Horizons, 52*, 357–365.

Manjoo, F. (2008). *True enough – Learning to live in a post fact society.* Hoboken, NJ: Wiley.

Manovich, L. (2001). *The language of new media.* Cambridge, MA: MIT Press.

Marres, N. (2012). *Material participation: Technology, the environment and everyday publics.* New York, NY: Palgrave Macmillan.

Marvin, C. (1988). *When old technologies were new: Thinking about electric communication in the late nineteenth century.* New York, NY: Oxford University Press.

Matusitz, J. (2013). *Terrorism and communication: A critical introduction.* Thousand Oaks, CA: Sage.

Mayfield, A. (2006). *What is social media?* London, UK: Spannerworks. Retrieved 5 May 2015 from http://openhouse.typepad.com/digital/files/What_is_Social_Media.pdf

Mazzei, A. & Ravazzani, S. (2011). Manager-employee communication during a crisis: The missing link. *Corporate Communications: An International Journal, 16*(3), 243–254.

McKinsey. (2013). Evolution of the networked enterprise: McKinsey global survey results. Retrieved 4 February 2015 from www.mckinsey.com/insights/business_technology/evolution_of_the_netnetwor_enterprise_mckinsey_global_survey_results

Merkelsen, H. (2011). The double-edged sword of legitimacy in public relations. *Journal of Communication Management, 15*(2), 125–143.

Merkel sichert Guttenberg "volles Vertrauen" zu. (2011, 18 February). *Die Welt Online.* Retrieved 5 February 2015 from www.welt.de/politik/deutschland/article12583321/Merkel-sichert-Guttenberg-volles-Vertrauen-zu.html

Merriam, S. B. (2006). *Fallstudien som forskningsmetod.* Lund, Sweden: Studentlitteratur.

Meyen, M. (2009). Medialisierung. *Medien & Kommunikationswissenschaft, 57*(1), 23–38.

Migration Board. (2013). *Aktuellt om ensamkommande barn.* Retrieved 5 May 2015 from www.migrationsverket.se/download/18.7c00d8e6143101d166d62/1388135859868/Aktuellt+om+dec+2013.pdf

Migration Board. (2013, April 12). *More asylums granted in Sweden.* Retrieved 5 May 2015 from www.migrationsverket.se/English/About-the-Migration-Board/News-archive/News-archive-2013/2013-04-12-More-asylums-granted-in-Sweden.html

Migration Board. (2014, June 30): *Ny lag om-särskilt ömmande omständigheter* [New law making it easier for children to grant protection in Sweden]. Retrieved 5 May 2015 from www.migrationsverket.se/Om-Migrationsverket/Nyhetsarkiv/Nyhetsarkiv-2014/2014-06-30-Ny-lag-om-sarskilt-ommande-omstandigheter.html.printable

Miller, G. R. & Steinberg, M. (1975). *Between people: A new analysis of interpersonal communication.* Chicago, IL: Science Research Associates.

Mirzoeff, N. (Ed.). (1998). *Visual culture reader.* London, UK: Routledge.

Moloney, K. (2000). *Rethinking public relations: The spin and the substance.* London, UK: Routledge.

Monbiot, G. (2003). *The age of consent: Manifesto for a new world order.* London, UK: Flamingo.

Morozov, E. (2011). *The net delusion: How not to liberate the world.* London, UK: Penguin.

Mouffe, C. (2000a). *Deliberative democracy or agonistic pluralism.* Reihe Politikwissenschaft, Political Science Series 72. Vienna: Department of Political Science, Institute for Advanced Studies (IHS).

―――. (2000b). *The democratic paradox.* London, UK: Verso.

―――. (2005). *On the political.* London, UK: Routledge.

―――. (2008). *Om det politiska* [On political]. Hägersten: Tankekraft Förlag.

―――. (2009). *The democratic paradox.* Manchester, UK: Verso.

Murray, S. (2008). Digital images, photo-sharing, and our shifting notions of everyday aesthetics. *Journal of Visual Culture, 7*(2), 147–163.

Neuman, P. R. (2009). *Old and new terrorism.* Cambridge, UK: Polity.

Nielsen, J. (2013). Intranet social features. Retrieved 4 February 2015 from www.nngroup.com/articles/intranet-social-features

Nielsen, R. K. (2011). Mundane internet tools, mobilizing practices, and the coproduction of citizenship in political campaigns. *New Media & Society, 13*(5), 775–771.

Nilsson, B. & Carlsson, E. (2014). Swedish politicians and new media: Democracy, identity and populism in a digital discourse. *New Media & Society, 16*(4), 655–671.

Niman, N. B. (2014). *The gamification of higher education: Developing a game-based business strategy in a disrupted marketplace.* New York, NY: Palgrave MacMillan.

Noelle-Neumann, E. (1973). Return to the concept of powerful mass media. *Studies of Broadcasting, 9,* 67–112.

―――. (1974). Spiral of silence: A theory of public opinion. *Journal of Communication, 24,* 43–51.

Nord, L. (2008). *Medier utan politik – en studie av de svenska riksdagspartiernas syn på press, radio och TV.* Stockholm: Lars Nord och Santérus Förlag.

Nordfront – Swedish Resistance Movement. (2014, November 28). *Der ewige Jude.* Retrieved 5 May 2015 from www.nordfront.se.

―――. (2014, December 1). *Of course it should be legal to label Hitler as a hero of the people.* Retrieved 5 May 2015 from www.nordfront.se.

Norén, M. (2008). *Designing for democracy.* Örebro: Örebro University Press.

Nørgaard-Kristensen, N. (2003). The professional cocktail: On the confusion of the role of the journalist and the role of public relations adviser. *Revista de Comunicación, 1,* 41–67.

Norris, P., Kern, M. & Just, M. (2003). *Framing terrorism: The news media, the government, and the public.* New York, NY: Routledge.

170 *Bibliography*

Bibliography

O'Leary

170 *Bibliography*

170 *Bibliography*

170 *Bibliography*

O'Leary, D. (2012, 22 July). Developing trust and relationships in the supply chain using social media. *European Business Review*.

Omilion-Hodges, L. M. & Baker, C. R. (2014). Everyday talk and convincing conversations: Utilizing strategic internal communication. *Business Horizons*, *57*, 435–445.

O'Reilly, T. (2005). What is Web 2.0: Design patterns and business models for the next generation of software. Retrieved 5 May 2015 from http://oreilly.com/web2/archive/what-is-web-20.html

Orlikowski, W. (2007). Sociomaterial practices: Exploring technology at work. *Organization Studies 28*(9), 1435–1448.

Orlikowski, W. J., Yates, J., Okamura, K. & Fujimoto, M. (1999). Shaping electronic communication: The metastructuring of technology in the context of use. In G. Desanctis & J. Fulk (eds.), *Shaping organization form: Communication, connection, and community* (pp. 133–171). Thousand Oaks, CA: Sage.

O'Shaughnessy, N. (1996). Social propaganda and social marketing. *European Journal of Marketing*, *30*(10–11), 62–75.

———. (2012). The death and life of propaganda. *Journal of Public Affairs*, *12*(1), 29–38.

Paine, K. D. (2011). *Measure what matters: Online tools for understanding customers, social media, engagement, and key relationships*. Hoboken, NJ: Wiley.

Palfrey, J. & Grasser, U. (2008). *Born digital: Understanding the first generation of digital natives*. New York, NY: Basic Books.

Panebianco, A. (1988). *Political parties: Organization and power*. Cambridge, UK: Cambridge University Press.

Papacharissi, Z. & de Fatima Oliveira, M. (2008). News frames terrorism: A comparative analysis of frames employed in terrorism coverage in U.S. and U.K. newspapers. *International Journal of Press/Politics*, *13*(1), 52–74.

Pariser, E. (2011). *The filter bubble: What the internet is hiding from you*. London, UK: Viking.

Patton, M. Q. (1990). *Qualitative evaluation and research methods*. Newbury Park, CA: Sage.

Petersson, O. (1991). *Makt – En sammanfattning av Maktutredningen*. Stockholm: Allmänna Förlaget.

Petersson, O., Djerf-Pierre, M., Strömbäck, J. & Weibull, L. (2005). *Demokratirådets rapport 2005 – Mediernas integritet*. Stockholm: SNS Förlag.

Petersson, O., et al. (1998). *SNS Demokratirådets rapport 1998 – Demokrati och medborgarskap*. Stockholm: SNS Förlag.

Phillips, D. (2001). *Online public relations*. London, UK: Kogan Page.

Phillips, D. & Young, P. (2009). *Online public relations* (2nd ed.). London, UK: Kogan Page.

Picard, R. G. (1989). Press relations of terrorist organizations. *Public Relations Review*, *15*(4), 12–23.

Pink, S. (2011). Amateur photographic practice, collective representation and the constitution of place. *Visual Studies*, *26*(2), 92–101.

PlagDoc & Kotynek, M. (2012, 8 June). Reflections on a swarm. *GuttenPlag Wiki*. Retrieved 5 May 2015 from http://de.guttenplag.wikia.com/wiki/Reflections_on_a_Swarm

Politbarometer: Februar II 2011. (2011, 25 February). *Forschungsgruppe Wahlen Online*. Retrieved 4 February 2015 from www.forschungsgruppe.de/Umfragen/Politbarometer/Archiv/Politbarometer_2011/Februar_II

Poole, M. S. & Van de Ven, A. H. (1989). Using paradox to build management and organization theories. *Academy of Management Review*, *14*(4), 562–578.

Powell, R. (2014, 25 June). Cats and Kalashnikovs: The ISIL social media strategy. *Sydney Morning Herald*. www.smh.com.au/world/cats-and-kalashnikovs-behind-the-isil-social-media-strategy-20140624-zsk50.htmlPrahalad, C. K. & Ramaswamy, V. (2004). Co-creation experiences: The next practice in value creation. *Journal of Interactive Marketing*, *18*(3), 5–14.

Prensky, M. (2001). Digital natives, digital immigrants. *On the Horizon*, *9*(5), 1–6.

Preuß, R. & Schultz, T. (2011, 16 February). Guttenberg soll bei Doktorarbeit abgeschrieben haben. *Süddeutsche Zeitung*. Retrieved 4 February 2015 from www.sueddeutsche.de/politik/plagiatsvorwurf-gegen-verteidigungsminister-guttenberg-soll-bei-doktorarbeit-abgeschrieben-haben-1.1060774

Prusher, I. (2014, 14 September). What the ISIS flag says about the militant group. *Time Magazine*. Retrieved 5 May 2015 from time.com/3311665/isis-flag-iraq-syria

Putnam, L. L. & Mumby, D. K. (2014). *The Sage handbook of organizational communication: Advances in theory, research, and methods*. Thousand Oaks, CA: Sage.

Quandt, T., Breuer, J., Festl, R. & Scharkow, M. (2013). Digitale Spiele: Stabile Nutzung in einem dynamischen Markt. Langzeitstudie GameStat: Repräsentativbefragungen zu digitalen Spielen in Deutschland 2010 bis 2013. *Media Perspektiven*, *10*, 483–492.

Radick, S. (2011). The power of social networks: Reviving the intranet. *Public Relations Tactics*, *18*, 18–18.

Rawls, J. (1971). *A theory of justice*. Oxford, UK: Oxford University Press.

Reckwitz, A. (2002). Toward a theory of social practices: A development in culturalist theorizing. *European Journal of Social Theory*, *5*(2), 243–263.

Reimer, J. & Ruppert, M. (2011). Das GuttenPlag-Wiki. *Medien Journal*, *4*, 4–17.

———. (2013). GuttenPlag-Wiki und Journalismus. In U. Dolata & J.-F. Schrape (eds.), *Internet, Mobile Devices und die Transformation der Medien* (pp. 303–330). Berlin: Edition Sigma.

Reputation Institute. (2012). CSR is not dead, it is just mismanaged. Retrieved 8 November 2014 from www.reputationinstitute.com/thought-leadership/csr-reptrak-100

Rest, J. (2011, 19 February). Abgekupfert beim Erstsemester. *Berliner Zeitung Online*. Retrieved 4 February 2015 from www.berliner-zeitung.de/archiv/guttenberg-affaere – der-unter-schummelverdacht-stehende-minister-erklaert-sich-nur-vor-ausgewaehlten-journalisten-und-brueskiert-damit-die-hauptstadtpresse—zugleich-steigt-und-steigt-die-zahl-der-zweifelhaften-passagen-in-seiner-doktorarbeit—abgekupfert-beim-erstsemester, 10810590,10772434.html

Rice, R. E. & Leonardi, P. M. (2014). Information and communication technologies in organizations. In L. L. Putnam & D. K. Mumby (eds.), *The Sage handbook of organizational communication: Advances in theory, research, and methods* (pp. 425–448). Thousand Oaks, CA: Sage.

Richards, B. (2004). Terrorism and public relations. *Public Relations Review*, *30*(2), 169–176.

Rothenberger, L. (2015). Terrorism as strategic communication. In D. Holtzhausen & A. Zerfass (eds.), *The Routledge handbook of strategic communication* (pp. 481–496). London, UK: Routledge.

Rothstein, B., Esaiasson, P., Hermansson, J., Micheletti, M. & Petersson, O. (1995). *SNS – Demokratirådets rapport 1995 – Demokrati som dialog*. Stockholm: SNS Förlag.

Ruck, K. & Welch, M. (2012). Valuing internal communication: Management and employee perspectives. *Public Relations Review*, *38*, 294–302.

Rücktritt wäre für Guttenberg "Unsinn". (2011, 19 February). *Focus Online.* Retrieved 5 May 2015 from www.focus.de/politik/deutschland/doktor-affaere-ruecktritt-waere-fuer-guttenberg-unsinn_aid_601467.html

Ruggiero, A. & Vos, M. (2013). Terrorism communication: Characteristics and emerging perspectives in the scientific literature 2002–2011. *Journal of Contingency and Crisis Management, 21*(3), 153–166.

Ruppert, M. & Reimer, J. (2011). Der Ex-Minister und sein Schwarm. *Journalist, 4.* Retrieved 4 February 2015 from www.journalist.de/aktuelles/meldungen/guttenplag-wiki-der-ex-minister-und-sein-schwarm.html

Rybalko, S. & Seltzer, T. (2010). Dialogic communication in 140 characters or less: How Fortune 500 companies engage stakeholders using Twitter. *Public Relations Review, 36*(4), 336–341.

Rydell, A. (2012). Gud är en hacker – Myten om den neutrala koden. In P. Snickars & P. Strömbäck (eds.), *Myten om Internet.* Stockholm: Volante Förlag, p. 57–81.

Sarvas, R. & Frohlich, D. M. (2011). *From snapshots to social media: The changing picture of domestic photography.* London, UK: Springer.

Schatzki, T. (1996). *Social practices: A Wittgensteinian approach to human activity and the social.* Cambridge, UK: Cambridge University Press.

———. (2001). Introduction: Practice theory. In T. Schatzki, K. Knorr-Cetina & E. Von Savigny (eds.), *The practice turn in contemporary theory* (pp. 1–15). London, UK: Routledge.

Schiappa, E., Allen, M. & Gregg, P. B. (2007). Parasocial relationships and television: A meta-analysis of the effects. In R. Preiss, B. Gayle, N. Burrell, M. Allen & J. Bryant (eds.), *Mass media effects research: Advances through meta-analysis* (pp. 301–314). New York, NY: Routledge

Schiappa, E., Allen, M. & Paine, K. D. (2011). *Measure what matters: Online tools for understanding customers, social media, engagement, and key relationships.* Hoboken, NJ: Wiley.

Schilling, A. & Strannegård, L. (2010). Osynliga händer och synligt resultat: Om kommunikationskonsulters arbete. In J. Pallas & L. Strannegård (eds.), *Företag och medier* (pp. 192–208). Malmö: Liber.

Schmid, A. P. (2011). 50 un- and under-researched topics in the field of (counter-) terrorism studies. *Perspectives on Terrorism, 5*(1), 76–78.

Schölzel, H. (2013). *Guerillakommunikation: Genealogie einer politischen Konfliktform.* Bielefeld: Transcript.

Schultz, F., Utz, S. & Göritz, A. (2011). Is the medium the message? Perceptions of and reactions to crisis communication via twitter, blogs and traditional media. *Public Relations Review, 37*(1), 20–27.

Scoble, R. & Israel, S. (2006). *Naked conversations: How blogs are changing the way businesses talk with customers.* Hoboken, NJ: John Wiley & Sons.

Seiffert, J. & Nothhaft, H. (2014). *Computer games: The missing media. The procedural rhetoric of computer games: A blind spot of public relations and strategic communication-research.* Paper presented at the 21st annual Bledcom Symposium, Bled Slovenia, 5 July.

Selbst Doktorvater distanziert sich von Guttenberg. (2011, 28 February). *Die Welt Online.* Retrieved 5 February 2015 from www.welt.de/politik/deutschland/article12663644/Selbst-Doktorvater-distanziert-sich-von-Guttenberg.html

Severin, W. J. & Tankard, J. W., Jr. (1997). *Communication theories: Origins, methods and uses in the mass media* (4th ed.). New York, NY: Longman.

Shea, T. (2014). *Gamification: Using gaming technology for achieving goals.* New York, NY: Rosen.

Sheppard, B., Rubin, G. J., Wardman, J. K. & Wessely, S. (2006). Viewpoint: Terrorism and dispelling the myth of a panic probe public. *Journal of Public Health Policy, 27*(3), 219–245.

Shils, E. (1960). *Political development in the new states.* The Hague: Mouton.

Shirky, C. (2009). *Here comes everybody: The power of organizing without organizations.* New York, NY: Penguin.

Shove, E. & Pantzar, M. (2007). Recruitment and reproduction: The careers and carriers of digital photography and floorball. *Human Affairs, 17*(2), 154–167.

Sieberer, U. (2006). Party unity in parliamentary democracies: A comparative analysis. *Journal of Legislative Studies, 12*(2), 150–178.

Simpson, B. & Carroll, B. (2008). Re-viewing role in processes of identity construction. *Organization, 15*(1), 29–50.

Smith, J. (2012). The companies with the best CSR reputation. Retrieved 4 May 2015 from www.forbes.com/sites/jacquelynsmith/2012/12/10/the-companies-with-the-best-csr-reputations/.

Smith, W. K. & Lewis, M. W. (2011). Toward a theory of paradox: A dynamic equilibrium model of organizing. *Academy of Management Review, 36*(2), 381–403.

Snickars, P. & Strömbäck, P. (2012). *Myten om Internet.* Stockholm: Volante Förlag.

Sohn, Y. J. & Lariscy, R. W. (2014). Understanding reputational crisis: Definition, properties, and consequences. *Journal of Public Relations Research, 26*(1), 23–43.

Solis, B. (2013). New digital influencers: The coming youthquake. Retrieved 5 February 2015 from www.briansolis.com/2013/05/new-digital-influencers-the-coming-youthquake

Somerville, I. & Purcell, A. (2011). A history of republican public relations in Northern Ireland from "Bloody Sunday" to the Good Friday agreement. *Journal of Communication Management, 15*(3), 192–209.

Spreng, M. (2011, 18 May). Schwarm-Intelligenz und Schwarm-Feigheit. *Sprengsatz.* Retrieved 5 February 2015 from www.sprengsatz.de/?p=3665

Staktson, B. (2011). *Gilla! Dela engagemang, passion och idéer via sociala medier.* Stockholm: Idealistas förlag.

Starck, K. & Kruckeberg, D. (2001). Public relations and community: A reconstructed theory revisited. In R. L. Heath (ed.), *Handbook of public relations* (pp. 51–60). Thousand Oaks, CA: Sage.

Strandberg, K. (2013). A social media revolution or just a case of history repeating itself? The use of social media in the 2011 Finnish parliamentary elections. *New Media & Society, 11*(5), 1329–1347.

Stiglitz, J., & Driffill, J. (2000). *Economics.* New York, NY: W.W. Norton.

Strömbäck, J. (2008). Four phases of mediatization: An analysis of the mediatization of politics. *International Journal of Press/Politics, 13*(3), 228–246.

———. (2010). *Makt, medier och samhälle.* Lund: Studentlitteratur.

Sturges, D. L. (1994). Communicating through crisis: A strategy for organizational survival. *Management Communication Quarterly, 7*, 297–316.

Sveriges Radio. (2012-09-05). *Gränspolis nekar Migrationsverket prövning.* www.sr.se.

Telleen, S. (1997a). Do you really want an intranet? Retrieved 4 February 2015 from www.iorg.com/papers/want.html

———. (1997b). The intranet paradigm. Retrieved 4 February 2015 from www.iorg.com/papers/paradigm.html

———. (1998). *Intranet organization: Strategies for managing change.* Retrieved 4 February 2015 from www.iorg.com/intranetorg

Theaker, A. & Yaxley, H. (2013). *The public relations strategic toolkit: An essential guide to successful public relations practice*. London, UK: Routledge

Thewalt, A. & Spieker, S. (2011, 21 February). Kampf um Guttenberg im Internet. *Bild.de*. Retrieved 4 February 2015 from www.bild.de/politik/2011/skandale/auf-facebook-bekriegen-sich-unterstuetzer-und-gegner-16287548.bild.html

Thomlison, T. D. (2000). An interpersonal primer with implications for public relations. In J. A. Ledingham & S. D. Bruning (eds.), *Public relations as relationship management: A relational approach to the study and practice of public relations* (pp. 177–203). Mahwah, NJ: Erlbaum.

Tourish, D. (2005). Critical upward communication: Ten commandments for improving strategy and decision making. *Long Range Planning, 38,* 485–503.

Tourish, D. & Robson, P. (2003). Critical upward feedback in organisations: Processes, problems and implications for communication management. *Journal of Communication Management, 8,* 150–168.

———. (2006). Sensemaking and the distortion of critical upward communication in organizations. *Journal of Management Studies, 43,* 711–730.

Tracey, K. (2002). *Everyday talk: Building and reflecting identities*. New York, NY: Guilford Press.

Tufekci, Z. (2008). Can you see me now? Audience and disclosure regulation in online social network sites. *Bulletin of Science, Technology and Society, 28*(1), 20–36.

Tuman, J. (2010). *Communicating terror: The rhetorical dimensions of terrorism* (2nd ed.). Thousand Oaks, CA: Sage.

Turban, D. B. & Cable, D. M. (2003). Firm reputation and applicant pool characteristics. *Journal of Organizational Behavior, 24*(6), 733–751.

Turner, J. R. (1993). Interpersonal and psychological predictors of parasocial interaction with different television performers. *Communication Quarterly, 41*(4), 443–453.

Twenge, J. (2009). Generational changes and their impact in the classroom: Teaching Generation Me. *Medical Education, 43,* 398–405.

Twenge, J. & Campbell, S. (2008). Generational differences in psychological traits and their impact on the workplace. *Journal of Managerial Psychology, 23*(8), 862–877.

Tyllström, A. (2013). *Legitimacy for sale: Constructing a market for PR consultancy.* (Unpublished doctoral thesis). Uppsala University.

Überraschungsbesuch am Hindukusch. (2011, 17 February). *Süddeutsche Zeitung Online*. Retrieved 5 May 2015 from www.sueddeutsche.de/politik/trotz-plagiatsvorwuerfen-guttenberg-reist-ueberraschend-nach-afghanistan-1.1061283

Ulmer, R. R., Seeger, M. W. & Sellnow, T. L. (2007). Post-crisis communication and renewal: Expanding the parameters of post-crisis discourse. *Public Relations Review, 33*(2), 130–134.

Uni Bayreuth erleichtert Guttenberg das politische Überleben. (2011, 24 February). *Zeit Online*. Retrieved 5 February 2015 from www.zeit.de/politik/deutschland/2011–02/guttenberg-plagiat-reaktionen

Uni Bayreuth prüft Vorwürfe gegen Guttenberg. (2011, 16 February). *Frankfurter Allgemeine Zeitung Online*. Retrieved 5 May 2015 from www.faz.net/aktuell/politik/inland/2.1673/dissertation-teilweise-abgeschrieben-uni-bayreuth-prueft-vorwuerfe-gegen-guttenberg-1588866.html

UNICEF. (2014). www.unicef.org.uk/UNICEFs-Work/UN-Convention/

Universität Bayreuth. (2011a). Stellungnahme zur heutigen Berichterstattung über Plagiatsvorwürfe im Zusammenhang mit der Dissertation von Dr. Karl-Theodor zu Guttenberg.

Retrieved 4 February 2015 from www.uni-bayreuth.de/presse/Aktuelle-Infos/2011/036–033-guttenberg.pdf

———. (2011b). Universität Bayreuth erkennt zu Guttenberg den Doktorgrad ab. Retrieved 5 May 2015 from www.uni-bayreuth.de/presse/Aktuelle-Infos/2011/040–037-gutten.pdf

Urry, J. (1990). *The tourist gaze*. London, UK: Sage.

———. (2002). *The tourist gaze* (2nd ed.). London, UK: Sage.

Utz, S., Schultz, F. & Glocka, S. (2013). Crisis communication online: How medium, crisis type and emotions affected public reactions in the Fukushima Daiichi nuclear disaster. *Public Relations Review*, *39*(1), 40–46.

Vaast, E. (2004). O brother, where are thou? From communities to networks of practice through intranet use. *Management Communication Quarterly*, *18*, 5–44.

Vaccari, C. & Nielsen, R. K. (2012). What drives politicians' online popularity? An analysis of the 2010 U.S. midterm elections. *Journal of Information Technology & Politics*, *10*(2), 208–222.

Valentini, C. & Romenti, S. (2011). Blogging about crises: The role of online conversations in framing Alitalia's performance during its crisis. *Journal of Communication Management*, *15*(4), 298–313.

van de Donk, W., Loader, B. D., Nixon, P. G. & Rucht, D. (2004). *Cyberprotest: New media, citizens and social movements*. London, UK: Routledge.

van Dijck, J. (2008). Digital photography: Communication, identity, memory. *Visual Communication*, *7*(1), 57–76.

van Dijk, J. (1999). *The network society: Social aspects of new media*. Thousand Oaks, CA: Sage.

Van House, N. A. (2011). Personal photography, digital technologies and the uses of the visual. *Visual Studies*, *26*(2), 125–134.

van Riel, C. (1995). *Principles of corporate communication*. Hemel Hempstead, UK: Prentice-Hall.

Verba, S. (1962). Political participation and strategies of influence: A comparative study. *Acta Sociologica*, *6*(1), 22–42.

Verčič, A. T. & Verčič, A. T. (2013). Digital natives and social media. *Public Relations Review*, *39*, 600–602.

von Bebenburg, P. (2011, 21 February). Den Überblick über die Quellen verloren. *Frankfurter Rundschau Online*. Retrieved 5 February 2015 from www.fr-online.de/politik/guttenberg-im-wortlaut—den-ueberblick-ueber-die-quellen-verloren-,1472596,7297946.html

Vygotsky, L. S. (1978). *Mind in society: The development of higher psychological processes*. Cambridge, MA: Harvard University Press.

Waddington, S. (ed.). (2012) *Share this: The social media handbook for PR professionals*. Chichester, UK: John Wiley & Sons.

Wagner, F. J. (2011, 17 February). Lieber Dr. zu Guttenberg. *Bild.de*. Retrieved 5 February 2015 from www.bild.de/news/standards/franz-josef-wagner/post-von-wagner-16015226.bild.html

Warde, A. (2005). Consumption and theories of practice. *Journal of Consumer Culture*, *5*(2), 131–153.

Watson, I. R. (2013). Digital natives or digital tribes. *Universal Journal of Educational Research*, *1*(2), 104–112.

Weber, M. (1978). *Economy and society: An outline of interpretative sociology*. Berkeley: University of California Press.

176 Bibliography

Bibliography

———. (1983). *Ekonomi och samhälle: Förståelsesociologins grunder. Band I: Sociologiska begrepp och definitioner.* Lund: Argos.

———. (1987). *Ekonomi och samhälle: Förståelsesociologins grunder. Band III: Politisk sociologi.* Lund: Argos.

Wedel, J. (2009). *Shadow elite: How the world's new powerbrokers undermine democracy, government and the free market.* New York, NY: Basic Books.

Weibull, L. & Wadbring, I. (2014). *Massmedier: nya villkor för press, radio och tv i det digitala medielandskapet.* Stockholm, Sweden: Ekerlids förlag.

Weick, K. E. (1969). *The social psychology of organizing.* Reading, MA: Addison-Wesley.

Weimann, G. (2008). The psychology of mass-mediated terrorism. *American Behavioral Scientist, 52*(1), 69–86.

Weinberg, B. D. & Pehlivan, E. (2011). Social spending: Managing the social media mix. *Business Horizons, 54,* 275–282.

Wenger, E. (1998). *Communities of practice: Learning, meaning, and identity.* Cambridge, MA: Cambridge University Press.

Wenger, E., McDermott, R. & Snyder, W. M. (2002). *Cultivating communities of practice: A guide to managing knowledge.* Boston, MA: Harvard Business School Press.

Wibeck, V. (2010). *Fokusgrupper: Om fokuserade gruppintervjuer som undersökningsmetod.* Lund: Studentlitteratur.

Wilkinson, P. (1997). The media and terrorism: A reassessment. *Terrorism and Political Violence, 9*(3), 51–64.

Williams, D. (2006). Virtual cultivation: Online worlds, offline perceptions. *Journal of Communication, 56,* 59–78.

Wood, R.T.A., Griffiths, M. D., & Parke, A. (2007). Experiences of time loss among videogame players: An empirical study. *Cyberpsychology and Behavior, 10,* 38–44.

Wright, D. K. & Hinson, M. D. (2008). How blogs and social media are changing public relations. *Public Relations Journal, 2*(2), 1–21.

Ybema, S., Keenoy, T., Oswick, C., Beverungen, A., Ellis, N. & Sabelis, I. (2009). Articulating identities. *Human Relations, 62*(3), 299–322.

Ye, L. & Ki, E-J. (2012). The status of online PR research: An analysis of published articles in 1992–2009. *Journal of Public Relations Research, 24*(5), 409–434.

Young, A. M. & Hinesly, M. D. (2014). Social media use to enhance internal communication: Course design for business students. *Business and Professional Communication Quarterly, 51*(5), 426–439.

Yuan, Y. C., Fulk, J., Monge, P. R. & Contractor, N. (2009). Expertise directory development, shared task interdependence, and strength of communication network ties as multilevel predictors of expertise exchange in transactive memory work groups. *Communication Research, 37,* 20–47.

Zichermann, G. & Cunningham, C. (2011). *Gamification by design: Implementing game mechanics in web and mobile apps.* Sebastopol, CA: O'Reilly Media.

Zichermann, G. & Linder, J. (2013). *The gamification revolution: How leaders leverage game mechanics to crush the competition.* New York, NY: McGraw-Hill.

Žižek, S. (2006, November). The political and its disavowal. *Palinurus: Engaging Political Philosophy, 9.*

Zuckerman, E. (2013). *Rewire: Digital cosmopolitans in the age of connection.* New York, NY: Norton.

Index

Bush, George W. 75, 147
business, separation from life 80–1
Butler, Judith 79
BuzzFeed 7

CA (corporate ability) crises 56
Campbell, Alastair 76
capitalism 78, 136; free-market 80; global 79; laissez-faire 73, 80; liberal 79–80; neo-liberal 79
Castells, Manuel 65, 81, 83
catalytic paradigm 82
Center for Strategic Counterterrorism Communication (CSCC) 149, 151
Chadwick, Andrew 95
channel effect 57
Chartered Institute of PR (CIPR) 26, 28
children: deportation of 124, 126; as unaccompanied minors 127
citizens: dialogue with authorities 83, 89; empowerment of 121; German 109–11; political engagement of 130, 144; right of to engage in politics 87
citizenship studies 34
city branding 35
civic engagement *see* engagement, civic
civic society *see* society, civic
Civilization (computer game) 136–7, 139, 141
Clash of Civilizations, The (Huntington) 67
"clicktivism" 90, 126
cloud computing 7, 28, 67
co-creation 5, 17, 27, 34, 47
collaboration 47, 49, 52, 107, 108, 113, 121
collective action 129, 154–5
collectivism 97, 100, 101
collectivity 129; loose 106; open 112, 115–17
comments and commenting 7, 22, 28–9, 50, 84, 89–91; on the case of Ali 123, 124, 126; and crisis management 54, 58, 59; damaging to reputations 54; on Swedish Instagram project 39, 42–3
Commodore 64 (computer) 132
common ground 91, 123, 128
communication: and contemporary media 120; cross-lateral 52; democratic 68; digital 5–6, 22–3; everyday 52–3; importance of 80; internal 45–6, 48, 50; Internet-based 26; interpersonal 7; manipulative 145; mass 144; negative 53; organisational 49–50, 53; political

83–5, 89, 98, 99; with politicians 90; and propaganda 144; strategic 49, 76, 81, 147–8, 153; synchronous vs. asynchronous 50; vector of 27; virtual strategies for 48; *see also* crisis communication
communism 73, 78, 149
community/ies: academic 25, 111; digital 129; formation of new 7, 53; online 91, 107, 112, 124, 128–9; of practice 49; in social media 29–30; virtual 30, 50, 52
companies *see* organisations
compulsion loop 133, 139, 141
computer games: addiction to 133, 142n2; as advertising space 132; and the cultivation effect 138; as dismissed media 133; immersive quality of 135; as missing media 132–3; and modern democracy 131; players' engagement with 135–6; and political culture 131–2, 134; as procedural media 136; as representation of reality 134; serious 130; sociopolitical implications of 130, 140–41; violent 133
computerisation movement 45
conferences: on interactive technology 29–30; PR 29
connectedness 29
consistency, in crisis response 16, 55, 58
Constitution of Society, The (Giddens) 74
constitutional state 122
content: antiterrorism 152; in computer games 131, 134, 138; editorial 17–18; media 144; professional 150; reposting 150; of social media 29, 34, 59, 96, 98, 103; user-created 5, 25, 27, 46–7, 66; visual 35, 37
contexts, collapsed 102
conversation 25, 29
co-production 150
core loop 139
corporate ability (CA) crises 56
corporate social responsibility (CSR) crises 56
Costa Concordia 62
counter-public activity 77, 79, 82
counterterrorism: communication units 143; social media strategies of 151–2
crises: challenge 56; corporate ability (CA) 56; corporate social responsibility (CSR) 56; management of 54–5; response phase 57–9; *see also* crisis communication; paracrises